W9-BWE-028

AUGUSTE COMTE:
The Foundation of Sociology

the Making of Sociology series
EDITOR: RONALD FLETCHER

The Making of Sociology
vol. 1 *Beginnings and Foundations*
vol. 2 *Developments*
vol. 3 *Reassessments: Consolidation and Advance?*
RONALD FLETCHER

Herbert Spencer
STANISLAV ANDRESKI

Max Weber
J. E. T. ELDRIDGE

John Stuart Mill
RONALD FLETCHER

Karl Marx
Z. A. JORDAN

L. T. Hobhouse
JOHN OWEN

Auguste Comte
KENNETH THOMPSON

Sociology and Industrial Life
J. E. T. ELDRIDGE

Deviance and Society
LAURIE TAYLOR

Forthcoming Titles
Vilfredo Pareto
Placido Bucolo
George Simmel
Peter Lawrence

AUGUSTE COMTE:
THE FOUNDATION OF SOCIOLOGY

Kenneth Thompson

A HALSTED PRESS BOOK

JOHN WILEY & SONS
NEW YORK

Published in the USA
by Halsted Press, a Division of
John Wiley & Sons, Inc., New York

First published in Great Britain by Thomas Nelson & Sons Ltd, 1975
Copyright © Kenneth Thompson 1975

All rights reserved. No part of this publication may be reproduced,
stored in a retrieval system, or transmitted in any form or by any
means, electronic, mechanical, photocopying, recording or
otherwise, without the prior permission of the publishers.

Auguste Comte
"A Halsted Press Book"
Includes Index.
1. Comte, Auguste, 1798–1857.

HM22.F8C75   1975   301'.092'4   75–12566
ISBN 0–470–85988–1

Printed in Great Britain

For
Margaret and Clare

Contents

Introduction by Ronald Fletcher ix

Preface xiii

Introductory Essay
Auguste Comte: Founder of Sociology 1

1 *Philosophy, Science and Sociology* 37

View of the nature and importance of the positive philosophy

Classification of the sciences

The sociological element

Relation of sociology to the other departments of positive philosophy

The intellectual character of positivism

The social aspect of positivism

2 *The Subject-matter and Methods of Sociology* 85

Characteristics of the positive method in its application to social phenomena

3 *Social Statics* 117

Social statics, or, theory of the spontaneous order of human society

Positive theory of the social forces

Limits of social variation

Theory of social existence

4 *Social Dynamics* 151

Social dynamics, or, theory of the natural progress of human society

Preparation of the historical question

Three interconnected laws of development

5 *Socialism and Communism* 175

6   *Sociology and Inequality of the Sexes: The Comte-Mill Correspondence*   189

Bibliography   211

Index   215

Introduction by Ronald Fletcher

The work of no man can have suffered more from the reputed extravagances of its author than that of Auguste Comte. Always, even from childhood, a person of extraordinary capacities of mind and character, of tremendous concentrations of effort in any task he undertook, it is undoubtedly true that as he grew older, Comte came to adopt extremes, in both his personal life and in his ideas, which were, and remain, greatly questionable. Undoubtedly, too, he was a contentious man: ready to do battle with those who, in his view, were gravely in error in their conceptions of sociology, and in the perspectives of knowledge and judgment with which they formulated their vision of the crisis of modern industrial society. For Comte was certain that it *was* a crisis; that it required all the responsibility, all the effort, that men had at their command if disaster was to be avoided; and he entered into his arguments with an appropriate degree of seriousness and commitment. To him, the quest for truth was not a matter for academic ivory towers, but the most crucial matter for life—in society—itself. Certainly, then, intense controversy attended him from the cradle to the grave.

Equally, however, nothing is more amusing than to hear some present-day sociologists—whose camp resembles nothing more than a carnival of the (professional!) animals—criticizing him for just those qualities out of which they appear to make their careers. In Comte's case there were at least (and this, too, is without doubt) the saving dimensions of genius. Nothing, similarly, is at once more comical and pathetic than to see the most travestied caricatures of Comte's positions passed from generation to generation, and with such aplomb, by scholars who clearly judge more by hearsay than by intellectual discrimination. Thus, to take one example, the almost universally taken-for-granted denunciation of 'positivism' and 'positivistic' sociology that forms the critical bedrock of so many post-war 'schools' rests on a misunderstanding of Comte so complete as to be almost unbelievable. But then one lesson that modern intellectual activity forces home is that *nothing—nothing* —is unbelievable! However, whatever the extremes of which Comte was guilty—and it is only fair to say that there were extremes of compassion, friendship, and loyalty, as well as of dogmatism and arrogance—his system of thought remains as one of the world's great achievements, and laid the foundations for that science of society for which many philosophers, such as Aristotle, Montesquieu, Hume and Kant, had paved the way.

Obviously, there were considerable thinkers before Comte who had devoted themselves to the study of man and society—even those (among the Scottish School, for example) who had pressed these studies towards the status of scientific exactitude. But it was Comte—while very fully, and in critical detail, acknowledging the contributions of all his predecessors—who actually articulated, with great clarity, that system of anaylsis which was distinctive of the new science and its subject-matter. Central matters of theory and method: the necessary care to state *testable* hypotheses; the use of the comparative method; the careful classification of societies; the new way of conceiving the relations between psychology and sociology; a systematic approach to the study of history; the study of the 'pathological' in relation to the under-standing of the 'normal' . . . these and many others found their first clarification in his work. The analysis of the essential nature of society—its major institutions and their historical changes and developments: the material basis of society (the formation, accumulation, concentration, and transmission of capital); the division of labour; language; the family; religion; the significant relation between Protestantism, Science, and the development of new patterns of property and enterprise in the development of industrial capitalism . . . all these, and many other themes that formed the starting-points of studies undertaken during the following 150 years, were initially laid down in his early essays, his *Positive Philosophy*, and then elaborated still further in his *System of Positive Polity*. Comte's *Positive Polity* is frequently discussed as though it was only Comte's megalomaniac construction of his vast 'Sociocracy'—but, in fact, no understanding of Comte's sociology proper is possible without an acquaintance with at least two volumes of this work: vol. 2 on *'Social Statics'* and vol. 3 on *'Social Dynamics'*. Certainly such a knowledge of Comte is a basic necessity for a satisfactory understanding of all the work of sociology that was to follow—from his day to our own.

That these misunderstandings of Comte's work have been able to survive for so long is largely because the translations of his work (including Harriet Martineau's abridgement of the *Positive Philosophy*) have been out of print and unavailable. For the same reason, students have not been in a position to formulate their own judgments about him. Gradually, however, Comte's work is being brought back into the picture of the making of sociology in the way that it deserves, and in this book, Kenneth Thompson's selections provide a systematic coverage of the major elements of his system, just as his introductory essay corrects some present-day misconceptions. Dr. Thompson, who now teaches in the Open University, has also lectured in the United States and is well aware of the current 'schools' of sociological theory—perhaps especially in the fields of the sociology of knowledge and the sociology of religion. In addition, he has had a long-standing special interest in French sociology, and in Comte in particular, and is therefore particularly well qualified to provide this new introduction to Comte's work. In his last section in particular, he also draws attention to the relevance of Comte's theories to present-day preoccupations. Comte's attitudes towards communism, and the relations between the ideas of Comte and Marx, are especially interesting; and Dr. Thompson also provides newly translated material on Comte's discussion, with John Stuart Mill, on the question of the status of women.

Here, then, is a new and reliable introduction to the thinker whose work constituted that crucial point of arrival and departure in the history of thought at which the study of man and society moved distinctively from the condition of speculative philosophy to that of testable science; that foundation statement from which, by way of agreement, disagreement, and continual critical assessment, almost all the major directions in the making of sociology were to grow. For an understanding of the distinctive nature and scope of the new science of society, no man's work is of greater importance.

Suffolk,
June 1974.

Preface

Auguste Comte (1798–1857) figures in some way in most introductory courses of sociology, but they are usually a very unsatisfactory experience from the students' point of view because of the unavailability of the translated works, most of which went out of print many years ago. It is therefore the first priority of this book to make available as many as possible of those key passages in Comte's multi-volumed works in which he sets out the first ever prospectus of a discipline of sociology. I believe these passages, setting out the proper subject matter of sociology and its appropriate logic and methods, can be regarded as the foundation of the discipline, and that they were accepted as such not only by the best-informed judges in Comte's own time, such as John Stuart Mill, but also in the next generation, as represented by Émile Durkheim.

Most of the extracts are taken from the following works:

The Positive Philosophy of Auguste Comte, translated and condensed by Harriet Martineau, three volumes, London: G. Bell (1913). This is a reprint of the first edition, published in two volumes, by John Chapman in 1853, and was the version which Comte himself recommended as the popular form of his six-volume *Cours de philosophie positive* (1830–42). This work will be referred to by the abbreviation *Pos. Phil.*

System of Positive Polity, four volumes, London: Longmans Green (1875–7). This is a translation by a team of scholars of *Système de politique positive* (1848–54) and will be referred to as *Pos. Pol.*

In the final section I have included some extracts from the correspondence between Comte and John Stuart Mill on a topic which is as contentious today as it was then—the inequality of the sexes and women's liberation. As far as I can ascertain these letters have not previously appeared in English, despite their obvious interest.[1] They reveal a great deal about the relationship between sociology and its social context, which is also part of its subject-matter. On the personal level they are very revealing about the factors that led to the eventual termination of one of the most promising instances of intellectual collaboration in the history of the social sciences.

Comte's prolixity renders almost impossible an editor's attempts to satisfy the competing demands of providing a comprehensive selection of the original work and of keeping a book cheap enough and short enough for the student to be able to afford and read. In practical terms I have followed a general rule of trying to give key passages in their entirety (allowing for small deletions) rather than providing a lot of very short extracts on many topics. My own criteria for evaluating Comte's work are set out in the Introduction. However, I must acknowledge with thanks the early influence of Professor Ilya Neustadt, who introduced me to Comte's sociology and whose knowledge of this subject far exceeds mine. More recently, I have been greatly influenced by the work of Pierre Arnaud, especially his short, but excellent, *Sociologie de Comte* (1969). Needless to say, neither of the above can be held responsible for any faults or blemishes in the following pages.

NOTES AND REFERENCES

1. The letters were published in *Lettres Inédites de John Stuart Mill à Auguste Comte avec les Responses de Comte*, Paris: Alcan (1899). I am grateful to Jane Kenrick for assistance in translating from the French.

Introductory Essay
Auguste Comte: Founder of Sociology

Who now reads Comte?[1] And why should they? An informed guess is probably all we need to answer the first question. In view of the fact that the English translations of Comte's two major works, his *Cours de philosophie positive* (1830–42, 6 volumes) and the *Système de politique positive* (1848–54, 4 volumes) have long been out of print, the answer is likely to be that very few people now read the works of the man who has been called the founder, or 'founder-in-chief'[2] of sociology. The second question presents more problems. It is all too easy to present quotations from notable sociologists that offer widely varying estimates of Comte's worth. Taken on its own terms, each judgment seems to have some validity, but in order to adjudicate between them it is essential to be clear about what Comte actually wrote and what are the underlying issues.

Underlying the various judgments about the contemporary relevance and worth of Comte's sociology, are issues concerning how an academic discipline should regard its past. Some would say 'forget it', on the grounds that all that is worthwhile has been incorporated in the present system of knowledge. They might quote A. N. Whitehead's comment: 'A science which hesitates to forget its founders is lost.' However, it can be said in reply to Whitehead's aphorism that it is also likely that a science that is ignorant of its founders does not know how far it has travelled nor in what direction, and so, in consequence, is lost.

Another related view is that the founding fathers can be treated as though they are our contemporaries, so that what they are providing are either true or false answers to the same problems that we ourselves are facing. This is a cumulative model of science. Thus Andreski, introducing a volume of selections from Herbert Spencer's *The Principles of Sociology*, in which everything 'mistaken or superseded' has been left out, says that it was 'inspired by the desire' to show that sociological knowledge has not become cumulative in this generation, but always was so. If we cut out from the works of the old masters what has become untenable in the light of later studies, their contributions dovetail like parts of a jigsaw puzzle.[3]

Opposed to this cumulative model of the development of sociology is the view which stresses the difference between the subject-matter of sociology and that of the physical sciences in this respect. It is well expressed in another book on Spencer by Peel, who, while not asserting that there is no 'accumulation' in sociology, insists that:

The history of sociology only becomes functionally necessary for the practice of sociology when sociology itself is conceived in ways radically distinct from natural science.

... Every age's sociology, our own as well as Spencer's, is irretrievably specific in its problems, both practical and theoretical. Despite its ambition to produce a universal theory of society after an *a priori* ideal drawn from natural science, it is necessarily attached to those models, metaphors and theories which best seem to capture the complex actuality which is each period of sociology's chief subject-matter: contemporary society.[4]

There is something in each of these views. On specific topics the observations provided by the early sociologists have been either absorbed or discarded in the light of their truth or falsity as revealed by further research. But matters concerning some of their more general models, theories and methodological tenets have not been so unequivocally settled. The problem here cannot be settled by demanding that sociologists should 'go back to the early fathers' or the 'gospels' (as some Christians exhort the Church), as though an addiction to contemporaneity is causing us to forget a previously laid down catechism. On the other hand, it is true, as Andreski says, that much that is said today with an air of discovery was said years ago by early sociologists like Comte and Spencer, and that if only their works were read more the tedious practice of 'rediscovering America' would be avoided.

Comte had a strong belief in the cumulative, systematic nature of sociology, and no doubt thought that he had provided the synthesis and systematization of all that was worthwhile in pre-sociological theorizing. Hence the title of his first major sociological work—*Cours de philosophie positive*. It was a *cours* because the work was first delivered as a course of lectures; it was *philosophie* because Comte used the word in the Aristotelian sense as a synthesis of knowledge; and it was *positive* because, believing that theological and metaphysical theories had been superseded, he wished to build his synthesis on a scientific basis. However, he did recognize that, for a time in the development of any new discipline, reflection on the history of the discipline and on systematization would have to go forward hand in hand until eventually the latter largely superseded the former.

Every science may be exhibited under two methods or procedures, the historical and the dogmatic ... A new science must be pursued historically, the only thing to be done being to study in chronological order the different works which have contributed to the progress of the science. But when such materials have become recast to form a general system, to meet the demand for a more natural logical order, it is because the science is too far advanced for the historical order to be practicable or suitable . . . Thus the dogmatic method is for ever superseding the historical, as we advance to a higher position in science. If every mind had to pass through all the stages that every predecessor in the study had gone through, it is clear that, however easy it is to learn rather than invent, it would be impossible to effect the purpose of education—to place the student on the vantage-ground gained by the labours of all the men who have gone before . . . It is true that a science cannot be completely understood without a knowledge of how it arose; and again, a dogmatic knowledge of any science is necessary to an understanding of its history . . . (*Pos. Phil.*, vol. 1, pp. 24–5)

Students of sociology would be well advised to read Comte for two reasons. First, as we will see, because he is an important figure in the history of the emergence of sociology as a discipline, and his contribution to that development helps us to understand what we possess now. Second, because we can only understand the relationship betwen sociology and its subject matter in the present-day, contemporary society, by comparing it with the relationship between sociological reasoning and its intellectual and social context in the past. The relevance of Comte's work to our understanding of the development of sociology and to an appreciation of the sociology of the present will become clearer if we keep in mind three underlying issues:

1. The part played by Comte in delimiting the subject matter of an autonomous discipline of sociology, and in suggesting appropriate methods of analysis;

2. His contribution to the founding of a tradition of self-analysis by the discipline of sociology, a sociology of sociology, or sociology of knowledge, which enables us to take account of the two-way relationship between sociology and its subject-matter;

3. His influence on the development of sociology as mediated through other important figures such as John Stuart Mill, Herbert Spencer and Émile Durkheim.

Comte and the Invention of Sociology

It is agreed that Comte invented the name *sociology* in 1839 to designate the new discipline that he had previously referred to as *social physics*.[5] Where there is less agreement is with regard to Comte's part in defining the new discipline and its methods. It has been suggested that Comte merely *synthesized* many of the ideas of other thinkers such as Turgot, Cordorcet, Montesquieu and Saint-Simon. Judgments such as this have served to retard an appreciation of the full scope of Comte's achievement in forging a viable academic discipline out of a mass of disjointed and previously unrelated theories and speculations. Comte was certainly a synthesizer of genius, and a great exponent of the art and aspirations of the eighteenth-century *Encyclopedists* who had set in motion the synthesizing effort to construct a unified scientific system. Where he surpassed them was in his ability to define the appropriate subject-matter and methods for this enterprise as it applied to the social sphere. What is most ironical is that full credit should have been denied to Comte's genius because of a tendency to evaluate him on the basis of those aspects of his work which were most derivative, such as the law of the three stages of intellectual development, and his organicist-functionalist model of the social order, whilst the more original aspects, such as his discussion of the epistemological and methodological bases of sociology, have been misunderstood or ignored. The currently fashionable denunciations of 'positive sociology' and the obvious misunderstanding of what that meant for Comte, are typical of this ill-informed criticism. It is a line of criticism worth examining, however, because it is at least directed to the central issue of Comte's definition of the appropriate subject-matter and method of sociology. We will discuss the substance of this criticism later. The issue is also relevant to arriving at a judgment of Comte's status as a founding father of sociology.

Alvin Gouldner, in the Introduction to Émile Durkheim's essay on *Socialism and Saint-Simon*, asserts that Durkheim there makes 'yeoman-like efforts to dispel the conception that Comte was the "father" of sociology', but still 'the belief in "Comte the father" persists, even among sociologists, as an almost indestructible myth'. He goes on to suggest why, in his opinion, the 'myth' persists:

> If the myth of 'Comte the founder of sociology' still persists in American sociology, despite long-standing evidence to the

contrary, this suggests that it performs certain on-going social functions for those holding it. There is an interesting problem here for a study in the sociology of knowledge. One hypothesis for such a study might be that acknowledgement of Comte as the putative father of sociology is less professionally damaging than acknowledgement of Saint-Simon who, as Durkheim points out, was also one of the founders of modern socialism . . . A 'founding father' is a professional symbol which can be treated as a trivial detail by no one who wishes to understand the profession as a social organization. Where there are conflicts, by later generations, concerning who their 'founding father' was, we suspect that this may be a serious question essentially reflecting a dispute over the character of the profession.[6]

Durkheim certainly sought to reach a balance between the claims of the Saint-Simonians and Comtists over the contributions of their respective masters in founding the positivist philosophy and sociology. But Gouldner's commentary misses the crucial distinction made by Durkheim. According to Durkheim, Saint-Simon had not received sufficient credit from Comte and his followers for the extent to which his ideas had influenced Comte, and so sown the seed for the growth of sociology. But he made it clear that it was Comte who patiently set about constructing an academic discipline, a science, whilst Saint-Simon dissipated his insights by a too-hasty application of them for utilitarian purposes. As Durkheim put it:

> In fact what differentiates Comte and Saint-Simon is that the former separated science from practice more clearly, but without disinteresting himself in the latter—at least during the better part of his career. Once given this idea of a positive science of societies, he undertook to realize it, not from the aspect of this or that immediate end, but in an abstract and disinterested manner.[7]

As there are some who favour the view that sociology only emerged as a distinct subject, with its own subject-matter and methods, in the work of Émile Durkheim, it is worth noting that Durkheim's *The Rules of Sociological Method* pays tribute to Comte for having provided 'almost the only original and important study we have on the matter'[8] of sociological methodology. Durkheim acknowledges that Comte was almost unique in this respect:

Thus, in the entire work of Spencer the problem of methodology occupies no place, for *The Study of Sociology*, perhaps a misleading title, is devoted to demonstrating the difficulties and possibilities of sociology, not to expounding the methods it ought to use. Mill, it is true, has dealt at great length with the question; but he has only refined with his dialectics what Comte had already expounded, without adding anything really original.[9]

It is clear then that Durkheim regarded Comte as having defined the method of the young science, even though he had reservations about some of his views. 'In spite of those reservations, a vivid feeling of social reality is ever present in Comte's works. No better initiation to sociology exists,' Durkheim concluded.

It is probably more for these reasons than from any embarrassment about Saint-Simon's socialism, that sociologists have acknowledged Comte as the founder of their discipline.[10] In fact, the periodic reluctance to make such a full acknowledgement, and the relative neglect of Comte's work, stem from the fact that some sociologists consider Comte to have shared the fault which Durkheim ascribed to Saint-Simon—a tendency to hurry too much, 'to prematurely use a hastily constructed science for utilitarian ends'.[11] It is worth examining the development of Comte's thought, and the various influences on it, including that of Saint-Simon, if we are to make a fair judgment of that issue.

The Development of Comte's Intellectual Position

Auguste Comte was born on 19 January 1798 in the city of Montpellier in the south of France. His father was a local government official, a Catholic and a Royalist. The son was almost always at odds with his father over their respective beliefs, although both seemed to have shared a strong attachment to *order* as a social priority. Auguste Comte made a brilliant start to his academic career by passing high on the list of successful candidates in the national entrance examinations for the prestigious École Polytechnique in Paris, which he entered in 1814. The École Polytechnique was the foremost centre of research and teaching in science and mathematics in the whole of Europe at that time. It was also a breeding ground for social reformers who believed that social reconstruction could only be accomplished by the application of scientific principles. Henri Gouhier, Comte's biographer, quotes one commentator's remark that these young *polytechnicians* believed that 'one could create a religion in the same way as one learned at the *École* to build a bridge'.[12] The remark is particularly apt in the case of Comte, because he added to the polytechnician's faith in social engineering, a great admiration for the emotional and moral unity that religion had provided for earlier societies. In fact, it is this aspect of Comte's thinking that has most alienated him from modern sociologists. However, it is worth mentioning at this point that Comte, in the fourth volume of his *System of Positive Polity* clearly separated sociology, as an autonomous discipline, from a yet to be developed, crowning discipline of *moral science*. And this 'final science' would relieve sociology of all the messianic missions which the first three volumes of the *System of Positive Polity* seemed to impose on it, and which subsequent sociologists feared would hamper its autonomous development.

After the École Polytechnique the next major influence brought to bear on Comte was that of Henri Saint-Simon.[13] Comte became his secretary in 1817 and soon his collaborator. The association lasted until 1824 when it was severed by a quarrel. Ever afterwards Comte was severe in his criticisms of the older man, and there is no doubt he felt he had been exploited. But he also gained much from his deep involvement as is suggested by the way in which he announced the break to a friend: 'I have nothing more to learn from M. Saint-Simon.'[14] He confessed earlier to his friend Valat that 'I certainly owe a great deal intellectually to Saint-Simon, that is to say, he contributed powerfully to launching me in the philosophic direction that I clearly created for myself today and which I will follow without hesitation all my life'.[15] But after the break he claimed that 'Later, I recognized that such a liaison had allowed no other result than to shackle my spontaneous reflections, previously guided by Condorcet'.[16] This raises the broader and more substantial issue about the more general influences on Comte's thinking and the kind of synthesis that he produced.

Condorcet was certainly a major influence in the development of Comte's thinking,[17] although his statement that 'from the outset of my career I have never ceased to represent the great Condorcet as my spiritual father' (*Pos. Phil.*, vol. 1, p. xviii) seems extravagant praise in the light of the severe criticisms which he made of Condorcet's ideas. What he took from Condorcet was the idea of laws of progress of civilization.

Condorcet it was who grasped the general conception of the operation fitted to raise politics to the rank of the sciences of observation. He first saw clearly that civilization is subject to a progressive course, every step of which is strictly connected with the rest by virtue of natural laws; discoverable through philosophic observation of the past, and which determine, in a positive manner for each epoch, the improvements adapted to the social state as a whole, and to each portion of it. (*Pos. Pol.*, Appendix, p. 570)

In tracing the outline of the successive steps of the progress of the human mind, however, Condorcet presented the sequence of epochs of civilization without any thought-out theory of their ordering principle.

He imagined that he could adequately co-ordinate facts by assuming, almost arbitrarily, for the commencement of each epoch some remarkable event now industrial, now scientific, now political. (*Pos. Pol.*, Appendix, p. 571)

Consequently his method was no better than that of the literary historians. Sociology needed systematic history based on a principle of classification of phenomena deriving from a general theory of development. Comte took examples of such principles of classification based on observation from the biologists of his day.

If Condorcet (and, to a lesser extent, Turgot[18]) impressed on Comte the need for a scientific explanation of *progress*, in keeping with the Enlightenment, he was also deeply influenced by the chief critics of that school, the traditionalists such as de Maistre[19] and de Bonald.[20] Comte said that Condorcet's contribution to the founding of sociology was deficient in two respects. Firstly, it was lacking in its 'scientific preparation', which was not surprising as it pre-dated the recent developments in biology which Comte thought supplied principles of classification which could be applied to social phenomena. Secondly, its theory of development was inadequate because it devalued the past and so provided no appreciation of the principles of the functioning of past social systems (or epochs). The result was that Condorcet placed himself in the contradictory position of explaining 'final progress as the result of an unbroken series of retrogressions' (*Pos. Pol.*, vol. 3, p. 527). De Maistre supplied what was lacking by showing how a previous system, such as feudalism in the Middle Ages, had functioned effectively in its own epoch. Comte spoke highly of this 'immortal school which arose at the beginning of the nineteenth century under the noble chairmanship of de Maistre, suitably accompanied by de Bonald', but he praised it chiefly for supplying the missing link for his theory of development. Once it had supplied that link, he had no further use for it. Although Condorcet and 'the ardour of the revolutionary spirit' had thrown 'dazzling light upon the future', it had at the same time

> . . . obscured our vision of the past . . . It encouraged that blind aversion to the Middle Ages which had been inspired by the emancipating process of modern times; a feeling which had once been necessary to induce us to abandon the old system . . . Right views upon the subject were impossible therefore until full justice had been rendered to the Middle Ages, which form at once the point of union and of separation between ancient and modern history. Now it was quite impossible to do this as long as the excitement of the first years of the revolution lasted. In this respect the philosophical reaction, organized at the beginning of the century by the great de Maistre, was of material assistance in preparing the true theory of progress. His school was of brief duration, and it was no doubt animated by a retrograde spirit; but it will always be ranked among the necessary antecedents of the positive system; although its works are now entirely superseded by the rise of the new philosophy, which in a more perfect form has embodied all their chief results. (*Pos. Pol.*, vol. 1, p. 50)

But positivism was the result of a combination of two impulses, one proceeding from philosophy, the other from science. (*Pos. Pol.*, vol. 3, p. 526)

> The first of these impulses emanated from the combination of the two opposite influences of Condorcet and de Maistre, the first revolutionary, the second retrograde; the one thinker having been influenced by the French crisis, the other by the reaction movement which followed it. (*Pos. Pol.*, vol. 3, p. 527)
>
> . . . Thenceforward the problem of constructing sociology was reduced to the question of how to effect a satisfactory reconciliation between the two antagonistic influences of Condorcet and de Maistre, the one furnishing the principal idea, the other the view essential to its completion . . . The reconciliation could only be accomplished in a region of speculation lying above both revolutionists and reactionists. Here it is that the philosophic root of positivism joins its

scientific root, which alone could furnish inspiration capable of becoming universal. (*Pos Pol.*, vol. 3, p. 525)

Comte had an extensive knowledge of current biological and medical science. The chief influence on his thinking was the work of Bichat, a biologist, author of *Recherches sur la vie et la mort* and *Traité d'anatomie générale*.

> This incomparable thinker now found himself in a position to establish directly the fundamental conception of life by combining once and for all the two aspects from which every being can be regarded, the statical and the dynamical. (*Pos. Pol.*, vol. 3, p. 528)

Comte regarded this theoretical framework, reconciling the structure and functioning of the parts by reference to their contribution to the whole, as applicable to social science and the reconciling of order and progress. Society can be viewed as a collective organism in which there is normally a harmony of structure and function working towards common ends through action and reaction among the parts and upon the environment. Social progress is marked by an increasing specialization of functions and a corresponding tendency towards an adaptation and perfection of organs. Social disturbances can be regarded as malfunctioning of the social organism and are the subject matter of social pathology.

Theory and Method

It was suggested earlier that the most enduring and remarkable contribution Comte made to sociology was in his discussion of the new discipline's proper subject-matter and methods, and in the manner in which he related the development of social science to conditions in society itself. We will return to this latter topic, which constitutes a veritable proto-sociology of knowledge analysis of sociology, but first we need to summarize the main elements in Comte's system of sociology.

Some of the elements that went into the Comtean synthesis have already been mentioned. There were many more antecedents that it would be tedious to relate in detail. We have seen that he believed that the main contributors to his own synthesis were the eighteenth-century philosophers of progress (Condorcet and Turgot), the opposing school of philosophers who reacted against the Enlightenment (de Bonald and de Maistre), and the scientists, especially those in biology and medicine (such as Bichat). But there were many others: the liberal political economists (Adam Smith and Jean Baptiste Say), the Greek philosophers (Plato and Aristotle), philosophers (such as Kant, Hume and Descartes), and social theorists and historians (such as Montesquieu, Bossuet and Adam Ferguson).

Comte never denied his sources, in fact he was constantly pre-occupied with reconstructing a genealogy of sociology, and relating its developments to historical circumstances. This 'sociology of knowledge' analysis of the development of sociology fits in with his two most celebrated conceptions—the Law of Three Stages (sometimes called the Law of Human Progress) and his Hierarchy of the Sciences. His underlying conception was that each successive stage or sub-stage in the evolution of the human mind necessarily grew out of the preceding one. He stated that a new system of thought could not be constituted until the old system had exhausted its potentialities and until social conditions were conducive to its establishment.

The Law of Three Stages stated that each branch of knowledge passes successively through three different theoretical conditions: the theological or fictitious; the metaphysical or abstract; and the scientific or positive. In the theological state the human mind searches for the origin and purpose of all effects and supposes that all phenomena are produced by the immediate action of super-natural beings. In the metaphysical state the mind supposes that abstract forces (personified abstractions, actual entities) produce all phenomena. In the final stage, the positive state, the mind gives up the vain search for absolute notions, the origin and destination of the universe, and the causes of phenomena, and studies their laws, that is, their relations of succession and resemblance. Comte also stressed that these stages and their sub-stages are correlated with parallel stages in the development of social organization, of types of social order, types of social units, and material conditions. The theological stage is accompanied by a social order in which priests are dominant and military men rule (he goes on to give a detailed set of sub-stages and their correlative changes in social organization). The metaphysical stage, which obtained, for example, during the Middle Ages and Renaissance, was under the sway of churchmen and lawyers. In the positive age, which was just beginning, society would be governed by industrial admini-strators and scientific moral guides. The prototypical social unit in each of these stages was first the family, then the state, and finally the whole human race. Social evolution was propelled not only by intellectual developments, but also by material factors such as population growth and the division of labour—ideas which were taken up by Durkheim in his first major work, *The Division of Labour in Society* (1893).

The hierarchy of the sciences is based on a similar notion of the stages of development of branches of knowledge, although these develop at different rates depending on their degree of generality, simplicity and independence. Astronomy, the most general, simple and independent of the sciences developed first, followed by physics, chemistry, biology and, finally, sociology. They each build on the prior developments of their predecessors in a hierarchy which is based on the criteria of increasing complexity and decreasing generality. Sociology could not emerge until its immediate neighbour in the hierarchy, biology, had begun to reach maturity. Biology and sociology are methodologically similar in that they both proceed from the study of organic wholes, unlike the preceding sciences such as physics and chemistry that proceed by isolating elements. Comte held that the social whole is more easily understood than its parts, and that there could be no successful scientific study of society if its parts are studied in isolation from their relations with the whole social system. It was for this very reason that he criticized the economists of his day because they examined the economic sector without reference to general social theory, and in isolation from other social institutions.

The methodological principle in biology of studying the parts in relation to the whole also included the useful procedure of separating anatomy from physiology. In sociology the parallel distinction was between statics and dynamics or social order and social progress. The study of social statics is concerned with the investigation of the laws of action and reaction of the different parts of the social system. There must always exist a 'spontaneous harmony' or consensus between the social system and its parts, except in certain pathological cases and in critical periods when the social system is in disequilibrium, which usually is the prelude to the development of a new organic state of affairs.

The components of the social system include as their basic unit not individuals, but *the family*, which is society in miniature, the precursor of all other social associations.

> . . . I shall treat the social organism as definitely composed of the families which are the true elements, or cells, next of the classes or castes which are its proper tissues, and lastly of the cities and communes which are its real organs. (*Pos. Pol.*, vol. 2, p. 242)

This conception has important functions in differentiating Comte's point of departure from that of utilitarian and contractualist social philosophers who derived man's social tendencies from supposed needs and propensities of individuals. But in utilizing the biological analogy Comte remained sensitive to the differences between the social organism and the biological organism. For example, whereas the biological organism is separated off and unified by its encasing skin, the social organism has to depend primarily on spiritual (cultural) unifying factors. It is for this reason that Comte's social statics give central importance to discussion of the functions of *language* and *religion*. Much of Comte's discussion is about the binding nature of culture. Language is a vital medium for the transmission of culture. Religion and morals supply the 'cement' that binds society together in a common *cult* and that excites affective attachments to the social order, and beliefs that legitimate the social order.

A final binding factor is the division of labour. The specialization of functions allowed men to utilize their individual talents and capacities to the full for the general good and, most importantly, created in each individual a sense of dependence on others. However, the modern division of labour could entail such a high degree of specialization and trivialization that individuals would lose all sense of their contribution to the overall interest and see only their private interests. It was to obviate this that Comte set forward his various proposals for developing a society based on a scientific moral code, and a positive religion, which would constitute a binding spiritual power directed by sociologist-priests. A science of morals would be the crowning discipline in the hierarchy of the sciences, but it needed the prior efforts of sociology to disclose the laws of social structure and functioning. On such a basis it would be possible to predict future trends of development and so to steer society by utilizing those currents, to row with the stream rather than against it or in ignorance of its tendencies. It was summed up in a famous sentence by Comte: *Savoir pour prévoir et prévoir pour pouvoir*—Knowledge for foreknowledge and foreknowledge for action.

The goal of orderly social development is the perfect distribution of functions and the perfect co-ordination of the social organs. The relations between these two aspects can be seen in the relations between society and government. Too much specialization in the distribution of functions could lead to loss of social unity, too little could represent an under-use of talents and capacities. It was the task of government to co-ordinate activities and to guard against divisive over-specialization. This task could only be successfully accomplished on the basis of scientific knowledge of the relations of the parts to the whole in society, and such knowledge could only be supplied by sociology.

If this was the vocation of sociology, what should be its methodology? Because Comte was committed to a synthesis of knowledge, he needed to lay down a methodology for sociology that would be appropriate to its subject-matter; and its subject-matter and methodology had to fit the position reserved for sociology in the hierarchy of the sciences. Sociology came after biology in the hierarchy and so it would obviously build on all that had been established about man's nature with regard to anatomy and physiology (which included much of what we would call psychology). It was not, however, the needs and propensities of the individual that constituted the subject-matter of the new discipline, but rather the development of those attributes which set man off from the lower species. The chief of these attributes was man's greater reasoning capacity, and this in turn was developed through his social organization and language.

> If we regard the course of human development from the highest scientific point of view, we shall perceive that it consists in educing, more and more, the characteristic faculties of humanity, in contrast with those of animality ... (*Pos. Phil.*, vol. 2, p. 299)

Sociology is thus interested in establishing the general course and the stages of development, of civilization. One strategy here might be to take economic development as the key factor and to define stages by developments in the means of production. This is often taken to be the distinctive standpoint of the Marxist theory of development. But although this may be an appropriate emphasis for some purposes, such as the analysis of causal factors in the development of the stage or epoch of capitalism, it is not on the same level as a theory of development which seeks to embrace the whole development of humanity from the animal level to that of the most scientifically advanced civilization.

Comte's emphasis is on man's intellectual development, which sets him off from the animals, enables him to control nature and so to rise above all-absorbing material concerns and to concentrate on developing still further his higher faculties.

> Civilization develops to an enormous degree, the action of man upon his environment: and thus, it may seem, at first, to concentrate our attention upon the cares of material existence,

the support and improvement of which appear to be the chief object of most social occupations. A closer examination will show, however, that this development gives the advantage to the highest human faculties, both by the security which sets free our attention from physical wants, and by the direct and steady excitement which it administers to the intellectual functions, and even the social feelings. (*Pos. Phil.*, vol. 2, p. 300)

The way in which Comte defined social evolution, therefore, made the development of man's (strictly speaking, *society's*) intellectual capacities the predominant factor, and this predominant factor forms the basis of his social statics and social dynamics. But in answer to some of Comte's critics on this point, it cannot be too heavily stressed that the emphasis that he places on intellectual development as the key factor in social development follows logically from his prior decision to deduce the proper study of *man* from the position which that science would occupy in the hierarchy of the sciences:

For man, properly so called, when regarded in his essential reality, and not by the light of materialist or spiritualist dreams, can only be understood by means of a previous knowledge of humanity, for on this man necessarily depends. And it would be needless to enlarge any further on the view already familiar to the reader, that the social existence of man is in necessary dependence on the vital (biological) and on the material order. We thus obtain, if we decompose into its parts the material order, the seven essential stages of knowledge: mathematical, astronomical, physical, chemical, vital, social, and finally moral. (*Pos Pol.*, vol. 2, p. 353)

Comte's general methodology, which is based on historical comparisons as its starting point, is to set out the general direction of human development in relation to man's fundamental conceptions about the natural and social order. However, although he regards this as the predominant factor, he warns against allowing this to blind us to the interconnections of this and other factors in any period.

The danger (which is inherent in every choice, and which is least in the choice that I have made) of losing sight of the interconnection of all the parts of human development, may be partly guarded against by frequently comparing them, to see if the variations in any one corresponds with equivalent variations in the others. (*Pos. Phil.*, vol. 2, p. 308)

Thus, he suggests that although we should bear in mind a *normal type*—where all the parts or factors vary together—we should also be prepared to find *deviations* from that type. Explanation would then be devoted to accounting for the deviation. However, it is also essential to try to deduce the likely limits to such variation or deviation. He agrees with Montesquieu that we should look for the effects of material conditions in modifying society, but criticizes him for not developing a theory about the limits of such modifiability. Montesquieu had forgotten a basic principle of logic, says Comte: 'that every examination of variations, must be a corollary of fundamental laws found in the normal type' (*Pos. Pol.*, vol. 2, p. 368). To arrive at a formulation of the normal type might seem to be a tall order for sociology in view of the greater complication and interdependence of social phenomena compared with the phenomena studied by sciences lower down the hierarchy. But, according to Comte, although there is 'inevitable increase in complication in proportion with the decrease of generality', it is also the case that 'as liability to imperfection increases, capacity for improvement increases' (*Pos. Pol.*, vol. 2, p. 376). He then shows how sources of variation that he had previously discussed—climatic, racial, national and individual—were each becoming less susceptible to producing variations from the 'normal state'; in each of these spheres 'man's activity is continually giving fresh ascendancy to the normal state over the different modifications of it' (*Pos Pol.*, vol. 2, p. 377). To take just one of these—the capacity of an individual to modify society's course of development—here too, as in the other three, the capacity for modifiability is becoming weaker and more regular.

Both of these results are yet more distinctly than before due to the growing domination of the dead over the living, a truth which is at the bottom of all sound explanations in sociology, as it is at the bottom of all harmony in practical life. In face of this irresistible pressure of our ancestors, the agitations of our contemporaries grow more and more idle; even in situations where they have the greatest scope . . . Human order exhibits a course of increasing regularity, by virtue of man's ever growing power to affect the sum of his destinies . . . For humanity is ever at work to assert its own high freedom of action, and thus triumphs over the blind fatality encompassing its life. (*Pos. Pol.*, vol. 2, pp. 379–80)

In other words, although the capacity for individuals (the 'great men of history') to make radical changes in society is decreasing, the possibility for society as a whole to make changes in keeping with knowledge of the laws of development is increasing.

It is clear then that, for Comte, sociology is fundamentally committed to a methodology which cannot ignore the historical dimension. Is it then nothing more than the established discipline of history? Comte's answer is that it must be more:

> Still, history has more of a literary and descriptive than of a scientific character. It does not yet establish a rational filiation in the series of social events so as to admit (as in other sciences, and allowing for its great complexity) of any degree of systematic prevision of their future succession. (*Pos. Phil.*, vol. 2, p. 208)

Some historians have taken Comte's strictures to heart and seek to produce 'systematic history', but they would still reject his aspiration to produce predictions of future trends on the basis of findings about past developments. But this is precisely where sociology must start if it is to be scientific.

> Perhaps the imputation of rashness cast upon the mere proposal of such a treatment of history is the strongest confirmation we could have of its present unscientific character: for such prevision is everywhere else admitted to be the ultimate scientific test. (*Pos. Phil.*, vol. 2, p. 208)

It was stated earlier that Comte's great contribution was to define the subject matter of sociology and to indicate its appropriate methods. In fact, for him, the two were inseparable. 'In every science, conceptions which relate to method are inseparable from those which relate to the doctrine under consideration' (*Pos. Phil.*, vol. 2, p. 210). He referred to history as the fourth method of sociology; the other three, which we shall discuss, were observation, experiment and comparison (*Pos. Phil.*, vol. 2, p. 256). But in addition to being a method it was also inseparable from sociology's basic conceptions:

> It asks from history something more than counsel and instruction to perfect conceptions which are derived from another source: it seeks its own general direction, through the whole system of historical conclusions. (*Pos. Phil.*, vol. 2, p. 257)

It was Comte's opinion that the social science of his day was still in the theologico-metaphysical infancy akin to what astrology had been to anatomy, alchemy to chemistry, and the search for a

universal panacea to medical science. There was too much speculation and not enough subjection of imagination to the discipline
of empirical observation. Scientific laws were also relative, in contrast to the search for absolute knowledge which accompanied the
use of theological and metaphysical notions. It is worth bearing in
mind this modest claim that Comte made for sociological laws:

> The study of the laws of phenomena must be relative, since
> it supposes a continuous progress of speculation subject to the
> gradual improvement of observation, without the precise
> reality being ever fully disclosed ... (*Pos. Phil.*, vol. 2, p. 213)

Critics have accused Comte of claiming too much for the
laws that he believed he had discovered, such as the Law of the
Three Stages, but he himself had provided the built-in corrective
to any such excess by his definition of laws as provisional and
relative. Similarly, when modern sociologists complain that
Comte's division of sociological study into social statics and social
dynamics is outmoded, they are often ignorant of Comte's own
discussion of the circumscribed and provisional nature of that
methodological device:

> This division, necessary for exploratory purposes, must not
> be stretched beyond that use: and as we saw in biology, that the
> distinction becomes weaker with the advance of science, so we
> shall see that when the science of social physics is fully
> constituted, this division will remain for analytical purposes,
> but not as a real separation of the science into two parts.
> (*Pos. Phil.*, vol. 2, p. 218)

Comte's general methodological principles for explaining social
phenomena have stood the test of time and sound remarkably
contemporary. What he calls 'political' or social facts are not to be
the subject of value judgments by sociologists, rather they are to be
explained by discovering the general relations which connect
phenomena in a system, and by locating that specific social
phenomena's connection with co-existing phenomena and also
with those that directly precede it.

> Thus then we see what is the function of social science.
> Without extolling or condemning political facts, science
> regards them as subjects of observation: it contemplates each
> phenomenon in its harmony with co-existing phenomena,
> and in its connection with the foregoing and the following
> state of human development: it endeavours to discover, from
> both points of view, the general relations which connect all

social phenomena: and each of them is *explained*, in the scientific sense of the word, when it has been connected with the whole of the existing situation, and the whole of the preceding movement. (*Pos. Phil.*, vol. 2, p. 240)

Having examined the general spirit of sociology, Comte then went on to discuss the methods of investigation which it could use. He said that we could expect to find in sociology a more varied set of methods than in other sciences because of the greater complexity of its phenomena, but this would not compensate for the increased 'imperfection' arising from its intricacy. The methods appropriate to sociology would be affected by the fact that it came late into the hierarchy of sciences, and so would be dependent on developments in the other sciences. The means of investigation would be of two kinds, those which were peculiar to itself, which he called 'direct', and those which arise from sociology's connections with other sciences, and are termed 'indirect'. The direct methods are observation, experiment and comparison.

Like much else in Comte's description of sociology and its methods, what he has to say about observation now strikes us as obvious and sensible. It requires an imaginative leap back into history on our part in order to appreciate how innovative and progressive his ideas were at that time. In fact, it is a tribute to the soundness of Comte's views that sociology should now take them for granted. Still, it might be asked: Why should it be necessary to single out observation as a method? It was necessary in order to oppose the previous tendencies for social theorizing to be theologically or metaphysically speculative and incapable of verification by empirical observation. But Comte had no time, either, for 'mindless empiricism'.

No real observation of any kind of phenomena is possible, except in as far as it is first directed, and finally interpreted, by some theory. (*Pos. Phil.*, vol. 2, p. 242)

Comte was not unaware of the difficulties this dual requirement would present to sociology.

I am not blind to the vast difficulty which this requisition imposes on the institution of positive sociology, obliging us to create at once, so to speak, observations and laws, on account of their indispensable connection, placing us in a sort of vicious circle, from which we can issue only by employing in the first instance materials which are badly elaborated, and doctrines which are ill-conceived. (*Pos. Phil.*, vol. 2, p. 243)

Nevertheless, an attempt had to be made. Facts were plentiful, it was their interconnection, and so their meaning, that could only be deduced by putting forward hypotheses relating them to laws of interconnection in social statics and to laws of development in social dynamics.

Similarly, in the second method, although it might seem as though experimentation was impossible for sociology, indirect experimentation (as distinct from the direct experiments in science like chemistry) was feasible. It consisted of an approach analogical to the comparison of pathological and normal cases in biology. Having posited a normal type as regards interconnection and succession of phenomena, the sociologist should then examine exceptions to this and seek to verify and improve his theory of the relations of co-existence and succession on the basis of the knowledge gained about the operations of the deviant case. This method could be used, for example, in analysing the exceptional factors operating in a revolutionary situation or with regard to a disastrous political policy.

The third method, comparison, could be employed in various ways. It could, for instance, be used to compare human society with the social state of the lower animals. This comparison obviously has its limitations, as Comte points out, but he suggests some useful benefits (*Pos Phil.*, vol. 2, pp. 247–9). The two main types of comparison, however, are the comparison of different co-existing states of human society so as to disclose different stages of evolution all at once, and comparison of societies at different consecutive stages in history. The purpose of these methods is to refine and verify laws of social interconnection and development.

Finally, Comte shows that he was aware of the difficulties that awaited the new science, and he issues a warning to those who might expect too much from their favourite methodologies— whether mathematical, historical, or what ever:

> The most perfect methods may, however, be rendered deceptive by misuse: and this we must bear in mind. We have seen that mathematical analysis itself may betray us into substituting signs for ideas, and that it conceals inanity of conception under imposing verbiage. The difficulty in the case of the historical method in sociology is in applying it, on account of the extreme complexity of the materials we have to deal with. (*Pos. Phil.*, vol. 2, p. 255)

Comte's Sociology of Sociology

The most remarkable and unique contribution made by Comte to the founding of sociology was his analysis of the social and intellectual developments that had made possible and necessary the emergence of the new discipline. He provided a sociology of sociology that was never matched by any of his contemporaries and has seldom been equalled since. At the same time he firmly instituted an approach to self-analysis by the discipline that is not found in any of the other social sciences—much to their detriment.

In presenting a history of social science in Book VI of his *Positive Philosophy*, Comte takes as an example of the convergence of the social and intellectual conditions necessary for the constitution of sociology, the case of the idea of progress. First of all he points out that, because of the complex and unique nature of social phenomena, it was impossible for sociology to develop until simpler sciences had become established, and also until a sufficiently wide range of social facts had been accumulated. Secondly, in addition to these intellectual developments, it was also necessary for certain facilitating social conditions to exist:

> It was not, in fact, till modern political revolutions, and especially the French, had proved the insufficiency of the old political system for the social needs of the age that the great idea of progress could acquire sufficient firmness, distinctness and generality, to serve a scientific purpose. (*Pos. Phil.*, vol. 2, pp. 194–5)

He also discusses the mutual interaction of science and industry as two key elements—theoretical and practical—in preparing the way for the political revolution and the ensuing development of sociology:

> Thus the two elements of modern civilization, the theoretic and the practical, tended separately to direct the revolution of the West. If we now consider their joint effect, we observe how each strengthened the proper action of the other, both in the positive and in the negative fields of operation. The natural affinity between the scientific spirit and industrial life, manifested itself gradually during their simultaneous career, which was preparing and even announcing their normal co-operation. Whilst science tended to systematize industry, industry gave to science an assumed object, in following which it gained a spontaneous discipline well qualified to check useless speculations. (*Pos. Phil.*, vol. 3, p. 442)

Comte provides an extensive account of the ways in which the revolution in the West, culminating in the French Revolution, paved the way for the development of positivism, social science, and sociology in particular. The whole of chapter 2 of the *System of Positive Polity* is given over to this subject, as its title indicates: 'The social aspect of positivism, as shown by its connection with the general revolutionary movement of western Europe.' Leaving aside his detailed analyses, the convergence of the three essential elements which formed the basis for the new discipline (a theory of order, a theory of progress, and a synthesizing conception based on developments in the other sciences) are summarized in relation to the revolution in one short passage:

> Now up to the time of the revolution, political development, on which the principal argument for the theory of progress must always be based, corresponded in its imperfection to the incapacity of the scientific spirit to frame the theory of it. A century ago, thinkers of the greatest eminence were unable to conceive of a really continuous progression; and humanity, as they thought, was destined to move in circles or in oscillations. But under the influence of the revolution a real sense of human development has arisen spontaneously and with more or less result, in minds of the most ordinary cast: first in France, and subsequently throughout the whole of western Europe. In this respect the crisis has been most salutary; it has given us that mental audacity as well as strength without which the conception could never have arisen. This conception is the basis of social science and therefore of all Positive Philosophy; since it is only from the social aspect that Positive Philosophy admits of being viewed as a connected whole. Without the theory of Progress, the theory of Order, even supposing it could be formed, would be inadequate as a basis for Sociology. It is essential that the two should be combined. The very fact that Progress, however viewed, is nothing but the development of Order, shows that Order cannot be fully manifested without Progress. The dependence of Positivism upon the French Revolution may now be understood more clearly. Nor was it by a merely fortuitous coincidence that by this time the introductory course of scientific knowledge by which the mind is prepared for Positivism should have been sufficiently completed. (*Pos. Pol.*, vol. 1, pp. 49–50)

In addition to providing detailed accounts of relationships between social conditions and the development of sociology,

Comte also pioneered the general field of the sociology of knowledge. He laid down as a fundamental premise of this sub-discipline recognition of 'the subordination of thought to social influences'.

> That is to say, the laws of thoughts can only be understood by the aid of sociology ... The direct proof of it may be found in the acknowledged influence which language exerts over all other intellectual operations. For no one can doubt how much language depends on the development of society ...
> (*Pos. Pol.*, vol. 2, p. 313)

He adds that mental action depends on social support or feedback, a notion that was to form the basis of Max Weber's social action theory, which has been influential in recent sociology of knowledge, but without there being any recognition of Comte's original statement of it:

> For Observation as for Reflection, each mind constantly depends on others to furnish it with materials on which to verify its results. In the morbid effect which the insane exert over the physicians devoting themselves to their care, we may see how the mind is shaken by earnestness of conviction, even when we know it to be mistaken. The boldest innovator rarely has full belief in his own discoveries, until they have won some amount of willing acceptance. (*Pos. Pol.*, vol. 2, p. 314)

There are many other passages and whole chapters on the relations between material, social and intellectual developments, some of which deal directly with conditions affecting the development of positive philosophy and sociology. He showed that the time was ripe for sociology to emerge both as regards prior intellectual developments and as a result of social pressures deriving principally from the French and Industrial Revolutions.

Criticisms

Two major criticisms need to be dealt with in presenting an account of Comte's sociology. The first is that which tends to devalue Comte's work because of his personal oddities and his elaborate and sometimes ludicrous schemes for a secular religion. The second criticism is directed against what is taken to be an inappropriate notion of science as it relates to sociology.

As far as the first criticism is concerned, I have never been able to see what relevance his personal oddities have in forming a judgment about the value of his sociological work. Some commentators seem to find more to say about his personal life than about his sociology. His love life and the fact that his wife Caroline was a former prostitute may excite the imagination of those who are more interested in biography than sociology, but it is difficult to see how any of this had the remotest impact on the *Cours de Philosophie Positive*. There is a case for showing that Comte's platonic love for Clothilde de Vaux, and the fact that she died of tuberculosis after only a year of the affair, caused him to elevate love and the affective side of life to the highest position in the *Système de politique positive*, but the sections which deal with such matters can be clearly distinguished from those parts in which he is still developing his account of the specific nature of sociology and its methods along the lines laid down in the *Cours de Philosophie Positive*, and even earlier in the *Prospectus des travaux scientifiques nécessaires pour réorganiser la Société* of 1822.[21]

There is a pronounced difference between the main emphases and ethos of the *Cours de philosophie positive* and the *Système de politique positive*, although Comte was anxious to persuade his readers otherwise. From the time of their first publication, the most perceptive and sympathetic readers of Comte's work, such as John Stuart Mill, remarked on the obvious differences. Whereas the first work is a cautious and relatively modest attempt to outline the subject area and methods of sociology and to trace its emergence as a discipline, the second great *opus* is more concerned overall with applying sociology and other sciences to preparing the way for the advent of the Religion of Humanity. This should not be taken as a dismissal of much that is of value in the later work. Very often Comte restates or develops points that he had made in his earlier work, and these subsequent developments add a great deal to our understanding of his sociology. But it is when Comte is tempted into trying to apply the infant discipline to tasks beyond its underdeveloped capacities, that the *Système de politique positive* begins to strain our credulity. It is ironic that Comte should have fallen into this trap, for it was one that he himself had warned against in his earlier writings:

> In its nascent state every science is implicated with its
> corresponding art; and remains implicated with it, as we have
> seen, the longer in proportion to the complexity of the
> phenomena concerned. If biological science, which is more
> advanced than social, is still too closely connected with the
> medical art, as we have seen that it is, we cannot be surprised

that men are insensible to the value of all social speculations which are not immediately connected with practical affairs. (*Pos. Phil.*, vol. 2, p. 139)

The other major criticism of Comte's sociology is directed against his view of the scientific character of sociology, and in particular his positivism. Unfortunately there is a great deal of confusion over the meaning of the term positivism and 'positivist sociology'. It derives from a mistaken notion that Comte failed to recognize that the actions of man in society could not be explained by the paradigms and methods appropriate to the natural sciences. Sometimes the charge is that positivist sociology must involve ignoring man's 'human' characteristics (such as his capacity for reflecting on his own motives, thoughts and actions) and that it must take a view of man as totally determined in his behaviour by forces beyond his control. None of this is true, and Comte's whole discussion of sociology's place in the hierarchy of sciences is devoted to showing the proper domains and distinctions between the study of the non-human and the human. The positive philosophy avoids exclusively 'materialist' or 'spiritualist' explanations.

Positive science was for a long time limited to the simplest subjects; it could not reach the highest except by a natural series of intermediate steps. As each of these steps is taken the student is apt to be influenced too strongly by the methods and results of the preceding stage. (*Pos. Pol.*, vol. 1, p. 39)

But far from positivism being such as to perpetuate or condoning that error, it provides the only way of combating it. It does this by establishing 'the encyclopedic scale, in which each science retains its own proper sphere of induction, while deductively it remains subordinate to the science which precedes it' (*Pos. Pol.*, vol. 1, p. 41). As the more 'special' phenomena depend upon the more general, it is to be expected that each science will exercise certain deductive influences upon those which follow it in the scale, that is, they will be influenced by its generalizations. But in order that the new science may assert the special character of its own subject-matter and make inductions specific to that, it must 'undergo a long struggle against the encroachments of the one preceding it' (*Pos. Pol.*, vol. 1, p. 39). Comte gives as an example the influence of biology upon sociology. The biologists often attempt to explain sociological facts by reference to race, for example, and show themselves ignorant of fundamental laws of sociology which can only be discovered by direct inductions from history (*Pos. Pol.*, vol. 1, p. 40).

Although Comte seldom discusses psychology as a separate science, he often includes parts of it in physiology/biology, and so it too can only explain certain aspects of man's behaviour, and any wider claim must be resisted. When it comes to explaining *social* phenomena, individual psychology must be supplemented by a sociology of interaction and of historical development:

> In all social phenomena we perceive the working of the physiological laws of the individual; and moreover something which modifies their effects, and which belongs to the influence of individuals over each other—singularly complicated in the case of the human race by the influence of generations on their successors. (*Pos. Phil.*, vol. 1, p. 29)

These factors set limits to the options and variations which can occur. But this view of laws of social phenomena in terms of limits is not a crude determinism (or 'fatalism' as Comte calls it) such as some critics have attributed to Comte's positivist sociology. Here too the hierarchy of the sciences shows that the subject-matter of the higher sciences is less determined, more modifiable and, in the case of human beings especially, permits intervention to guide the course of events.

Comte's positivist sociology does not have any of the inevitable 'dehumanizing' consequences attributed to it by those who, knowing little of what he actually wrote, simply use him as a straw-man, to be knocked down so that some other new perspective can be put in its place. There is little that could be objected to in Comte's careful relating of sociology to the natural sciences, on the one hand, which tell us about man's environment and his own physical constitution, and to history, on the other hand, which enables us to discover principles or trends in the development of societies. The one area that Comte did neglect was that of face-to-face interaction and social psychology, and this was to a large degree due to his critical attitude towards the inadequate psychology prevailing at the time.

One group of present-day sociologists who have considered themselves in opposition to 'positivist sociology' are those who derive inspiration from the phenomenological school of philosophy. But, here too, the references to 'positivism' do little justice to what Comte intended. Alfred Schultz, who provided perhaps the strongest inspiration for phenomenology in sociology, had a better appreciation of the similarities between Comte's sociology of knowledge and his own ideas and those of another prominent exponent of phenomenology, Max Scheler. Schutz's references to Comte and Scheler on the sociology of knowledge set out very well the real position which Comte adopted on the interrelationship between ideas and material factors, and on the issue of determinism and social development.

It is worth quoting Schutz in concluding this section on the criticisms of Comte, because the account which he gives is true to the main emphases of Comte's sociology, and illustrates not only its topicality, but also its soundness and continuing relevance. Schutz was discussing the influence of philosophical ideas upon the self-interpretation of the group, and vice versa. Like Comte, he asserts that philosophical or theological systems have a considerable influence on the meaning structure of the world-taken-for-granted. He then draws on Scheler and Comte to explain the interrelationship of material factors (*Realfactoren*, such as race, geopolitical structure, political power relationships, conditions of economic production) and ideas (*Idealfactoren*). Beginning with a reference to Scheler (although it becomes clear that it holds equally for Comte), he states:

> According to this philosopher, an idea or a philosophy or even a scientific concept can become effective within the social reality only if the *Realfactoren*—corresponding in our terminology to the structure of the social group as interpreted by the group itself—are ready for it. The *Realfactoren* open and close, so to speak, the sluice gates through which the stream of *Idealfactoren* has to pass. On the other hand, the blind material forces can be guided and directed by the ideal factors. If, according to Comte the history of the material factors is characterized by a *fatalité modifiable*, the stream of ideal factors exhibits a *liberté modifiable*, namely, a freedom that is conditioned in its translation into social reality by the resistance of the material factors.[22]

It is hard to imagine a better re-statement of Comte's sociological concerns, emphasizing the historical method, theories of development, the indispensability of taking account of the *total social phenomenon* and the interrelationships of the factors within it, and the centrality of the sociology of knowledge.

Influence on the Development of Sociology

Having examined some of the criticisms of Comte's sociology, which have limited acceptance of his work and so reduced his influence, it remains to look at his positive influence on the development of sociology. Much of what Comte outlined as the proper subject-matter and methods of sociology has been accepted by the discipline and taken for granted, so much so that it is often not attributed to Comte. The fact that Comte often does not receive the credit which is his due is of no great importance in itself. He himself 'far from claiming any originality not really belonging to him, was eager to connect his own most original thoughts with every germ of anything similar which he observed in previous thinkers'.[23] The comment is John Stuart Mill's, and it points out the real significance of Comte and his work. Comte was important in the foundation of sociology because he brought together from diverse sources all the ideas that could be of value in constructing such a social science, and his achievement influenced others who played a major role in the subsequent development of sociology. He influenced the development of Anglo-American sociology through the mediation of such key figures as John Stuart Mill, Herbert Spencer and Lester F. Ward; and French sociology, primarily through Émile Durkheim.

We have already examined the argument about the relative weights of the influence of Saint-Simon and Comte on Durkheim's sociology. Durkheim's own writings state quite clearly that he was greatly influenced by both, but when he comes to discuss explicitly the subject-matter, logic and methods of sociology in *The Rules of Sociological Method,* he is chiefly concerned with Comte's statement on these matters, closely followed by those of Spencer and Mill. There can be no doubt that he regarded the foundation of the discipline as having been laid down by Comte, and like many others of the first generation of university sociologists, he looked to Comte, Mill and Spencer as the chief architects of that discipline. A similar picture emerges if one examines the work of Lester Ward (1841–1913), an American contemporary of Durkheim's, who was the first systematic sociologist in America, and developed a sociology which synthesized the ideas of Comte and Spencer.

What then was Comte's relationship to his two contemporaries, Spencer and Mill? There is no difficulty in discovering the nature of the influence he exerted on Mill because Mill wrote extensively on that subject and corresponded freely with Comte for several years.[24] It is quite different with Spencer who, unlike Comte and Mill, was extremely reluctant to acknowledge intellectual debts.

Mill testified to the early and profound influence that Comte's writings had on his thought, when he began their correspondence on 8 November 1841, by stating:

> It was in 1828, Sir, that I first read your small *Traité de politique positive*; and the experience of reading it gave my ideas a serious jolt which, along with other causes, though of far greater importance than them, finally determined me to break with the Benthamite section of the revolutionary school in which I was brought up, and into which I can almost say I was born . . . Since the time when I became aware of the first outlines of your sociological ideas, I believe I can say that the seeds sown by that small work have not lain idle in my mind.[25]

By the time Mill had read the sixth volume of the *Cours de philosophie positive* in 1842 he was led to inform Comte that he regarded him as the founder of sociology:

> This volume is the proper conclusion to a work which is necessarily unique in the development of humanity, for even supposing that you had not laid the first fundamental bases of the positive sociological doctrine you would still remain the founder of the true sociological ethos in all that is most characteristic of it and, as a result, that of the definitive systematization of human knowledge.[26]

Relations between the two men cooled in later years and Mill found his secondary disagreements with Comte's views assuming greater proportions when he read the *Système de politique positive*. The tragedy of the relationship was that the two men were at such different stages in their development when it started that there was little chance of a real mutual collaboration developing. The French sociologist, Lucien Levy-Bruhl, has pointed out that at the same time that Mill and Comte were entering into correspondence, Comte was writing to his friend Valat that 'the age for discussion is now over for me'.[27] He was 43 years old, eight years older than Mill, and his mind was turning away from laying the foundations of a new intellectual discipline towards the implementation of schemes for social re-organization.

Although Comte and Mill were similar in their aptitude for unravelling the logic of the sciences, Comte had a closer affinity to Spencer in his role as a system builder. Unlike Comte and Spencer, Mill always had more of a collection of 'opinions' than a closed and complete system. Mill once suggested to Comte that they should discuss their 'opinions' on various subjects. But Comte had no 'opinions', in the sense which Mill intended. He had a body of doctrine, a system. He constructed his system expressly in order to put an end to the ebb and flow of shifting 'opinions', which he believed had given rise to the anarchy which characterized society after the old certainties had been undermined by the critical philosophies of the Enlightment, and when the political and industrial revolutions had overthrown established authorities and hierarchies.

It was because of this comprehensive system-building tendency that, for a short while in the nineteenth century, Comte and Spencer enjoyed reputations almost as cult figures. Their systems attracted adherents all over the world. They influenced governments as well as individuals in all classes of society. Spencer had the wider reputation: hundreds of thousands of copies of his books were sold in America, for instance, and his social evolutionary doctrines were an acknowledged pressure on legislation there.[28] But Comte too had his teachings widely disseminated, partly through the writings of those influenced by him and in magazine articles and tracts. There were also positivist groups or churches in several countries, and in Brazil positivism even became the quasi-official doctrine of the state, and Comte's doctrines were taught in the schools.

The widespread appeal of the intellectual systems of Comte and Spencer in the nineteenth century was due to the fact that they promised to bring order to what seemed to be intellectual and social chaos. The unification of knowledge and the discovery of laws of man and society appeared to be within reach in view of the impressive progress made by the natural sciences. Although Spencer's synthetic philosophy eclipsed Comte's positive philosophy and swept all before it because of the affinity of Spencer's social evolutionary theory with Darwin's theory of evolution, in the long term Comte's specifically sociological teachings have proved sounder than Spencer's.

The reasons for Comte's superiority over Spencer in sociology were revealed in the dispute which they had over the classification (or hierarchy) of the sciences. And the judgment in favour of Comte was delivered in the most delicate, but firm fashion by Mill. There was a strong suspicion among their contemporaries that Spencer's sociology had been derived in some key aspects from the earlier writings of Comte, and Spencer went to great lengths to deny this.[29] Spencer's arguments were set out in a publication entitled, *The Classification of the Sciences to which are added Reasons for Dissenting from the Philosophy of M. Comte* (1864). Mill in turn gave his judgment in a series of articles in the *West-*

minster Review in 1865.[30] He pronounced that Spencer 'does scant justice to what he rejects' in Comte, and implied that Spencer was ill-informed on the subject.

The dispute is significant because, apart from the issue of who influenced whom, it reveals a crucial difference in the foundations of sociology as laid down by Comte and Spencer. Granted that both were system-builders and synthesizers at a time when such enterprises were socially desired, we are still left with the question of what there was of permanent value to sociology once the systems became outmoded or undermined by the accumulation of deviant findings. The crucial difference between the classifications of the sciences of Comte and Spencer, and so also between their sociologies, was that Comte rejected the notion of discovering a uniform law or single method to explain all phenomena. While Comte sought to apply a theory of intellectual and historical evolution to the development of society, Spencer's sweeping law of evolution claimed to explain the nature and course of the universe and everything in it. For Comte this was inadequate and misleading for understanding man and society when what was required was an appreciation of *historical* laws of co-existence and development.

And so we are left with the essential merit of Comte's contribution to the founding of sociology. It was his lasting achievement to have staked out a claim for a social science which, both in the definition of its subject-matter and its proper methods of study, would respect the position of humanity as an integral part of the world of nature and yet unique in that world. Furthermore, whereas Spencer's sociology led to the conclusion that nothing could be done to improve society, Comte's sociology encourages us to believe that—on the basis of knowledge we are able to establish—enlightened and informed social action can hasten the movement of society towards a more just and harmonious state.

NOTES AND REFERENCES

1. The form of this question has a special significance for the history of sociology. Talcott Parsons' influential account of the development of sociology begins with the quotation: 'Who now reads Spencer? . . . We have evolved beyond Spencer.' According to Parsons, Comte and Spencer represented an outdated 'mechanistic positivism' which had been superseded by a 'voluntaristic theory of action' more appropriate to the sociological study of social action. Cf. T. Parsons, *The Structure of Social Action*, 2 volumes, New York: Free Press, paperback edn (1968), pp. 3, 11 and 293.

2. The title 'founder-in-chief' was bestowed on Comte in an article commemorating the centenary of Comte's invention of the term 'Sociology'. Cf. Frank Hankins, 'A Comtean Centenary: Invention of the Term "Sociology"', in *American Sociological Review* (1939), **4**, 16.

3. S. Andreski (ed.), *Herbert Spencer: The Principles of Sociology*, London: Macmillan (1969), p. xii.

4. J. D. Y. Peel, *Herbert Spencer: The Evolution of a Sociologist*, London: Heinemann (1971), p. x.

5. Comte dropped the term 'social physics' because of what he considered to be its misleading use by the Belgian statistician, Adolphe Quetelet (1796–1874), in a book published in 1835, *On Man and the Development of Human Faculties: An Essay on Social Physics*.

6. Alvin W. Gouldner, Introductory Essay to Emile Durkheim, *Socialism*, New York: Collier Books (1962), pp. 11–12.

7. Durkheim, *op. cit.*, p. 146.

8. Émile Durkheim, *The Rules of Sociological Method*, New York: Free Press, paperback edn (1964), p. lix. First published in French in 1895.

9. *Ibid.*

10. Saint-Simon was more religious than socialist in his later writings, which was one reason why Comte broke with him.

11. Durkheim, *Socialism*, p. 146.

12. Henri Gouhier, *Le Jeunesse d'Auguste Comte*, 3 volumes, Paris: Vrin (1933–41), vol. 1, p. 146.

13. Comte Henri de Saint-Simon (1760–1825), French aristocrat and utopian socialist, prolific writer on social matters.

14. Letter to d'Eichtal, 1 May 1824, quoted in Pierre Arnaud, *Sociologie de Comte*, Paris: Presses Universitaires de France (1969), p. 63.

15. Quoted in Durkheim, *Socialism*, p. 144.

16. *Ibid.*

17. The Marquis de Condorcet (1743–94), in his book *Historical Essay on the Progress of Human Reason* (1794), set forward a theory of human progress and held out the possibility of a science which might foresee the future progress of mankind and so accelerate and direct it.

18. Jacques Turgot (1727–81), a protagonist of progress, wrote that man's intellectual development passed through three stages: anthropomorphism; a period of explanation positing abstract essences; and scientific explanation.

19. Comte Joseph Marie de Maistre (1753–1821), leader of post-revolutionary French traditionalists, author of *Considerations on France* (1796) and *Essay on the Generative Principle of Political Constitutions* (1814).

20. Louis Gabriel Ambroise Vicomte de Bonald (1754–1840), author of *Theory of Political and Religious Authority in Civil Society* (1796) and *Primitive Legislation* (1802).

21. This essay was first published in a volume by Saint-Simon entitled *Suite des travaux ayant pour objet de fonder le système industriel* (1822); the fact that he still held to it as his fundamental and unchanged statement of his doctrine was specifically affirmed by Comte when he republished it as an Appendix in vol. 4 of the *Système de politique positive* under the title *Plan des travaux scientifiques nécessaires pour réorganiser la Société*.

22. A. Schutz, *Collected Papers*, 3 volumes, The Hague: Martinus Nijhoff (1964), vol. 2, p. 249.

23. John Stuart Mill, *Auguste Comte and Positivism*, London: N. Trübner (1865), pp. 5–6.

24. Specially translated excerpts from that correspondence are included on pp. 193–210 of this book.

25. *Lettres Inédites de John Stuart Mill à Auguste Comte avec les Responses de Comte*, Paris: Alcan (1899), p. 2.

26. *Lettres Inédites . . .*, p. 119, letter dated 23 October 1842.

27. Quoted by Levy-Bruhl, in his Introduction to the *Lettres Inédites . . .*, p. xii.

28. Cf. R. Hofstadter, *Social Darwinism in American Thought*, Boston (1955 edn), pp. 31–50.

29. Not very convincingly according to some commentators. Cf. the review of the evidence in S. Eisen, 'Herbert Spencer and the Spectre of Comte' in *The Journal of British Studies* (1967), **7**, 48–67.

30. Published in J. S. Mill, *Auguste Comte and Positivism*, London: N. Trübner (1865).

I   Philosophy, Science and Sociology

View of the Nature and Importance of the Positive Philosophy*

A general statement of any system of philosophy may be either a sketch of a doctrine to be established, or a summary of a doctrine already established. If greater value belongs to the last, the first is still important, as characterizing from its origin the subject to be treated. In a case like the present, where the proposed study is vast and hitherto indeterminate, it is especially important that the field of research should be marked out with all possible accuracy. For this purpose, I will glance at the considerations which have originated this work, and which will be fully elaborated in the course of it.

In order to understand the true value and character of the positive philosophy, we must take a brief general view of the progressive course of the human mind, regarded as a whole; for no conception can be understood otherwise than through its history.

Law of human progress

From the study of the development of human intelligence, in all directions, and through all times, the discovery arises of a great fundamental law, to which it is necessarily subject, and which has a solid foundation of proof, both in the facts of our organization and in our historical experience. The law is this: that each of our leading conceptions—each branch of our knowledge—passes successively through three different theoretical conditions: the theological, or fictitious; the metaphysical, or abstract; and the scientific, or positive. In other words, the human mind, by its nature, employs in its progress three methods of philosophizing, the character of which is essentially different, and even radically opposed: viz., the theological method, the metaphysical and the positive. Hence arise three philosophies, or general systems of conceptions on the aggregate of phenomena, each of which excludes the others. The first is the necessary point of departure of the human understanding; and the third is its fixed and definitive state. The second is merely a state of transition.

First stage

In the theological state, the human mind, seeking the essential nature of beings, the first and final causes (the origin and purpose) of all effects—in short, absolute knowledge—supposes all

* Extracts from *Pos. Phil.*, vol. 1, pp. 1–35.

phenomena to be produced by the immediate action of super-natural beings.

Second stage

In the metaphysical state, which is only a modification of the first, the mind supposes, instead of supernatural beings, abstract forces, veritable entities (that is, personified abstractions) inherent in all beings, and capable of producing all phenomena. What is called the explanation of phenomena is, in this stage, a mere reference of each to its proper entity.

Third stage

In the final, the positive state, the mind has given over the vain search after absolute notions, the origin and destination of the universe, and the causes of phenomena, and applies itself to the study of their laws—that is, their invariable relations of succession and resemblance. Reasoning and observation, duly combined, are the means of this knowledge. What is now understood when we speak of an explanation of facts is simply the establishment of a connection between single phenomena and some general facts, the number of which continually diminishes with the progress of science.

Ultimate point of each

The theological system arrived at the highest perfection of which it is capable when it substituted the providential action of a single being for the varied operations of the numerous divinities which had been before imagined. In the same way, in the last stage of the metaphysical system, men substitute one great entity (nature) as the cause of all phenomena, instead of the multitude of entities at first supposed. In the same way, again, the ultimate perfection of the positive system would be (if such perfection could be hoped for) to represent all phenomena as particular aspects of a single general fact, such as gravitation, for instance.

The importance of the working of this general law will be established hereafter. At present, it must suffice to point out some of the grounds of it.

Evidences of the law

There is no science which, having attained the positive stage, does not bear marks of having passed through the others. Some time since it was (whatever it might be) composed, as we can now perceive, of metaphysical abstractions, and, further back in the course of time, it took its form from theological conceptions. We shall have only too much occasion to see, as we proceed, that our most advanced sciences still bear very evident marks of the two earlier periods through which they have passed.

Actual

The progress of the individual mind is not only an illustration, but an indirect evidence of that of the general mind. The point of departure of the individual and of the race being the same, the phases of the mind of a man correspond to the epochs of the mind of the race. Now, each of us is aware, if he looks back upon his own history, that he was a theologian in his childhood, a metaphysician in his youth, and a natural philosopher in his manhood. All men who are up to their age can verify this for themselves.

Besides the observation of facts, we have theoretical reasons in support of this law.

Theoretical

The most important of these reasons arises from the necessity that always exists for some theory to which to refer our facts, combined with the clear impossibility that, at the outset of human knowledge, men could have formed theories out of the observation of facts. All good intellects have repeated, since Bacon's time, that there can be no real knowledge but that which is based on observed facts. This is incontestible, in our present advanced stage; but, if we look back to the primitive stage of human knowledge, we shall see that it must have been otherwise then. If it is true that every theory must be based upon observed facts, it is equally true that facts cannot be observed without the guidance of some theory. Without such guidance, our facts would be desultory and fruitless; we could not retain them: for the most part we could not even perceive them.

Thus, between the necessity of observing facts in order to form a theory, and having a theory in order to observe facts, the human mind would have been entangled in a vicious circle, but for the natural opening afforded by theological conceptions. This is the fundamental reason for the theological character of the primitive philosophy. This necessity is confirmed by the perfect suitability of the theological philosophy to the earliest researches of the human mind. It is remarkable that the most inaccessible questions —those of the nature of beings, and the origin and purpose of phenomena—should be the first to occur in a primitive state, while those which are really within our reach are regarded as almost unworthy of serious study. The reason is evident enough: that experience alone can teach us the measure of our powers; and if men had not begun by an exaggerated estimate of what they can do, they would never have done all that they are capable of. Our organization requires this. At such a period there could have been no reception of a positive philosophy, whose function is to discover the laws of phenomena, and whose leading characteristic it is to regard as interdicted to human reason those sublime mysteries which theology explains, even to their minutest details, with the most attractive facility. It is just so under a practical view of the nature of the researches with which men first occupied themselves. Such inquiries offered the powerful charm of unlimited empire over the external world, a world destined wholly for our use, and involved in every way with our existence. The theological philosophy, presenting this view, administered exactly the stimulus necessary to incite the human mind to the irksome labour without which it could make no progress. We can now scarcely conceive of such a state of things, our reason having become sufficiently mature to enter upon laborious scientific researches, without needing any such stimulus as wrought upon the imaginations of astrologers and alchemists. We have motive enough in the hope of discovering the laws of phenomena, with a view to the confirmation or rejection of a theory. But it could not be so in the earliest days; and it is to the chimeras of astrology and alchemy that we owe the long series of observations and experiments on which our positive science is based. Kepler felt this on behalf of astronomy, and Berthollet on behalf of chemistry. Thus was a spontaneous philosophy, the theological, the only possible beginning, method and provisional system, out of which the positive philosophy could grow. It is easy, after this, to perceive how metaphysical methods and doctrines must have afforded the means of transition from the one to the other.

The human understanding, slow in its advance, could not step at once from the theological into the positive philosophy. The two are so radically opposed, that an intermediate system of conceptions has been necessary to render the transition possible. It is only in doing this, that metaphysical conceptions have any utility whatever. In contemplating phenomena, men substitute for supernatural direction a corresponding entity. This entity may have been supposed to be derived from the supernatural action: but it is more easily lost sight of, leaving attention free for the facts themselves, till, at length, metaphysical agents have ceased to be anything more than the abstract names of phenomena. It is not easy to say by what other process than this our minds could have passed from supernatural considerations to natural; from the theological system to the positive.

The law of human development being thus established, let us consider what is the proper nature of the positive philosophy.

Character of the positive philosophy

As we have seen, the first characteristic of the positive philosophy is that it regards all phenomena as subjected to invariable natural *laws*. Our business is—seeing how vain is any research into what are called *causes*, whether first or final—to pursue an accurate discovery of these laws, with a view to reducing them to the smallest possible number. By speculating upon causes, we could solve no difficulty about origin and purpose. Our real business is to analyse accurately the circumstances of phenomena, and to connect them by the natural relations of succession and resemblance. The best illustration of this is in the case of the doctrine of gravitation. We say that the general phenomena of the universe are *explained* by it, because it connects under one head the whole immense variety of astronomical facts . . .

History of the positive philosophy

Before ascertaining the stage which the positive philosophy has reached, we must bear in mind that the different kinds of our knowledge have passed through the three stages of progress at different rates, and have not therefore arrived at the same time. The rate of advance depends on the nature of the knowledge in question, so distinctly that, as we shall see hereafter, this consideration constitutes an accessory to the fundamental law of progress. Any kind of knowledge reaches the positive stage early in proportion to its generality, simplicity, and independence of other departments. Astronomical science, which is above all made up of facts that are general, simple, and independent of other sciences, arrived first; then terrestrial physics; then chemistry; and, at length, physiology.

It is difficult to assign any precise date to this revolution in science. It may be said, like everything else, to have been always going on; and especially since the labours of Aristotle and the school of Alexandria; and then from the introduction of natural science into the west of Europe by the Arabs. But, if we must fix upon some marked period, to serve as a rallying point, it must be that, about two centuries ago, when the human mind was astir under the precepts of Bacon, the conceptions of Descartes, and the discoveries of Galileo. Then it was that the spirit of the positive philosophy rose up in opposition to that of the superstitious and scholastic systems which had hitherto obscured the true character of all science. Since that date, the progress of the positive philosophy, and the decline of the other two, have been so marked that no rational mind now doubts that the revolution is destined to go on to its completion—every branch of knowledge being, sooner or later, brought within the operation of positive philosophy. This is not yet the case. Some are still lying outside: and not till they are brought in will the positive philosophy possess that character of universality which is necessary to its definite constitution.

New department of positive philosophy

In mentioning just now the four principal categories of phenomena —astronomical, physical, chemical and physiological—there was an omission which will have been noticed. Nothing was said of social phenomena. Though involved with the physiological, social phenomena demand a distinct classification, both on account of their importance and of their difficulty. They are the most individual, the most complicated, the most dependent on all others; and therefore they must be the latest—even if they had no special obstacle to encounter. This branch of science has not hitherto entered into the domain of positive philosophy. Theological and metaphysical methods, exploded in other departments, are as yet exclusively applied, both in the way of inquiry and discussion, in all treatment of social subjects, though the best minds are heartily weary of eternal disputes about divine right and the sovereignty of the people. This is the great, while it is evidently the only gap which has to be filled, to constitute, solid and entire, the positive philosophy. Now that the human mind has grasped celestial and terrestrial physics, mechanical and chemical and organic physics, both vegetable and animal, there remains one science, to fill up the series of sciences of observation—social physics. This is what men have now most need of: and this it is the principal aim of the present work to establish.

Social physics

It would be absurd to pretend to offer this new science at once in a complete state. Others, less new, are in very unequal conditions of forwardness. But the same character of positivity which is impressed on all the others will be shown to belong to this. This once done, the philosophical system of the moderns will be in fact complete, as there will then be no phenomenon which does not naturally enter into some one of the five great categories. All our fundamental conceptions having become homeogeneous, the positive state will be fully established. It can never again change its character, though it will be for ever in course of development by additions of new knowledge. Having acquired the character of universality which has hitherto been the only advantage resting with the two preceding systems, it will supersede them by its natural superiority, and leave to them only an historical existence.

Secondary aim of this work

We have stated the special aim of this work. Its secondary and general aim is this: to review what has been effected in the sciences, in order to show that they are not radically separate, but all branches from the same trunk. If we had confined ourselves to the first and special object of the work, we should have produced merely a study of social physics: whereas, in introducing the second and general, we offer a study of positive philosophy, passing in review all the positive sciences already formed.

The purpose of this work is not to give an account of the natural sciences. Besides that it would be endless, and that it would require a scientific preparation such as no one man possesses, it would be apart from our object, which is to go through a course of not positive science, but positive philosophy. We have only to consider each fundamental science in its relation to the whole positive system, and to the spirit which characterizes it; that is, with regard to its methods and its chief results.

The two aims, though distinct, are inseparable; for, on the one hand, there can be no positive philosophy without a basis of social science, without which it could not be all-comprehensive; and, on the other hand, we could not pursue social science without having been prepared by the study of phenomena less complicated than those of society, and furnished with a knowledge of laws and anterior facts which have a bearing upon social science. Though the fundamental sciences are not all equally interesting to ordinary minds, there is no one of them that can be neglected in an inquiry like the present; and, in the eye of philosophy, all are of equal value to human welfare. Even those which appear the least interesting have their own value, either on account of the perfection of their methods, or as being the necessary basis of all the others.

Speciality

Lest it should be supposed that our course will lead us into a wilderness of such special studies as are at present the bane of a true positive philosophy, we will briefly advert to the existing prevalence of such special pursuit. In the primitive state of human knowledge there is no regular division of intellectual labour. Every student cultivates all the sciences. As knowledge accrues, the sciences part off; and students devote themselves each to some one branch. It is owing to this division of employment, and concentration of whole minds upon a single department, that science has made so prodigious an advance in modern times; and the perfection of this division is one of the most important characteristics of the positive philosophy. But, while admitting all the merits of this change, we cannot be blind to the eminent disadvantages which arise from the limitation of minds to a particular study. It is inevitable that each should be possessed with exclusive notions, and be therefore incapable of the general superiority of ancient students, who actually owed that general superiority to the inferiority of their knowledge. We must consider whether the evil can be avoided without losing the good of the modern arrangement; for the evil is becoming urgent. We all acknowledge that the divisions established for the convenience of scientific pursuit are radically artificial; and yet there are very few who can embrace in idea the whole of any one science: each science moreover being itself only a part of a great whole. Almost every one is busy about his own particular section, without much thought about its relation to the general system of positive knowledge. We must not be blind to the evil, nor slow in seeking a remedy. We must not forget that this is the weak side of the positive philosophy, by which it may yet be attacked, with some hope of success, by the adherents of the theological and metaphysical systems. As to the remedy, it certainly does not lie in a return to the ancient confusion of pursuits, which would be mere retrogression, if it were possible, which it is not. It lies in perfecting the division of employments itself—in carrying it one degree higher—in constituting one more speciality from the study of scientific generalities.

Proposed new class of students

Let us have a new class of students, suitably prepared, whose business it shall be to take the respective sciences as they are, determine the spirit of each, ascertain their relations and mutual connection, and reduce their respective principles to the smallest number of general principles, in conformity with the fundamental rules of the positive method. At the same time, let other students be prepared for their special pursuit by an education which recognizes the whole scope of positive science, so as to profit by the labours of the students of generalities, and so as to correct reciprocally, under that guidance, the results obtained by each. We see some approach already to this arrangement. Once established, there would be nothing to apprehend from any extent of division of employments. When we once have a class of learned men, at the disposal of all others, whose business it shall be to connect each new discovery with the general system, we may dismiss all fear of the great whole being lost sight of in the pursuit of the details of knowledge. The organization of scientific research will then be complete; and it will henceforth have occasion only to extend its development, and not to change its character. After all, the formation of such a new class as is proposed would be merely an extension of the principle which has created all the classes we have. While science was narrow, there was only one class: as it expanded, more were instituted. With a further advance a fresh need arises, and this new class will be the result.

Advantages of the positive philosophy

The general spirit of a course of positive philosophy having been thus set forth, we must now glance at the chief advantages which may be derived, on behalf of human progression, from the study of it . . .

Illustrates the intellectual function

The study of the positive philosophy affords the only rational means of exhibiting the logical laws of the human mind, which have hitherto been sought by unfit methods. To explain what is meant by this, we may refer to a saying of M. de Blainville, in his work on comparative anatomy, that every active, and especially every living being, may be regarded under two relations—the statical and the dynamical; that is, under conditions or in action. It is clear that all considerations range themselves under the one or the other of these heads. Let us apply this classification to the intellectual functions.

If we regard these functions under their statical aspect—that is, if we consider the conditions under which they exist—we must determine the organic circumstances of the case, which inquiry involves it with anatomy and physiology. If we look at the dynamic aspect, we have to study simply the exercise and results of the intellectual powers of the human race, which is neither more nor less than the general object of the positive philosophy. In short, looking at all scientific theories as so many great logical facts, it is only by the thorough observation of these facts that we can arrive at the knowledge of logical laws . . .

This, then, is the first great result of the positive philosophy—
the manifestation by experiment of the laws which rule the intellect
in the investigation of truth; and, as a consequence the knowledge
of the general rules suitable for that object.

Must regenerate education

The second effect of the positive philosophy, an effect not less
important and far more urgently wanted, will be to regenerate
education.

The best minds are agreed that our European education, still
essentially theological, metaphysical and literary, must be superseded by a positive training, conformable to our time and needs . . .

Advances sciences by combining them

The same special study of scientific generalities must also aid the
progress of the respective positive sciences: and this constitutes our
third head of advantages.

The divisions which we establish between the sciences are,
though not arbitrary, essentially artificial. The subject of our researches is one: we divide it for our convenience, in order to deal
the more easily with its difficulties. But it sometimes happens, and
especially with the most important doctrines of each science, that
we need what we cannot obtain under the present isolation of the
sciences—a combination of several special points of view; and for
want of this, very important problems wait for their solution much
longer than they otherwise need do . . .

Such is the advantage which, in the third place, we shall owe to
positive philosophy—the elucidation of the respective sciences by
their combination.

Must reorganize society

In the fourth place the positive philosophy offers the only solid
basis for that social reorganization which must succeed the critical
condition in which the most civilized nations are now living.

It cannot be necessary to prove to anybody who reads this work
that ideas govern the world, or throw it into chaos; in other words,
that all social mechanism rests upon opinions. The great political
and moral crisis that societies are now undergoing is shown by a
rigid analysis to arise out of intellectual anarchy. While stability
in fundamental maxims is the first condition of genuine social
order, we are suffering under an utter disagreement which may be
called universal. Till a certain number of general ideas can be
acknowledged as a rallying-point of social doctrine, the nations

will remain in a revolutionary state, whatever palliatives may be devised; and their institutions can be only provisional. But whenever the necessary agreement on first principles can be obtained, appropriate institutions will issue from them, without shock or resistance; for the causes of disorder will have been arrested by the mere fact of the agreement. It is in this direction that those must look who desire a natural and regular, a normal state of society.

Now, the existing disorder is abundantly accounted for by the existence, all at once, of three incompatible philosophies—the theological, the metaphysical and the positive. Any one of these might alone secure some sort of social order; but while the three co-exist, it is impossible for us to understand one another upon any essential point whatever. If this is true, we have only to ascertain which of the philosophies must, in the nature of things, prevail; and, this ascertained, every man, whatever may have been his former views, cannot but concur in its triumph. The problem once recognized cannot remain long unsolved; for all considerations whatever point to the positive philosophy as the one destined to prevail. It alone has been advancing during a course of centuries, throughout which the others have been declining. The fact is incontestable . . .

No hope of reduction to a single law

Because it is proposed to consolidate the whole of our acquired knowledge into one body of homogeneous doctrine, it must not be supposed that we are going to study this vast variety as proceeding from a single principle, and as subjected to a single law. There is something so chimerical in attempts at universal explanation by a single law, that it may be as well to secure this work at once from any imputation of the kind, though its development will show how undeserved such an imputation would be. Our intellectual resources are too narrow, and the universe is too complex, to leave any hope that it will ever be within our power to carry scientific perfection to its last degree of simplicity. Moreover, it appears as if the value of such an attainment, supposing it possible, were greatly overrated . . .

The only necessary unity is that of method, which is already in great part established. As for the doctrine, it need not be *one*; it is enough that it should be *homogeneous*. It is, then, under the double aspect of unity of method and homogeneousness of doctrine that we shall consider the different classes of positive theories in this work. While pursuing the philosophical aim of all science, the lessening of the number of general laws requisite for the explanation of natural phenomena, we shall regard as presumptuous every attempt, in all future time, to reduce them rigorously to one.

Having thus endeavoured to determine the spirit and influence of the positive philosophy, and to mark the goal of our labours, we have now to proceed to the exposition of the system; that is, to the determination of the universal, or encyclopedic order, which must regulate the different classes of natural phenomena, and consequently the corresponding positive sciences.

Classification of the Sciences

. . . Classification must proceed from the study of the things to be classified, and must by no means be determined by *a priori* considerations. The real affinities and natural connections presented by objects being allowed to determine their order, the classification itself becomes the expression of the most general fact. And thus does the positive method apply to the question of classification itself, as well as to the objects included under it.

True principle of classification

It follows that the mutual dependence of the sciences—a dependence resulting from that of the corresponding phenomena—must determine the arrangement of the system of human knowledge. Before proceeding to investigate this mutual dependence, we have only to ascertain the real bounds of the classification proposed: in other words, to settle what we mean by human knowledge, as the subject of this work.

Boundaries of our field

The field of human labour is either speculation or action: and thus, we are accustomed to divide our knowledge into the theoretical and the practical. It is obvious that, in this inquiry, we have to do only with the theoretical. We are not going to treat of all human notions whatever, but of those fundamental conceptions of the different orders of phenomena which furnish a solid basis to all combinations, and are not founded on any antecedent intellectual system. In such a study, speculation is our material, and not the application of it—except where the application may happen to throw back light on its speculative origin . . .

There can be no doubt that man's study of nature must furnish the only basis of his action upon nature; for it is only by knowing the laws of phenomena, and thus being able to foresee them, that we can, in active life, set them to modify one another for our advantage. Our direct natural power over everything about us is extremely weak, and altogether disproportioned to our needs. Whenever we effect anything great it is through a knowledge of natural laws, by which we can set one agent to work upon another, even very weak modifying elements producing a change in the results of a large aggregate of causes. The relation of science to art may be summed up in a brief expression: From science comes prevision: from prevision comes action.

We must not, however, fall into the error of our time, of regarding science chiefly as a basis of art. However great may be the services rendered to industry by science; however true may be the saying that knowledge is power, we must never forget that the sciences have a higher destination still—and not only higher but more direct—that of satisfying the craving of our understanding to know the laws of phenomena . . .

Natural science

We must distinguish between the two classes of natural science— the abstract or general, which have for their object the discovery of the laws which regulate phenomena in all conceivable cases: and the concrete, particular, or descriptive, which are sometimes called natural sciences in a restricted sense, whose function it is to apply these laws to the actual history of existing beings. The first are fundamental; and our business is with them alone, as the second are derived, and, however important, not rising into the rank of our subjects of contemplation. We shall treat of physiology, but not of botany and zoology, which are derived from it. We shall treat of chemistry, but not of mineralogy, which is secondary to it . . .

We have now considered : first, that science being composed of speculative knowledge and of practical knowledge, we have to deal only with the first, and second, that theoretical knowledge, or science properly so called, being divided into general and particular, or abstract and concrete science, we have again to deal only with the first.

Being thus in possession of our proper subject, duly prescribed, we may proceed to the ascertainment of the true order of the fundamental sciences.

Difficulty of classification

The classification of the sciences is not so easy a matter as it may appear. However natural it may be, it will always involve something, if not arbitrary, at least artificial; and in so far, it will always involve imperfection. It is impossible to fulfil, quite rigorously, the object of presenting the sciences in their natural connection, and according to their mutual dependence, so as to avoid the smallest danger of being involved in a vicious circle. It is easy to show why.

Historical and dogmatic methods

Every science may be exhibited under two methods or procedures, the historical and the dogmatic. These are wholly distinct from each other, and any other method can be nothing but some combination of these two. By the first method, knowledge is presented in the same order in which it was actually obtained by the human mind, together with the way in which it was obtained. By the second, the system of ideas is presented as it might be conceived of at this day, by a mind which, duly prepared and placed at the right point of view, should begin to reconstitute the science as a whole. A new science must be pursued historically, the only thing to be done being to study in chronological order the different works which have contributed to the progress of the science. But when such materials have become recast to form a general system, to meet the demand for a more natural logical order, it is because the science is too far advanced for the historical order to be practicable or suitable. The more discoveries are made, the greater becomes the labour of the historical method of study, and the more effectual the dogmatic, because the new conceptions bring forward the earlier ones in a fresh light. Thus, the education of an ancient geometer consisted simply in the study, in their due order, of the very small number of original treatises then existing on the different parts of geometry. The writings of Archimedes and Apollonius were, in fact, about all. On the contrary, a modern geometer commonly finishes his education without having read a single original work dating further back than the most recent discoveries, which cannot be known by any other means. Thus the dogmatic method is for ever superseding the historical, as we advance to a higher position in science. If every mind had to pass through all the stages that every predecessor in the study had gone through, it is clear that, however easy it is to learn rather than invent, it would be impossible to effect the purpose of education—to place the student on the vantage-ground gained by the labours of all the men who have gone before. By the dogmatic method this is done, even though the living student may have only an ordinary intellect, and the dead may have been men of lofty genius. By the dogmatic method, therefore, must every advanced science be attained, with so much of the historical combined with it as is rendered necessary by discoveries too recent to be studied elsewhere than in their own records. The only objection to the preference of the dogmatic method is that it does not show how the science was attained; but a moment's reflection will show that this is the case also with the historical method. To pursue a science historically is quite a different thing from learning the history of its progress. This last pertains to the study of human history, as we shall see when we reach the final division of this work. It is true that a science cannot be completely understood without a knowledge of how it arose; and again, a dogmatic knowledge of any science is necessary to an understanding of its history; and therefore we shall notice, in treating of the fundamental sciences, the incidents of their origin, when distinct and illustrative; and we shall use their history, in a scientific sense, in our treatment of social physics; but the historical study, important, even essential, as it is, remains entirely distinct from the proper dogmatic study of science. These considerations, in this place, tend to define more precisely the spirit of our course of inquiry, while they more exactly determine the conditions under which we may hope to succeed in the construction of a true scale of the aggregate fundamental sciences. Great confusion would arise from any attempt to adhere strictly to historical order in our exposition of the sciences, for they have not all advanced at the same rate; and we must be for ever borrowing from each some fact to illustrate another, without regard to priority of origin. Thus, it is clear that, in the system of the sciences, astronomy must come before physics, properly so called: and yet, several branches of physics, above all, optics, are indispensable to the complete exposition of astronomy. Minor defects, if inevitable, cannot invalidate a classification which, on the whole, fulfils the principal conditions of the case. They belong to what is essentially artificial in our division of intellectual labour. In the main, however, our classification agrees with the history of science; the more general and simple sciences actually occurring first and advancing best in human history, and being followed by the more complex and restricted, though all were, since the earliest times, enlarging simultaneously.

A simple mathematical illustration will precisely represent the difficulty of the question we have to resolve, while it will sum up the preliminary considerations we have just concluded.

We propose to classify the fundamental sciences. They are six, as we shall soon see. We cannot make them less; and most scientific men would reckon them as more. Six objects admit of 720 different dispositions, or, in popular language, changes. Thus we have to choose the one right order (and there can be but one right) out of 720 possible ones. Very few of these have ever been proposed; yet we might venture to say that there is probably not one in favour of which some plausible reason might not be assigned; for we see the wildest divergences among the schemes which have been proposed—the sciences which are placed by some at the head of the scale being sent by others to the further extremity. Our problem is, then, to find the one rational order, among a host of possible systems.

True principle of classification

Now we must remember that we have to look for the principle of classification in the comparison of the different orders of phenomena, through which science discovers the laws which are her object. What we have to determine is the real dependence of scientific studies. Now, this dependence can result only from that of the corresponding phenomena. All observable phenomena may be included within a very few natural categories, so arranged as that the study of each category may be grounded on the principal laws of the preceding, and serve as the basis of the next ensuing. This order is determined by the degree of simplicity, or, what comes to the same thing, of generality of their phenomena. Hence results their successive dependence, and the greater or lesser facility for being studied.

It is clear, *a priori*, that the most simple phenomena must be the most general; for whatever is observed in the greatest number of cases is of course the most disengaged from the incidents of particular cases. We must begin then with the study of the most general or simple phenomena, going on successively to the more particular or complex. This must be the most methodical way, for this order of generality or simplicity fixes the degree of facility in the study of phenomena, while it determines the necessary connection of the sciences by the successive dependence of their phenomena. It is worthy of remark in this place that the most general and simple phenomena are the furthest removed from man's ordinary sphere, and must thereby be studied in a calmer and more rational frame of mind than those in which he is more nearly implicated; and this constitutes a new ground for the corresponding sciences being developed more rapidly.

We have now obtained our rule. Next we proceed to our classification.

Inorganic and organic phenomena

We are first struck by the clear division of all natural phenomena into two classes—of inorganic and of organic bodies. The organized are evidently, in fact, more complex and less general than the inorganic, and depend upon them, instead of being depended on by them. Therefore it is that physiological study should begin with inorganic phenomena; since the organic include all the qualities belonging to them, with a special order added, viz., the vital phenomena, which belong to organization. We have not to investigate the nature of either; for the positive philosophy does not inquire into natures. Whether their nature be supposed different or the same, it is evidently necessary to separate the two studies of inorganic matter and of living bodies. Our classification will stand through any future decision as to the way in which living bodies are to be regarded; for, on any supposition, the general laws of inorganic physics must be established before we can proceed with success to the examination of a dependent class of phenomena.

Inorganic

Each of these great halves of natural philosophy has subdivisions. Inorganic physics must, in accordance with our rule of generality and the order of dependence of phenomena, be divided into two sections—of celestial and terrestrial phenomena. Thus we have astronomy, geometrical and mechanical, and terrestrial physics. The necessity of this division is exactly the same as in the former case.

Astronomy

Astronomical phenomena are the most general, simple, and abstract of all; and therefore the study of natural philosophy must clearly begin with them. They are themselves independent, while the laws to which they are subject influence all others whatsoever. The general effects of gravitation preponderate, in all terrestrial phenomena, over all effects which may be peculiar to them, and modify the original ones. It follows that the analysis of the simplest terrestrial phenomenon, not only chemical, but even purely mechanical, presents a greater complication than the most compound astronomical phenomenon. The most difficult astronomical question involves less intricacy than the simple movement of even a solid body, when the determining circumstances are to be computed. Thus we see that we must separate these two studies and proceed to the second only through the first, from which it is derived.

Physics

In the same manner, we find a natural division of terrestrial physics into two, according as we regard bodies in their mechanical or their chemical character. Hence we have physics, properly so called, and chemistry. Again, the second class must be studied through the first.

Chemistry

Chemical phenomena are more complicated than mechanical, and depend upon them, without influencing them in return. Every one knows that all chemical action is first submitted to the influence of weight, heat, electricity, etc., and presents moreover something which modifies all these. Thus, while it follows physics, it presents itself as a distinct science.

Such are the divisions of the sciences relating to inorganic matter. An analogous division arises in the other half of natural philosophy—the science of organized bodies.

Organic

Here we find ourselves presented with two orders of phenomena: those which relate to the individual, and those which relate to the species, especially when it is gregarious. With regard to man, especially, this distinction is fundamental. The last order of phenomena is evidently dependent on the first, and is more complex. Hence we have two great sections in organic physics—physiology, properly so called, and social physics, which is dependent on it.

Physiology

In all social phenomena we perceive the working of the physiological laws of the individual; and moreover something which modifies their effects, and which belongs to the influence of individuals over each other—singularly complicated in the case of the human race by the influence of generations on their successors. Thus it is clear that our social science must issue from that which relates to the life of the individual.

Sociology

On the other hand, there is no occasion to suppose, as some eminent physiologists have done, that social physics is only an appendage to physiology. The phenomena of the two are not

identical, though they are homogeneous; and it is of high importance to hold the two sciences separate. As social conditions modify
the operation of physiological laws, social physics must have a set
of observations of its own ...

Five natural sciences

Thus we have before us five fundamental sciences in successive
dependence: astronomy, physics, chemistry, physiology and finally
social physics. The first considers the most general, simple, abstract
and remote phenomena known to us, and those which affect all
others without being affected by them. The last considers the most
particular compound, concrete phenomena, and those which are
most interesting to man. Between these two, the degrees of
speciality, of complexity, and individuality are in regular proportion to the place of the respective sciences in the scale exhibited ...

Defects are in us, not in science

There is one liability to be guarded against, which we may mention
here. We must beware of confounding the degrees of precision
which we are able to attain in regard to any science, with the certainty of the science itself. The certainty of science, and our precision in the knowledge of it, are two very different things, which
have been too often confounded; and are so still, though less than
formerly. A very absurd proposition may be very precise; as if we
should say, for instance, that the sum of the angles of a triangle is
equal to three right angles; and a very certain proposition may be
wanting in precision in our statement of it; as, for instance, when
we assert that every man will die. If the different sciences offer to
us a varying degree of precision, it is from no want of certainty in
themselves, but of our mastery of their phenomena ...

Mathematics

It cannot but have been observed that in our enumeration of the
sciences there is a prodigious omission. We have said nothing of
mathematical science. The omission was intentional; and the
reason is no other than the vast importance of mathematics ...

It needs scarcely be pointed out that in placing mathematics at
the head of positive philosophy, we are only extending the application of the principle which has governed our whole classification.
We are simply carrying back our principle to its first manifestation.
Geometrical and mechanical phenomena are the most general,
the most simple, the most abstract of all—the most irreducible to
others, the most independent of them; serving, in fact, as a basis

to all others. It follows that the study of them is an indispensable preliminary to that of all others. Therefore must mathematics hold the first place in the hierarchy of the sciences . . . The order that results is this; an order which of all possible arrangements is the only one that accords with natural manifestation of all phenomena, mathematics, astronomy, physics, chemistry, physiology, social physics.

Addition of moral science to the hierarchy*

. . . If this immense classification of phenomena be grouped under its three leading branches, we find that the material order at the lower end, and the social order at the upper, are indirectly modified only by the vital order which separates them and unites them. The latter, on the contrary, is at once subject to the two kinds of indirect variations. In the same way, in distinguishing the three successive modes of material existence, we see that the mathematical laws by themselves, that is geometry and mechanics, the great field of which is the heavens, are indirectly affected only by the laws of physics and chemistry. But the operation of physical phenomena (properly so-called) is affected at the same time by the variations of the astronomical and of the chemical order, between which the physical forms the natural junction.

Human order divisible into (1) social and (2) moral

We must now apply to the human order these general principles as to the limits of variation. For this purpose, we will first separate the human order finally into its two necessary modes: the one collective, the other individual; forming respectively social existence and moral existence. I introduced this distinction between sociology and morals in the first chapter of this volume as needed to complete my encyclopedic classification of the sciences; and this, the concluding chapter, may be now devoted to fill up and establish this prime doctrine; while in the rest of the treatise it will be constantly applied, especially in implicit form.

Thus forming seven sciences

This final conception of seven, instead of six, degrees for the encyclopedic scale of the sciences was in my thought, when I sketched the general scheme of positive education; so that of the two latter years of the seven years course, one year should be devoted to sociology, and then one year to morals. That I should have suggested it in that connection illustrates the religious purpose

* *Pos. Pol.*, vol. 2, pp. 352–3.

involved in sound philosophy, and further shows how real and opportune is the distinction itself. Its value is further shown by the agreement between the subject chosing the encyclopedic course in the systematic wisdom of modern reason and the admirable instinct of the genius of antiquity to regard morals as the master science.

The venerable theocracies with which civilization opened, of which the spirit long survived in the oracles of Greece, proclaimed forty centuries ago that the knowledge of man was the true end of all science. Now that we have completed the immense objective education in science which has been accomplished since the date of this luminous aphorism, the subjective synthesis irrevocably brings us back to the same starting-point; for it gives us at once the general result of that knowledge and the principle of the synthesis. For man, properly so called, when regarded in his essential reality, and not by the light of materialist or spiritualist dreams, can only be understood by means of a previous knowledge of humanity, for on this man necessarily depends. And it would be needless to enlarge any further on the view already familiar to the reader, that the social existence of man is in necessary dependence on the vital and on the material order. We thus obtain, if we decompose into its parts the material order, the seven essential stages of knowledge, mathematical, astronomical, physical, chemical, vital, social, and finally moral. In the positive system, these will henceforth be the steps in the great encyclopedic series of the sciences.

The Sociological Element*

The only really universal point of view is the human, or speaking more exactly, the social. This is the only one which recurs and is perpetually renewed, in every department of thought; in regard to the external world as well as to man. Thus, if we want to conceive of the rights of the sociological spirit to supremacy, we have only to regard all our conceptions, as I have explained before, as so many necessary results of a series of determinate phases, proper to our mental evolution, personal and collective, taking place according to invariable laws, statical and dynamical, which rational observation is competent to disclose. Since philosophers have begun to meditate deeply on intellectual phenomena, they have always been more or less convinced, in spite of all prepossession, of the

* *Pos. Phil.*, vol. 3, pp. 351–75.

inevitable reality of these fundamental laws; for their existence is always supposed in every study, in which any conclusion whatever would be impossible if the formation and variation of our opinions were not subject to a regular order, independent of our will, and the pathological change of which is known to be in no way arbitrary. But, besides the extreme difficulty of the subject, and its vicious management hitherto, human reason being capable of growth only in social circumstances, it is clear that no decisive discovery could be made in this way till society should have attained a generality of view which was not possible till our day. Imperfect as sociological study may yet be, it furnishes us with a principle which justifies and guides its intervention, scientific and logical, in all the essential parts of the speculative system, which can thus alone be brought into unity. It appears to me that the mere existence of this book is a sufficient testimony to the reality and fertility of the new general philosophy; for it presents the spectacle of the whole range of sciences subjected to one point of view, without interference with the independence of any, and with a confirmation instead of a weakening of their respective characters, by the power of a single thought—by the application of a single general law. Brief as my expositions have necessarily been, thoughtful readers cannot but be aware of the new light, generated by the creations of sociology, cast upon all the foregoing sciences . . .

Solves antagonisms

This unity, thus established and regarded both historically and dogmatically, puts an end to the long and fatal antagonism between the conceptions which relate to man, and those which concern the external world. Hitherto they have been concluded to be irreconcilable; but my philosophical solution combines them entirely and for ever . . .

To make this connection perfectly clear, it is necessary to strip away the last metaphysical illusions, and show what is the true human point of view—that it is not individual but social; for under either the statical or the dynamical aspect, man is a mere abstraction, and there is nothing real but humanity, regarded intellectually or, yet more, morally. It is only through its holding this view, that the theological philosophy has retained any of its influence to this day; and the fate of the metaphysical philosophy is decided by its inability to treat of man otherwise than individually. The same vice marked the positive system, while it was directed by the mathematical spirit alone; and this compelled philosophers, as

Cabanis and Gall, for instance, to fix on biology as the centre of scientific unity. This was so far a good as that it brought the modern centre of organization much nearer to its real seat; but it would not answer further than for a necessary transition; and it protracted the old intellectual system by impeding the development of sound social speculation, which it looked upon as merely a natural corollary of biological studies. Whether the science of the individual is instituted metaphysically or positively, it must be utterly ineffectual for the construction of any general philosophy, because it is excluded from the only universal point of view. The evolution of the individual mind can disclose no essential law: and it can afford neither indications nor verifications of any value unless brought under the methods of observation taught by the evolution of the human mind in general. Thus, the biological phase is only the last introductory stage, as each of the preceding sciences had been before, to the development of the positive spirit, by which its own scientific and logical constitution must be consolidated . . .

Spirit of the method

Such is the relation of this solution to the present and the past. As to the future—I need not point out the unreasonableness of any fears that the supremacy of the sociological philosophy can injure any of the anterior sciences. That supremacy would be compromised by the neglect of any one of them, even if such neglect were possible. It may and will be the case that irrational and undisciplined labours will meet with less favour and less impunity than hitherto; and also that the highest scientific capacity, and the most earnest public attention, will be directed to sociological researches, as the best ability and interest always are at the command of the needs of their time. But there is nothing to lament in either of these results. As to the effect on private education, there is no greater cause for anxiety. The sociological theory requires that the education of the individual should be a reproduction, rapid but accurate, of that of the race. In his brief career, he must pass through the three stages which an aggregate of nations has wrought out with infinite comparative slowness; and if any material part of the experience is evaded, his training will be abortive. For the individual then, as for the race, mathematical speculation will be the cradle of rational positivity; and the claims of geometers are certain, therefore, of just consideration—and the more, as the order and urgency of the needs of the human mind become better understood. But it will not be forgotten that a cradle is not a throne; and that the first demand of positivity, in its humblest degree, is to have free way, and to pursue it up to the point of universality, which is the only limit of genuine education.

These are the considerations which prove the fitness of the positive philosophy to reconcile the antagonistic methods of connecting our various speculations—the one taking man and the other the external world for its starting-point. Here we find the solution of the great logical conflict which, from the time of Aristotle and Plato, has attended the entire evolution, intellectual and social, of the human race; and which, once indispensable to the double preparatory movement, has since been a chief obstacle to the fulfilment of its destination.

Having thus ascertained the spirit of the positive method, I have to indicate briefly its nature and destination, and then, its institution and development, in its complete and indivisible state; that its attributes, hitherto spontaneous, may be duly systematized, from the sociological point of view.

Nature of the method

The positive philosophy is distinguished from the ancient, as we have seen throughout, by nothing so much as its rejection of all inquiring into causes, first and final; and its confining research to the invariable relations which constitute natural laws. Though this mature view is yet too recent to be fully incorporated with all our studies, it is applied to every class of elementary conceptions, and is firmly established in regard to the most simple and perfect, showing that a similar prevalence in the more complex and incomplete is merely a question of time. The true idea of the nature of research being thus attained, the next step was to determine the respective offices of observation and reasoning, so as to avoid the danger of empiricism on the one hand, and mysticism on the other. We have accordingly sanctioned, in the one relation, the now popular maxim of Bacon, that observed facts are the only basis of sound speculation; so that we agree to what I wrote a quarter of a century ago—that no proposition that is not finally reducible to the enunciation of a fact, particular or general, can offer any real and intelligible meaning.

Inquiry into laws

On the other hand, we have repudiated the practice of reducing science to an accumulation of desultory facts, asserting that science, as distinguished from learning, is essentially composed, not of facts, but of laws, so that no separate facts can be incorporated with science till it has been connected with some other, at least by the aid of some justifiable hypothesis. Besides that, sound theoretical indications are necessary to control and guide observation, the positive spirit is for ever enlarging the logical province at the expense of the experimental, by substituting the prevision of phenomena more and more for the direct exploration of them; and scientific progress essentially consists in gradually diminishing the number of distinct and independent laws, while extending their mutual connection. I have explained before that our geometers have been led, by contemplating only the wonderful scope of the law of gravitation, and exaggerating even that, to expect and strive after an impracticable unity. Our intellectual weakness, and the scientific difficulties with which we have to cope, will always leave us in the midst of irreducible laws, even in regard to the interior of each science. The universality which is proper to the sociological point of view instructs us how to establish as wide a connection as our means admit, without repressing the spirit of each science under a factitious mathematical concentration. In this way, while sound generalization will be for ever reducing the number of really independent laws, it will not be forgotten that such progress can have no value whatever, except in its subordination to the reality of the conceptions which guide it.

Accordance with common sense

The next important feature of the positive method is the accordance of its speculative conclusions with the development of popular good sense. The time is past for speculation, awaiting divine information, to look down upon the modest course of popular wisdom. As long as philosophers were searching into causes, while the multitude were observing indications, there was nothing in common between them: but now that philosophers are inquiring for laws, their loftiest speculations are in essential combination with the simplest popular notions, differing in degree of mental occupation, but not in kind. I have repeatedly declared in this work that the philosophical spirit is simply a methodical extension of popular good sense to all subjects accessible to human reason—practical wisdom having been unquestionably the agency by which the old speculative methods have been converted into sound ones, by human contemplations having been recalled to their true objects, and subjected to due conditions. The positive method is, like the theological and metaphysical, no invention of any special mind, but the product of the general mind; and the positive philosopher takes the spontaneous wisdom of mankind for his radical type, and generalizes and systematizes it, by extending it to abstract speculations, which have thus obtained the advancement that they exhibit, both in their nature and treatment. It is only by the popular determination that the field of scientific research can be marked out, because that determination alone can be perfectly and certainly free from personal bias of every kind, and directed upon impressions common to all men; and it is in fact impossible to conceive of either the origin or the final unanimous propagation of positive speculations apart from the general impulse and interest in them. The commonest facts are, as I have often said, the most important, in all orders of knowledge; and we have seen that the best instrumentalities of rational positivity are the systematized logical procedures given out by common sense. We see how modern psychology, setting out from the opposite point—from the dogmatic formation of the first principles of human knowledge, and proceeding to analyse complex phenomena by the method which we now reject in the case of the simplest—has never yet, with all its toil and perplexity, risen to the level of popular knowledge derived from general experience. Public reason determines the aim as well as the origin of science, directing it towards previsions which relate to general needs, as when, for instance, the founder of astronomy foresaw that, as a whole, it would afford a rational determination of the longitudes, though that result was not realized till Hipparchus had been dead two thousand years. The proper task of positive philosophers is then simply to institute and develop the intermediate processes which are to connect the two extremes indicated by popular wisdom; and the real superiority of the philosophical spirit over common sense results from its special and continuous application to familiar speculations, duly abstracting them, ascertaining their relations, and then generalizing and co-ordinating them—this last process being the one in which popular wisdom fails the most, as we see by the ease with which the majority of men entertain incompatible notions. Thus we perceive that positive science is, in fact, the result of a vast general elaboration, both spontaneous and systematic, in which the whole human race has borne its share, led on by the specially contemplative class. The theological view was widely different from this; and it is one of the distinctive characters of the positive philosophy that it implicates the thinking multitude with the scientific few in the general progress—not only past but future; showing how familiar a social incorporation is reserved for a speculative system which is a simple extension of general wisdom. And here we recognize a fresh evidence that the sociological point of view is the only philosophical one.

Conception of natural laws

So much has been said about the fundamental principle of sound philosophy being the subjection of all phenomena to invariable laws, that I need advert to it here only because it must occupy its place in the statement of our general conclusions. We have seen how late and partial was the development of the germs of this truth; how the principle was long recognized only in geometrical and numerical subjects, which seemed naturally placed beyond the theological pale that included everything else: how it began to show its value when it made its way into astronomy: how it afforded the intellectual ground of transition from polytheism to monotheism: how it was introduced, by means of alchemy and astrology, into physico-chemical speculations: how scholasticism then took it up, and extended it into a new field by its transient doctrine of a providence submitting its action to rules: a doctrine which, by its apparent reconciling tendency, has protected the positive principle to this day, while it was spreading through all the provinces of inorganic philosophy, and taking possession at last of the science of man, with all his intellectual and moral attributes. Here its progress stopped, till I extended it to social phenomena. Some metaphysical speculation there has been about the existence of general laws of society; but their germs have never been brought to light, nor their application to the most common and interesting phenomena been exhibited; but the exposition made in this work leaves no doubt of the universal presence of the principle, the generality of which is in the way henceforth of being proved, both by its philosophical ascendancy and its agreement with the general mind, to the satisfaction of all thinking men. Nothing but the protracted influence of monotheistic conceptions could have thus long prevented its universal acceptance amidst the overwhelming evidence of law afforded by the fulfilment of rational human prevision; and now, the nascent discovery of sociological laws will extinguish all remaining opposition by withdrawing its last province from theological explanation, and uniting it with the rest of the empire of human knowledge. While completing and consolidating the great mental revolution begun by the preceding sciences, this sociological recognition of laws perfects the conception of law in all the other provinces, by securing to them that independence in the case of each science which they could not obtain under the supremacy of the mathematical spirit; for, instead of being regarded as an indirect consequence, in the later sciences, of their action in the earlier, and as even growing weaker and more remote, they are suddenly reinforced in importance and dignity by being found in full action in a region inaccessible to mathematical conceptions. The sense of the presence of invariable laws, which first arose in the mathematical province, is fully matured and developed in high sociological speculation, by which it is carried on to universality.

As to the scientific nature of these laws, our ignorance of anything by something else, in now explaining and now foreseeing cerdoes not at all interfere with our power of prevision under any laws, but which divides them into two classes, for practical use. Our positive method of connecting phenomena is by one or other of two relations—that of similitude or that of succession—the mere fact of such resemblance or succession being all that we can pretend to know, and all that we need to know; for this perception comprehends all knowledge, which consists in elucidating something by something else, in now explaining and now foreseeing certain phenomena by means of the resemblance or sequence of other phenomena. Such prevision applies to past, present and future alike, consisting as it does simply in knowing events in virtue of their relations, and not by direct observation. This general distinction between the laws of resemblance and those of succession has been employed in this work in the equivalent form of the statical and dynamical study of subjects—that is, the study of their existence first, and then of their action. This distinction is not due to mathematics, in the geometrical part of which it cannot exist. It only begins to be possible in the mechanical portion of mathematics; manifests its character when the study of living bodies is arrived at, and organization and life are separately considered; and finally, is completely established in sociological science, where it attains its full practical use in its correspondence with the ideas of order and of progress.

Logically considered, these laws offer one more distinction, according as their source is experimental or logical. The force and dignity of the laws are in no way affected by the different degrees of credit attached to the modes of ascertaining them. And it is usually a mistake to assign different degrees of credit to two modes of ascertainment which are necessary to each other, and each preferable in some portion or other of the field of knowledge. What the one finds, the other confirms and elucidates; what the one indicates, the other searches for and finds. The positive system requires, on the whole, that deduction should be preferred for special researches, and induction reserved for fundamental laws. The different sciences present varying facilities for the application of the two methods, of which I will only briefly say that they go far to compensate each other. Sociology, for instance, might seem to be too complex for the deductive method, and, at the same time less adapted to the inductive than the simpler sciences which admit of the broadest extension of positive argumentation: yet, through the dependence of the more complex sciences on the simpler, the latter yield *a priori* considerations to the former, which actually render the greater number of fundamental ideas deductive, which would be inductive in sciences that are more independent. Another consideration is that the more recent sciences, which are the more complex, have the advantage of being born at a more advanced stage of the human mind, when mental habits are improved by a stronger prevalence of the philosophical spirit. Thus, if a comparison were fairly established between the first and last terms of the scale of sciences, I will venture to say, that sociological science, though only established by this book, already rivals mathematical science itself, not in precision and fecundity, but in positivity and rationality. It is more completely emancipated from metaphysical influence; and it is so interconnected as to issue in unity, as I have shown by deducing from a single law the general explanation of each of the successive phases of the human evolution. There is nothing comparable to this in the whole range of the anterior sciences, except the perfect systematization achieved by Lagrange in his theory of equilibrium and motion, with regard to a subject much less difficult and much better prepared: and this proves the natural aptitude of sociology for a more complete co-ordination, notwithstanding its recency and complexity, in virtue simply of its natural position at the close of the encyclopedical scale.

Logical method

These considerations point out to us the correlative characters which distinguish the positive method of philosophizing—the logical and the scientific. The first consists in the preponderance of observation over imagination, contrary to the earliest mode of proceeding. We have no longer anything to fear from theological appeals to the imagination: but the metaphysical procedure, which follows neither fictions nor facts, but its own train of entities, is still too attractive to minds which are not sufficiently established in positive practices. It is still necessary to point out that laws are the true subject of investigation, and that the function of imagination in philosophizing is to create or perfect the means of connection between established facts, but not, in any case, to meddle with the point of departure or the direction of the inquiry. Even in the *a priori* mode of proceeding, the general considerations which direct the case have been derived from observation in the science concerned or in some other. To see in order to foresee is the business of science: to foresee everything without having seen anything is only an absurd metaphysical utopia, which still obtains too much favour.

Scientific method

The scientific view which corresponds with this logical one is, that the positive philosophy substitutes the relative for the absolute in the study of qualities. Every inquiry for causes and modes of production involves the tendency to absolute notions; and the tendency therefore existed throughout the theological and metaphysical periods. The greatest of modern metaphysicians, Kant, deserves immortal honour for being the first to attempt an escape from the absolute in philosophy, by his conception of a double reality, at once objective and subjective; an effort which shows a just sense of sound philosophy. Placed as he was, however, between the Cartesian philosophy behind and the positive philosophy in its completion before him, he could not give a truly relative character to his view; and his successors lapsed into the absolute tendencies which he had restrained for a time. Now that the scientific evolution comprehends social speculations, nothing can stop the decay of the absolute philosophy. Inorganic science, presenting the external world, where man appears only as a spectator of phenomena independent of him, shows that all ideas in that sphere are essentially relative—as I have before remarked, especially with regard to weight, for one instance. Biology confirms the testimony by showing, with regard to individual man, that the mental operations, regarded as vital phenomena, are subject, like all other human phenomena, to the fundamental relation between the organism and its medium, the dualism of which constitutes life, in every sense. Thus, all our knowledge is necessarily relative, on the one hand, to the medium, in as far as it is capable of acting on us, and on the other to the organism, in as far as it is susceptible of that action; so that the inertia of the one or the insensibility of the other at once destroys the continuous reciprocity on which every genuine idea depends. This is especially noticeable in instances in which the communication is of a single kind, as in astronomical philosophy, where ideas cease in the case of dark stars or of blind men. All our speculations, as well as all other phenomena of life, are deeply affected by the external constitution which regulates the mode of action, and the internal constitution which determines its personal result, without our being able in any case to assign their respective influences to each class of conditions thus generating our impressions and our ideas. Kant attained to a very imperfect equivalent of this biological conception: but, if it could have been better accomplished, it would have been radically defective, because it relates only to the individual mind; a point of view much too remote from philosophical reality to occasion any decisive revolution. The only natural and sound view was obviously one which should present a dynamical estimate of collective human intelligence, through its whole course of development. This is at length done by the creation of sociology, on which the entire elimination of the absolute in philosophy now depends . . .

Speculative life

Whenever, in the course of this work, we have noticed the intellectual needs that relate to practical life, we have found them confirmatory of my view of the positive philosophy. It is as the basis of rational action that science has hitherto been universally prized; and that attribute will never lose any of its value. We have seen throughout how practical needs have generated science in all departments; though the science could not have been thus generated if our mental tendencies had not been favourable to it; since the practical aptitude of positive theories could be discovered only by adequate culture, driving out theological and metaphysical chimeras which made much larger promises. When once the relation of science to practical wants was made clear in a few cases, it became a very effectual stimulus to the philosophical spirit by exposing the impotence of the system of arbitrary wills and entities in directing man's action upon nature; and the rationality and positivity of our conceptions were proved, to the eminent advantage of lofty scientific speculation, when prevision was made the ground of action, and the humblest practical problems were seen to be connected with the highest theoretical researches; as in the arts which relate to astronomy. Though some few minds find sufficient stimulus to the philosophical labour which is repugnant to our nature in the need to know phenomena and to connect them, the philosophical discipline would have been considerably retarded if practical exigencies had not afforded a more general instigation. By completing the system of natural philosophy, the creation of sociology must prodigiously extend the relation between speculation and practice, which must henceforth embrace all possible cases . . .

Liberty of method

One more suggestion remains, with regard to the destination of the positive method; that, from its relative spirit, it determines the kind of liberty of option left to our understandings in the formation of conceptions, as long as we respect the reality of external laws. In the construction of scientific works, we may give them the most suitable form, as we would in the æsthetic province . . .

Relation of Sociology to the Other Departments of Positive Philosophy*

The conditions of the positive philosophy with regard to this science are not fulfilled till its relations with the other sciences are ascertained. Its establishment in its proper place in the hierarchy is a principle of such importance that it may be seen to comprehend all the philosophical requisites for its institution as a science: and it is for want of this that all attempts in our time to treat social questions in a positive manner have failed. Whether we consider the indispensable data of various kinds supplied to sociology by the other sciences, or the yet more important requisite of the sound speculative habits formed by the preparatory study of them, the daily spectacle of abortive attempts to construct a social science leaves no doubt that this grand omission is the cause of the failure, and of the wrong direction always taken, sooner or later, by minds which seemed fitted to accomplish something better. We must, then, review the relation of this last of the sciences to all the rest; but our examination of each of them, and of biology especially, has so anticipated this part of my subject, that I may pass over it very briefly.

It is a new idea that the science of society is thus connected with the rest: yet in no case is the relation more unquestionable or more marked. Social phenomena exhibit, in even a higher degree, the complexity, speciality, and personality which distinguish the higher phenomena of the individual life. In order to see how this establishes the connection in question, we must remember that in the social, as in the biological case, there are two classes of considerations: that of man or humanity, which constitutes the phenomenon, and that of the medium or environment, which influences

* *Pos. Phil.*, vol. 2, pp. 258–74.

this partial and secondary development of one of the animal races. Now, by the first term of this couple, sociology is subordinated to the whole of the organic philosophy, which discloses to us the laws of human nature: and by the second, it is connected with the whole system of inorganic philosophy, which reveals to us the exterior conditions of human existence. One of the two great divisions of philosophy, in short, determines the agent concerned in sociological phenomena, and the other the medium in which it is developed. It is clear that we here take together, and treat as one, the three sections of inorganic philosophy—chemistry, physics and astronomy—as they all relate equally to the social medium. It will be enough if we point out the participation of each, as the occasion arises. As to the method, properly so called, it is, as we have seen, more and more necessary to subject studies to the graduated system of prior studies, in proportion to their increasing complexity. These are the two points we have to consider in surveying once more the encyclopedical scale, beginning, as before, with the relations which are the closest and most direct. We shall afterwards have to exhibit the reaction, scientific and logical, which sociology, once instituted, must exercise, in its turn, on the whole of the preceding sciences: a reaction which is, as yet, even less suspected than the primary action itself.

Relation to biology

The subordination of social science to biology is so evident that nobody denies it in statement, however it may be neglected in practice . . .

The whole social evolution of the race must proceed in entire accordance with biological laws; and social phenomena must always be founded on the necessary invariableness of the human organism, the characteristics of which, physical, intellectual and moral, are always found to be essentially the same, and related in the same manner, at every degree of the social scale—no development of them attendant upon the social condition ever altering their nature in the least, nor, of course, creating or destroying any faculties whatever, or transposing their influence. No sociological view can therefore be admitted, at any stage of the science, or under any appearance of historical induction, that is contradictory to the known laws of human nature. No view can be admitted, for instance, which supposes a very marked character of goodness or wickedness to exist in the majority of men; or which represents the sympathetic affections as prevailing over the personal ones; or the intellectual over the affective faculties, etc. In cases like these, which are more common than the imperfection of the biological theory would lead us to expect, all sociological principles must be as carefully submitted to ulterior correction as if they supposed human life to be extravagantly long, or contravened, in any other way, the physical laws of humanity; because the intellectual and moral conditions of human existence are as real and as imperative as its material conditions, though more difficult to estimate, and therefore less known. Thus, in a biological view, all existing political doctrines are radically vicious, because, in their irrational estimate of political phenomena, they suppose qualities to exist among rulers and the ruled—here an habitual perverseness or imbecility, and there a spirit of concert or calculation—which are incompatible with positive ideas of human nature, and which would impute pathological monstrosity to whole classes; which is simply absurd. An example like this shows what valuable resources positive sociology must derive from its subordination to biology; and especially in regard to cerebral physiology, whenever it comes to be studied as it ought.

The students of biology have, however, the same tendency to exalt their own science at the expense of that which follows it, that physicists and chemists have shown in regard to biology. The biologists lose sight of historical observation altogether, and represent sociology as a mere corollary of the science of man; in the same way that physicists and chemists treat biology as a mere derivative from the inorganic philosophy. The injury to science is great in both cases. If we neglect historical comparison, we can understand nothing of the social evolution; and the chief phenomenon in sociology—the phenomenon which marks its scientific originality—that is, the gradual and continuous influence of generations upon each other, would be disguised or unnoticed, for want of the necessary key—historical analysis. From the time that the influence of former generations becomes the cause of any modification of the social movement, the mode of investigation must accord with the nature of the phenomena; and historical analysis therefore becomes preponderant, while biological considerations, which explained the earliest movements of society, cease to be more than a valuable auxiliary and means of control . . .

Relation to inorganic philosophy

If sociology is thus subordinated to biology, it must be scientifically related to the whole system of inorganic philosophy, because biology is so. But it is also connected with that system by immediate relations of its own.

In the first place, it is only by the inorganic philosophy that we can duly analyse the entire system of exterior conditions, chemical, physical and astronomical, amidst which the social evolution proceeds, and by which its rate of progress is determined. Social phenomena can no more be understood apart from their environment than those of individual life. All exterior disturbances which could affect the life of individual man must change his social existence; and, conversely, his social existence could not be seriously disturbed by any modifications of the medium which should not derange his separate condition . . .

Man's action on the external world

One consideration remains, of the more importance because it applies especially to physico-chemical knowledge, which we seem to have rather neglected in this sketch for astronomical doctrine: I mean the considerations of man's action on the external world, the gradual development of which affords one of the chief aspects of the social evolution, and without which the evolution could not have taken place as a whole, as it would have been stopped at once by the preponderance of the material obstacles proper to the human condition. In short, all human progress, political, moral or intellectual, is inseparable from material progression, in virtue of the close interconnection which, as we have seen, characterizes the natural course of social phenomena. Now, it is clear that the action of man upon nature depends chiefly on his knowledge of the laws of inorganic phenomena, though biological phenomena must also find a place in it. We must bear in mind, too, that physics, and yet more chemistry, form the basis of human power, since astronomy, notwithstanding its eminent participation in it, concurs not as an instrument for modifying the medium, but by prevision. Here we have another ground on which to exhibit the impossibility of any rational study of social development otherwise than by combining sociological speculations with the whole of the doctrines of inorganic philosophy . . .

Reaction of sociology

To complete the account of these encyclopedic relations, we must look at the connection in an inverse way, estimating the philosophical reaction of social physics on all the foregoing sciences, in regard both to doctrine and method. It must be at the end of the work that I must treat of sociology as completing the whole body of philosophy, and showing that the various sciences are branches from a single trunk; and thereby giving a character of unity to the variety of special studies that are now scattered abroad in a fatal dispersion. In this place I can only point out, in a more special manner, the immediate reaction of sociology on all the rest of natural philosophy in virtue of its own scientific and logical properties.

As to doctrine

In regard to the doctrine, the essential principle of this reaction is found in the consideration that all scientific speculations whatever, in as far as they are human labours, must necessarily be subordinated to the true general theory of human evolution. If we could conceive of such a thing as this theory being so perfected as that no intellectual obstacle should limit the abundance of its most exact deductions, it is clear that the scientific hierarchy would be, as it were, inverted, and would present the different sciences, in an *a priori* way, as mere parts of this single science. We have no power to realize such a state of things; but the mere supposition may enable us to comprehend the legitimate general intervention of true social science in all possible classes of human speculation. At first sight, it appears as if this high intervention must belong to the biological theory of our nature; and it was by that avenue that philosophers first caught a glimpse of the conception: and it is perfectly true that the knowledge of the individual man must exert a secret, but inevitable influence over all the sciences, because our labours bear the ineffaceable impress of the faculties which produce them. But a close examination will convince us that this universal influence must belong more to the theory of social evolution than to that of individual man, for the reason that the development of the human mind can take place only through the social state, the direct consideration of which must therefore prevail whenever we are treating of any results of that development. This is, then, in the briefest form, the first philosophical ground of the intellectual intervention of social physics in the cultivation of all the parts of natural philosophy. There will be more to say about it hereafter.

It is evident that sociology must perfect the study of the essential relations which unite the different sciences, as this inquiry constitutes an essential part of social statics, directly intended to disclose the laws of such a connection, in the same way as in all cases of connection between any of the elements of our civilization. The most marked instance of this operation of social science is in the direct study of social dynamics, in virtue of the principle, so familiar to us by this time, that true co-ordination must be disclosed by the natural course of the common development. All scientific men who have viewed their own particular subject in a large way have felt what important benefit might be afforded by corresponding historical information, by regulating the spontaneous expansion of scientific discoveries, and warning away from deceptive or premature attempts. I need not set forth the value that there would be in a history of the sciences, which is keenly felt by all who have made any important discovery in any science whatever: but, as my last chapter proves, no real scientific history, no theory of the true filiation of eminent discoveries, at present exists, in any form or degree. We have only compilations of materials more or less rational, which may be of some provisional use, but which cannot be afterwards employed in the construction of any historical doctrine without strict revision, and which are certainly in their present state unfit to yield any happy scientific suggestions. When a true social science shall have been founded, such labours will assume the philosophical direction of which they are at present destitute, and will aid that development of human genius which now, in the form of unorganized erudition, they merely impede. If we remember that no science can be thoroughly comprehended till its history is understood, we shall see what special improvements this new science must introduce into each of the rest, as well as into the co-ordination of them all.

As to method

This leads us to consider the reaction of sociology on the other sciences in regard to method. Without entering at present upon the great subject of a general theory of the positive method, I must just point out the established truth that each of the fundamental sciences specially manifests one of the chief attributes of the universal positive method, though all are present, in more or less force, in each science. The special resource of sociology is that it participates directly in the elementary composition of the common ground of our intellectual resources. It is plain that this logical co-operation of the new science is as important as that of any of the anterior sciences. We have seen that sociology adds to our other means of research that which I have called the *historical method*, and which will hereafter, when we are sufficiently habituated to it, constitute a fourth fundamental means of observation. But, though sociology has given us this resource, it is more or less applicable to all orders of scientific speculation. We have only to regard every

discovery, at the moment it is effected, as a true social phenomenon, forming a part of the general series of human development,
and, on that ground, subject to the laws of succession, and the
methods of investigation which characterize that great evolution.
From this starting-point, indisputable in its rationality, we comprehend immediately the whole necessary universality of the
historical method, thenceforth disclosed in all its eminent intellectual dignity. We can even see that, by this method, scientific
discoveries become in a certain degree susceptible of rational prevision, by means of an exact estimate of the anterior movement of
the science, interpreted by the laws of the course of the human
mind. The historical precision can hardly become very precise; but
it may furnish preparatory indications of the general direction of
the contemporary progress, so as to save the vast waste of intellectual forces which is occasioned by conjectural attempts, usually
doomed to failure. By this process of comparison of the present
with the past, in regard to each science, it must become possible
to subject the art of discovery to a kind of rational theory which
may guide the instinctive efforts of individual genius, which cannot hold its course apart from the general mind, however per-
suaded it may be of its separation. The historical method will thus,
by governing the systematic use of all other scientific methods,
impart to them an amplitude of rationality in which they are now
deficient, by transferring to the whole that regulated progression
which at present belongs only to the details: and the choice of
subjects for investigation, till now almost arbitrary, or, at least
thoroughly empirical, will acquire, in a certain degree, that
scientific character which now belongs only to the partial investigation of each of them. The method itself must, if it is to accomplish these purposes, be subject to the philosophical conditions
imposed by the positive spirit of sociology. It must never consider
the development of each complete science, separately from the
total progression of the human mind, or even from the fundamental evolution of humanity. Thus social physics, which supplies
this method, must superintend its gradual application, at least, in
so far as the general conception of human development is concerned ...

Thus we see that the reaction of sociology on the other sciences
is as important in a logical as in a scientific view. On the one hand,
positive sociology mutually connects all the sciences, and on the
other hand, it adds to all resources for investigation, a new and a
higher method. While, from its nature, dependent on all that went
before, social physics repays as much as it receives by its two kinds

of service towards all other knowledge. We can already perceive that such a science must form the principal band of the scientific sheaf, from its various relations, both of subordination and of direction, to all the rest.

The Intellectual Character of Positivism*

The charge of materialism which is often made against positive philosophy is of more importance. It originates in the course of scientific study upon which the positive system is based. In answering the charge, I need not enter into any discussion of impenetrable mysteries. Our theory of development will enable us to see distinctly the real ground of the confusion that exists upon the subject.

Positive science was for a long time limited to the simplest subjects; it could not reach the highest except by a natural series of intermediate steps. As each of these steps is taken, the student is apt to be influenced too strongly by the methods and results of the preceding stage. Here, as it seems to me, lies the real source of that scientific error which men have instinctively blamed as materialism. The name is just, because the tendency indicated is one which degrades the higher subjects of thought by confounding them with the lower. It was hardly possible that this usurpation by one science of the domain of another should have been wholly avoided. For since the more special phenomena do really depend upon the more general, it is perfectly legitimate for each science to exercise a certain deductive influence upon that which follows it in the scale. By such influence the special inductions of that science were rendered more coherent. The result, however, is that each of the sciences has to undergo a long struggle against the encroachments of the one preceding it; a struggle which even in the case of the subjects which have been studied longest, is not yet over. Nor can it entirely cease until the controlling influence of sound philosophy be established over the whole scale, introducing juster views of the relations of its several parts, about which at present there is such irrational confusion. Thus it appears that materialism is a danger inherent in the mode in which the scientific studies necessary as a preparation for positivism were pursued. Each science tended to absorb the one next to it, on the ground of having reached the positive stage earlier and more thoroughly. The evil then is really deeper and more extensive than is imagined by most

* *Pos. Pol.*, vol. 1, pp. 39–45.

of those who deplore it. It passes generally unnoticed except in the highest class of subjects. These doubtless are more seriously affected, inasmuch as they undergo the encroaching process from all the rest; but we find the same thing in different degrees, in every step of the scientific scale . . .

But the biologists who resist this encroachment most energetically, are often guilty of the same mistake. They not unfrequently attempt, for instance, to explain all sociological facts by the influence of climate and race, which are purely secondary; thus showing their ignorance of the fundamental laws of sociology, which can only be discovered by a series of direct inductions from history.

This philosophical estimate of materialism explains how it is that it has been brought as a charge against positivism, and at the same time proves the deep injustice of the charge. Positivism, far from countenancing so dangerous an error, is, as we have seen, the only philosophy which can completely remove it. The error arises from certain tendencies which are in themselves legitimate, but which have been carried too far; and positivism satisfies these tendencies in their due measure. Hitherto the evil has remained unchecked, except by the theologico-metaphysical spirit, which, by giving rise to what is called spiritualism, has rendered a very valuable service. But useful as it has been, it could not arrest the active growth of materialism, which has assumed in the eyes of modern thinkers something of a progressive character, from having been so long connected with the cause of resistance to a retrograde system. Notwithstanding all the protests of the spiritualists, the lower sciences have encroached upon the higher to an extent that seriously impairs their independence and their value. But positivism meets the difficulty far more effectually. It satisfies and reconciles all that is really tenable in the rival claims of both materialism and spiritualism; and, having done this, it discards them both. It holds the one to be as dangerous to order as the other to progress. This result is an immediate consequence of the establishment of the encyclopedic scale, in which each science retains its own proper sphere of induction, while deductively it remains subordinate to the science which precedes it. But what really decides the matter is the paramount importance, both logically and scientifically, given by positive philosopy to social questions. For these being the questions in which the influence of materialism is most mischievous, and also in which it is most easily introduced, a system which gave them the precedence over all others necessarily considers materialism as obstructive as spiritualism, both alike retarding the growth of that science for the sake of which all other sciences are studied. Further advance in the work of social regeneration implies the elimination of both of them, because it cannot proceed without exact knowledge of the laws of moral and social phenomena . . .

The charge of fatalism has accompanied every fresh extension of positive science, from its first beginnings. Nor is this surprising; for when any series of phenomena passes from the dominion of wills, whether modified by metaphysical abstractions or not, to the dominion of laws the regularity of the latter contrasts so strongly with the instability of the former, as to present an appearance of fatality, which nothing but a very careful examination of the real character of scientific truth can dissipate. And the error is the more likely to occur from the fact that our first types of natural laws are derived from the phenomena of the heavenly bodies. These, being wholly beyond our interference, always suggest the notion of absolute necessity, a notion which it is difficult to prevent from extending to more complex phenomena, as soon as they are brought within the reach of the positive method. And it is quite true that positivism holds the order of nature to be in its primary aspects strictly invariable. All variations, whether spontaneous or artificial, are only transient and of secondary import. The conception of unlimited variations would in fact be equivalent to the rejection of law altogether. But while this accounts for the fact that every new positive theory is accused of fatalism, it is equally clear that blind persistence in the accusation shows a very shallow conception of what positivism really is. For unchangeable as the order of nature is in its main aspects, yet all phenomena, except those of astronomy, admit of being modified in their secondary relations, and this the more as they are more complicated. The positive spirit when confined to the subjects of mathematics and astronomy, was inevitably fatalist; but this ceased to be the case when it extended to physics and chemistry, and especially to biology, where the margin of variation is very considerable. Now that it embraces social phenomena, the reproach, however it may have been once deserved, should be heard no longer, since these phenomena, which will for the future form its principal field, admit of larger modification than any others, and that chiefly by our own intervention. It is obvious then that positivism, far from encouraging indolence, stimulates us to action, especially to social action, far more energetically than any theological doctrine. It removes all groundless scruples, and prevents us from having recourse to chimeras. It encourages our efforts everywhere, except where they are manifestly useless . . .

The phenomena in question are those of intelligent beings who are always occupied in amending the defects of their economy. It is obvious, therefore, that they will show less imperfection than if, in a case equally complicated, the agents could have been blind. The standard by which to judge of action is always to be taken relatively to the social state in which the action takes place. Therefore all historical positions and changes must have at least some grounds of justification; otherwise they would be totally incomprehensible, because inconsistent with the nature of the agents and of the actions performed by them . . .

The object of sociology is to explain all historical facts; not to justify them indiscriminately, as is done by those who are unable to distinguish the influence of the agent from that of surrounding circumstances.

On reviewing this brief sketch of the intellectual character of positivism, it will be seen that all its essential attributes are summed up in the word *positive*, which I applied to the new philosophy at its outset. All the languages of western Europe agree in understanding by this word and its derivatives the two qualities of *reality* and *usefulness*. Combining these, we get at once an adequate definition of the true philosophic spirit, which, after all, is nothing but good sense generalized and put into a systematic form. The term also implies in all European languages, *certainty* and *precision*, qualities by which the intellect of modern nations is markedly distinguished from that of antiquity. Again, the ordinary acceptation of the term implies a directly *organic* tendency. Now the metaphysical spirit is incapable of organizing; it can only criticize. This distinguishes it from the positive spirit, although for a time they had a common sphere of action. By speaking of positivism as organic, we imply that it has a social purpose; that purpose being to supersede theology in the spiritual direction of the human race.

But the word will bear yet a further meaning. The organic character of the system leads us naturally to another of its attributes, namely, its invariable *relativity*. Modern thinkers will never rise above that critical position which they have hitherto taken up towards the past, except by repudiating all absolute principles. This last meaning is more latent than the others, but is really contained in the term. It will soon become generally accepted, and the word *positive* will be understood to mean *relative* as much as it now means *organic, precise, certain, useful* and *real* . . .

The Social Aspect of Positivism, as Shown by its Connection with the General Revolutionary Movement of Western Europe*

As the chief characteristic of positive philosophy is the preponderance of the social point of view through the whole range of speculation, its efficiency for the purposes of practical life is involved in the very spirit of the system. When this spirit is rightly understood, we find that it leads at once to an object far higher than that of satisfying our scientific curiosity; the object, namely, of organizing human life. Conversely, that practical aspect of positive philosophy exercises the most salutary influence upon its speculative character. By keeping constantly before us the necessity of concentrating all scientific efforts upon the social object which constitutes their value, we take the best possible means of checking the tendency inherent in all abstract enquiries to degenerate into useless digressions. But this general connection between theory and practice would not by itself be sufficient for our purpose. It would be impossible to secure the acceptance of a mental discipline, so new and so difficult, were it not for considerations derived from the general conditions of modern society; considerations calculated to impress philosophers with a more definite sense of obligation to do their utmost towards satisfying the wants of the time. By thus arousing public sympathies and showing that the success of positivism is a matter of permanent and general importance, the coherence of the system as well as the elevation of its aim will be placed beyond dispute. We have hitherto been regarding positivism as the issue in which intellectual development necessarily results. We have now to view it from the social side; for until we have done this, it is impossible to form a true conception of it.

Relation of positivism to the French Revolution

And to do this, all that is here necessary is to point out the close relation in which the new philosophy stands to the whole course of the French Revolution. This Revolution has now been agitating western nations for sixty years. It is the final issue of the vast

* *Pos. Pol.*, vol. 1, pp. 46–51.

transition through which we have been passing during the five previous centuries.

In this great crisis there are naturally two principal phases; of which only the first, or negative, phase has yet been accomplished. In it we gave the last blow to the old system, but without arriving at any fixed and distinct prospect of the new. In the second or positive phase, which is at last beginning, a basis for the new social state has to be constructed. The first phase led as its ultimate result to the formation of a sound philosophical system: and by this system the second phase will be directed. It is this twofold connection which we are now to consider.

The strong reaction which was exercised upon the intellect by the first great shock of Revolution was absolutely necessary to rouse and sustain our mental efforts in the search for a new system. For the greatest thinkers of the eighteenth century had been blinded to the true character of the new state by the effete remnants of the old. And the shock was especially necessary for the foundation of social science. For the basis of that science is the conception of human progress, a conception which nothing but the Revolution could have brought forward into sufficient prominence.

Social order was regarded by the ancients as stationary: and its theory under this provisional aspect was admirably sketched out by the great Aristotle. In this respect the case of sociology resembles that of biology. In biology statical conceptions were attained without the least knowledge of dynamical laws. Similarly, the social speculations of antiquity are entirely devoid of the conception of progress. Their historical field was too narrow to indicate any continuous movement of humanity. It was not till the Middle Ages that this movement became sufficiently manifest to inspire the feeling that we were tending towards a state of increased perfection ...

Now up to the time of the Revolution, political development, on which the principal argument for the theory of progress must always be based, corresponded in its imperfection to the incapacity of the scientific spirit to frame the theory of it. A century ago, thinkers of the greatest eminence were unable to conceive of a really continuous progression; and humanity, as they thought, was destined to move in circles or in oscillations. But under the influence of the Revolution a real sense of human development has arisen spontaneously and with more or less result, in minds of the most ordinary cast; first in France, and subsequently throughout the whole of western Europe. In this respect the crisis has been most salutary; it has given us that mental audacity as well as strength without which the conception could never have arisen. This conception is the basis of social science and therefore of all positive philosophy; since it is only from the social aspect that positive philosophy admits of being viewed as a connected whole. Without the theory of progress, the theory of order, even supposing that it could be formed, would be inadequate as a basis for sociology. It is essential that the two should be combined. The very fact that progress, however viewed, is nothing but the development of order, shows that order cannot be fully manifested without progress. The dependence of positivism upon the French Revolution may now be understood more clearly. Nor was it by a merely fortuitous coincidence that by this time the introductory course of scientific knowledge by which the mind is prepared for positivism should have been sufficiently completed.

But we must here observe that, beneficial as the intellectual reaction of this great crisis undoubtedly was, its effects could not be realized until the ardour of the revolutionary spirit had been to some extent weakened. The dazzling light thrown upon the future for some time obscured our vision of the past. It disclosed, though obscurely, the third term of the social progression; but it prevented us from fairly appreciating the second term. It encouraged that blind aversion to the Middle Ages, which had been inspired by the emancipating process of modern times; a feeling which had once been necessary to induce us to abandon the old system. The suppression of this intermediate step would be as fatal to the conception of progress as the absence of the last; because this last differs too widely from the first to admit of any direct comparison with it. Right views upon the subject were impossible therefore until full justice had been rendered to the Middle Ages, which form at once the point of union and of separation between ancient and modern history. Now it was quite impossible to do this as long as the excitement of the first years of the Revolution lasted. In this respect the philosophical reaction, organized at the beginning of our century by the great de Maistre, was of material assistance in preparing the true theory of progress. His school was of brief duration, and it was no doubt animated by a retrograde spirit; but it will always be ranked among the necessary antecedents of the positive system; although its works are now entirely superseded by the rise of the new philosophy, which in a more perfect form has embodied all their chief results . . .

Thus it appears that the revolutionary movement, and the long period of reaction which succeeded it, were alike necessary, before the new general doctrine could be distinctly conceived of as a whole. And if this preparation was needed for the establishment of positivism as a philosophical system, far more needful was it for the recognition of its social value. For it guaranteed free exposition and discussion of opinion: and it led the public to look to positivism as the system which contained in germ the ultimate solution of social problems. This is a point so obvious that we need not dwell upon it further.

2   *The Subject-matter and Methods of Sociology*

Characteristics of the Positive Method in its Application to Social Phenomena*

In every science, conceptions which relate to method are insepar-able from those which relate to the doctrine under consideration. The method has to be so varied in its application, and so largely modified by the complexity and special nature of the phenomena, in each case, that any general notions of method would be too indefinite for actual use. If, therefore, we have not separated the method from the doctrine in the simpler departments of science, much less should we think of doing so when treating of the com-plex phenomena of social life, to say nothing of the great feature of this last case—its want of positivity. In the formation of a new science the general spirit of it must be seized before its particular parts can be investigated: that is, we must have some notion of the doctrine before examining the method, and then the method can-not be estimated in any other way than by its use. Thus, I have not to offer a logical exposition of method in social physics before proceeding to the science itself; but I must follow the same plan here as in the case of the anterior sciences—ascertaining its general spirit, and what are the collective resources proper to it. Though these subjects may be said to belong to the science itself, we may consider them as belonging to the method, as they are absolutely necessary to direct our understandings in the pursuit of this diffi-cult study.

In the higher order of sciences, in those which are the simplest and the most advanced, the philosophical definition of each was almost sufficient to characterize their condition and general re-sources, to which no doubt could attach. But the case is otherwise with a recent and extremely complex study, the very nature of which has to be settled by laborious discussions, which are happily needless in regard to the preceding sciences. In treating of biology, we found it necessary to dwell upon preparatory explanations which would have seemed puerile in any of the foregoing depart-ments, because the chief bases of a science about which there were still so many disputes must be indisputably settled before it could take rank in the positive series. It is evident that the same process is even more needful, and must be more laborious, in the case of the science of social development, which has hitherto had no character of positivity at all, and which some of the ablest minds of our time sentence never to have any. We must not be surprised then if, after applying here the simplest and most radical ideas of positive

* *Pos. Phil.*, vol. 2, pp. 210–57.

philosophy, such as would indeed appear trivial in their formal application to the more advanced sciences, the result should appear to many, even among the enlightened, to constitute too bold an innovation, though the conditions may be no more than the barest equivalent of those which are admitted in every other case.

Infantile state of social science

If we look with a philosophical eye upon the present state of social science, we cannot but recognize in it the combination of all the features of that theologico-metaphysical infancy which all the other sciences have had to pass through. The present condition of political science revives before our eyes the analogy of what astrology was to astronomy, alchemy to chemistry, and the search for the universal panacea to the system of medical studies. We may, for our present purpose, consider the theological and the metaphysical polities together, the second being only a modification of the first in its relation to social science. Their attributes are the same, consisting, in regard to method, in the preponderance of imagination over observation; and, in regard to doctrine, in the exclusive investigation of absolute ideas; the result of both of which is an inevitable tendency to exercise an arbitrary and indefinite action over phenomena which are not regarded as subject to invariable natural laws. In short, the general spirit of all speculation at that stage is at once ideal in its course, absolute in its conception, and arbitrary in its application; and these are unquestionably the prevailing characteristics of social speculation at present, regarded from any point of view whatever. If we reverse all the three aspects, we shall have precisely the spirit which must actuate the formation of positive sociology, and which must afterwards direct its continuous development. The scientific spirit is radically distinguished from the theological and metaphysical by the steady subordination of the imagination to observation; and though the positive philosophy offers the vastest and richest field to human imagination, it restricts it to discovering and perfecting the co-ordination of observed facts, and the means of effecting new researches: and it is this habit of subjecting scientific conceptions to the facts whose connection has to be disclosed, which it is above all things necessary to introduce into social researches; for the observations hitherto made have been vague and ill-circumscribed, so as to afford no adequate foundation for scientific reasoning; and they are usually modified themselves at the pleasure of an imagination stimulated by the most fluctuating passions . . .

The relative superseding the absolute

If we contemplate the positive spirit in its relation to scientific conception, rather than the mode of procedure, we shall find that this philosophy is distinguished from the theologico-metaphysical by its tendency to render relative the ideas which were at first absolute. This inevitable passage from the absolute to the relative is one of the most important philosophical results of each of the intellectual revolutions which has carried on every kind of speculation from the theological or metaphysical to the scientific state. In a scientific view, this contrast between the relative and the absolute may be regarded as the most decisive manifestation of the antipathy between the modern philosophy and the ancient. All investigation into the nature of beings, and their first and final causes, must always be absolute; whereas the study of the laws of phenomena must be relative, since it supposes a continuous progress of speculation subject to the gradual improvement of observation, without the precise reality being ever fully disclosed: so that the relative character of scientific conceptions is inseparable from the true idea of natural laws, just as the chimerical inclination for absolute knowledge accompanies every use of theological fictions and metaphysical entities. Now, it is obvious that the absolute spirit characterizes social speculation now, wherever it exists, as the different schools are all agreed in looking for an immutable political type, which makes no allowance for the regular modification of political conceptions according to the variable state of civilization ...

Prevision of social phenomena

The last of the preliminary considerations that we have to review is that of the scientific prevision of phenomena, which, as the test of true science, includes all the rest. We have to contemplate social phenomena as susceptible of prevision, like all other classes, within the limits of exactness compatible with their higher complexity. Comprehending the three characteristics of political science which we have been examining, prevision of social phenomena supposes first, that we have abandoned the region of metaphysical idealities, to assume the ground of observed realities by a systematic subordination of imagination to observation; secondly, that political conceptions have ceased to be absolute, and have become relative to the variable state of civilization, so that theories, following the natural course of facts, may admit of our foreseeing them; and, thirdly, that permanent political action is limited by determinate laws, since, if social events were always exposed to disturbance by the accidental intervention of the legislator, human or divine, no scientific prevision of them would be possible. Thus, we may concentrate the conditions of the spirit of positive social philosophy on this one great attribute of scientific prevision.

Spirit of social science

The philosophical principle of the science being that social phenomena are subject to natural laws, admitting of rational prevision, we have to ascertain what is the precise subject, and what the peculiar character of those laws. The distinction between the statical and dynamical conditions of the subject must be extended to social science; and I shall treat of the conditions of social existence as, in biology, I treated of organization under the head of anatomy; and then of the laws of social movement, as in biology of those of life, under the head of physiology. This division, necessary for exploratory purposes, must not be stretched beyond that use: and, as we saw in biology, that the distinction becomes weaker with the advance of science, so shall we see that when the science of social physics is fully constituted, this division will remain for analytical purposes, but not as a real separation of the science into two parts. The distinction is not between two classes of facts, but between two aspects of a theory. It corresponds with the double conception of order and progress: for order consists (in a positive sense) in a permanent harmony among the conditions of social existence; and progress consists in social development; and the conditions in the one case, and the laws of movement in the other, constitute the statics and dynamics of social physics . . .

Statical study

The statical study of sociology consists in the investigation of the laws of action and reaction of the different parts of the social system—apart, for the occasion, from the fundamental movement which is always gradually modifying them. In this view, sociological prevision, founded upon the exact general knowledge of those relations, acts by judging by each other the various statical indications of each mode of social existence, in conformity with direct observation—just as is done daily in the case of anatomy. This view condemns the existing philosophical practice of contemplating social elements separately, as if they had an independent existence; and it leads us to regard them as in mutual relation, and forming a whole which compels us to treat them in combination. By this method, not only are we furnished with the only possible basis for the study of social movement, but we are put in possession of an important aid to direct observation; since many social elements which cannot be investigated by immediate observation may be estimated by their scientific relation to others already known . . .

The scientific principle of the relation between the political and the social condition is simply this: that there must always be a spontaneous harmony between the whole and the parts of the social system, the elements of which must inevitably be, sooner or later, combined in a mode entirely conformable to their nature. It is evident that not only must political institutions and social manners on the one hand, and manners and ideas on the other, be always mutually connected; but, further, that this consolidated whole must be always connected, by its nature, with the corresponding state of the integral development of humanity, considered in all its aspects, of intellectual, moral and physical activity; and the only object of any political system whatever, temporal or spiritual, is to regulate the spontaneous expansion so as best to direct it towards its determinate end. Even during revolutionary periods, when the harmony appears furthest from being duly realized, it still exists: for without it there would be a total dissolution of the social organism. During those exceptional seasons, the political regime is still, in the long run, in conformity with the corresponding state of civilization, as the disturbances which are manifest in the one proceed from equivalent derangements in the other. It is observable that when the popular theory attributes to the legislator the permanent power of infringing the harmony we are speaking of, it supposes him to be armed with a sufficient authority. But every social power, whether called authority or anything else, is constituted by a corresponding assent, spontaneous or deliberate, explicit or implicit, of various individual wills, resolved, from certain preparatory convictions, to concur in a common action, of which this power is first the organ, and then the regulator. Thus, authority is derived from concurrence, and not concurrence from authority (setting aside the necessary reaction) so that no great power can arise otherwise than from the strongly prevalent disposition of the society in which it exists: and when there is no strong preponderance, such powers as exist are weak accordingly: and the more extensive the society, the more irresistible is the correspondence. On the other hand, there is no denying the influence which, by a necessary reaction, the political system, as a whole, exercises over the general system of civilization, and which is so often exhibited in the action, fortunate or disastrous, of institutions, measures, or purely political events, even upon the course of the sciences and arts, in all ages of society, and especially the earliest. We need not dwell on this; for no one denies it. The common error, indeed, is to exaggerate it, so as to place the reaction before the primary action. It is evident, considering their scientific relation to each other, that both concur in creating that fundamental agreement of the social organism which I propose to set forth in a brief manner, as the philosophical principle of statical sociology . . .

In brief, it is our business to contemplate order, that we may perfect it; and not to create it; which would be impossible. In a scientific view, this master-thought of universal social interconnection becomes the consequence and complement of a fundamental idea established, in our view of biology, as eminently proper to the study of living bodies. Not that this idea of interconnection is peculiar to that study: it is necessarily common to all phenomena; but amidst immense differences in intensity and variety, and therefore in philosophical importance. It is, in fact, true that wherever there is any system whatever, a certain interconnection must exist . . .

It follows from this attribute that there can be no scientific study of society, either in its conditions or its movements, if it is separated into portions, and its divisions are studied apart. I have already remarked upon this, in regard to what is called political economy. Materials may be furnished by the observation of different departments; and such observation may be necessary for that object: but it cannot be called science. The methodical division of studies which takes place in the simple inorganic science is thoroughly irrational in the recent and complex science of society, and can produce no results. The day may come when some sort of subdivision may be practicable and desirable; but it is impossible for us now to anticipate what the principle of distribution may be; for the principle itself must arise from the development of the science; and that development can take place no otherwise than by our formation of the science as a whole. The complete body will indicate for itself, at the right season, the particular points which need investigation; and then will be the time for such special study as may be required. By any other method of proceeding, we shall only find ourselves encumbered with special discussions, badly instituted, worse pursued, and accomplishing no other purpose than that of impeding the formation of real science. It is no easy matter to study social phenomena in the only right way—viewing each element in the light of the whole system. It is no easy matter to exercise such vigilance as that no one of the number of contemporary aspects shall be lost sight of. But it is the right and the only way . . .

Order of statical study

Before we go on to the subject of social dynamics, I will just remark that the prominent interconnection we have been considering prescribes a procedure in organic studies different from that which suits inorganic. The metaphysicians announce as an aphorism that we should always, in every kind of study, proceed from the simple to the compound: whereas, it appears most rational to suppose that we should follow that or the reverse method, as may best suit our subject. There can be no absolute merit in the method enjoined, apart from its suitableness. The rule should rather be (and there probably was a time when the two rules were one) that we must proceed from the more known to the less. Now, in the inorganic sciences, the elements are much better known to us than the whole which they constitute: so that in that case we must proceed from the simple to the compound. But the reverse method is necessary in the study of man and of society; man and society as a whole being better known to us, and more accessible subjects of study, than the parts which constitute them. In exploring the universe, it is as a whole that it is inaccessible to us; whereas, in investigating man or society, our difficulty is in penetrating the details . . .

Dynamical study

Passing on from statical to dynamical sociology, we will contemplate the philosophical conception which should govern our study of the movement of society. Part of this subject is already dispatched, from the explanations made in connection with statics having simplified the chief difficulties of the case. And social dynamics will be so prominent throughout the rest of this work, that I may reduce within very small compass what I have to say now under that head.

Though the statical view of society is the basis of sociology, the dynamical view is not only the more interesting of the two, but the more marked in its philosophical character, from its being more distinguished from biology by the master-thought of continuous progress, or rather, of the gradual development of humanity. If I were writing a methodical treatise on political philosophy, it would be necessary to offer a preliminary analysis of the individual impulsions which make up the progressive force of the human race, by referring them to that instinct which results from the concurrence of all our natural tendencies, and which urges man to develop the whole of his life, physical, moral and intellectual, as far as his circumstances allow. But this view is admitted by all enlightened philosophers; so that I must proceed at once to consider the continuous succession of human development, regarded in the whole race, as if humanity were one. For clearness, we may take advantage of Condorcet's device of supposing a single nation to which we may refer all the consecutive social modifications actually witnessed among distinct peoples. This rational fiction is nearer the reality than we are accustomed to suppose; for, in a political view, the true successors of such or such a people are certainly those who, taking up and carrying out their primitive endeavours, have prolonged their social progress, whatever may be the soil which they inhabit, or even the race from which they spring. In brief, it is political continuity which regulates sociological succession, though the having a common country must usually affect this continuity in a high degree. As a scientific artifice merely, however, I shall employ this hypothesis, and on the ground of its manifest utility.

Social continuity

The true general spirit of social dynamics then consists in conceiving of each of these consecutive social states as the necessary result of the preceding, and the indispensable mover of the following, according to the axiom of Leibnitz: 'the present is big with the future.' In this view, the object of science is to discover the laws which govern this continuity, and the aggregate of which determines the course of human development. In short, social dynamics studies the laws of succession, while social statics inquires into those of co-existence; so that the use of the first is to furnish the true theory of progress to political practice, while the second performs the same service in regard to order; and this suitability to the needs of modern society is a strong confirmation of the philosophical character of such a combination.

Produced by natural laws

If the existence of sociological laws has been established in the more difficult and uncertain case of the statical condition, we may assume that they will not be questioned in the dynamical province . . .

Now, in whichever of these ways we regard, as a whole, the movement of humanity, from the earliest periods till now, we shall find that the various steps are connected in a determinate order; as we shall hereafter see, when we investigate the laws of this succession. I need refer here only to the intellectual evolution, which is the most distinct and unquestionable of all, as it has been the least impeded and most advanced of any, and has therefore been usually taken for guidance. The chief part of this evolution, and that which has most influenced the general progression, is no doubt the development of the scientific spirit, from the primitive labours of such philosophers as Thales and Pythagoras to those of men like Lagrange and Bichat. Now, no enlightened man can doubt that, in this long succession of efforts and discoveries, the human mind has pursued a determinate course, the exact preparatory knowledge of which might have allowed a cultivated reason to foresee the progress proper to each period. Though the historical considerations cited in my former volume were only incidental, any one may recognize in them numerous and indisputable examples of this necessary succession, more complex perhaps, but not more arbitrary than any natural law, whether in regard to the development of each separate science, or to the mutual influence of the different branches of natural philosophy. In accordance with the principles laid down at the beginning of this work, we have already seen in various signal instances, that the chief progress of each period, and even of each generation, was a necessary result of the immediately preceding state; so that the men of genius, to whom such progression has been too exclusively attributed, are essentially only the proper organs of a predetermined movement, which would, in their absence, have found other issues. We find a verification of this in history, which shows that various eminent men were ready to make the same great discovery at the same time, while the discovery required only one organ. All the parts of the human evolution admit of analogous observations, as we shall presently see, though they are more complex and less obvious than that which I have just cited . . .

Notion of human perfectibility

We have nothing to do here with the metaphysical controversy about the absolute happiness of man at different stages of civilization. As the happiness of every man depends on the harmony between the development of his various faculties and the entire system of the circumstances which govern his life; and as, on the other hand, this equilibrium always establishes itself spontaneously to a certain extent, it is impossible to compare in a positive way, either by sentiment or reasoning, the individual welfare which belongs to social situations that can never be brought into direct comparison: and therefore the question of the happiness of different animal organisms, or of their two sexes, is merely impracticable and unintelligible. The only question therefore is of the effect of the social evolution, which is so undeniable that there is no reasoning with any one who does not admit it as the basis of the inquiry. The only ground of discussion is whether development and improvement—the theoretical and the practical aspect—are one; whether the development is necessarily accompanied by a corresponding amelioration, or progress, properly so called. To me it appears that the amelioration is as unquestionable as the development from which it proceeds, provided we regard it as subject, like the development itself, to limits, general and special, which science will be found to prescribe. The chimerical notion of unlimited perfectibility is thus at once excluded. Taking the human race as a whole, and not any one people, it appears that human development brings after it, in two ways, an ever-increasing amelioration, first, in the radical condition of man, which no one disputes; and next, in his corresponding faculties, which is a view much less attended to . . .

Adhering to our relative, in opposition to the absolute, view, we must conclude the social state, regarded as a whole, to have been as perfect, in each period, as the co-existing condition of humanity and of its environment would allow. Without this view, history would be incomprehensible; and the relative view is as indispensable in regard to progress, as, in considering social statics, we saw it to be in regard to order . . .

Social phenomena modifiable

We must observe, in the first place, that social phenomena may, from their complexity, be more easily modified than any others, according to the law which was established to that effect in my first volume. Thus, the limits of variations are wider in regard to sociological than any other laws. If, then, human intervention holds the same proportionate rank among modifying influences as it is natural at first to suppose, its influence must be more considerable in the first case than in any other, all appearances to the contrary notwithstanding. This is the first scientific foundation of all rational hopes of a systematic reformation of humanity; and on this ground illusions of this sort certainly appear more excusable than on any other subject. But though modifications, from all causes, are greater in the case of political than of simpler phenomena, still they can never be more than modifications: that is, they will always be in subjection to those fundamental laws, whether statical or dynamical, which regulate the harmony of the social elements, and the filiation of their successive variations. There is no disturbing influence, exterior or human, which can make incompatible elements co-exist in the political system, nor change in any way the natural laws of the development of humanity. The inevitable gradual preponderance of continuous influences, however imperceptible their power may be at first, is now admitted with regard to all natural phenomena; and it must be applied to social phenomena, whenever the same method of philosophizing is extended to them. What then are the modifications of which the social organism and social life are susceptible, if nothing can alter the laws either of harmony or of succession? The answer is that modifications act upon the intensity and secondary operation of phenomena, but without affecting their nature or their filiation. To suppose that they could, would be to exalt the disturbing above the fundamental cause, and would destroy the whole economy of laws. In the political system this principle of positive philosophy shows that, in a statical view, any possible variations can affect only the intensity of the different tendencies belonging to each social situation, without in any way hindering or producing, or, in a word, changing the nature of, those tendencies; and, in the same way, in a dynamical view, the progress of the race must be considered susceptible of modification only with regard to its speed, and without any reversal in the order of development, or any interval of any importance being overleaped. These variations are analogous to those of the animal organism, with the one difference that in sociology they are more complex; and, as we saw that the limits of variation remain to be established in biology, it is not to be expected that sociology should be more advanced. But all we want here is to obtain a notion of the general spirit of the law, in regard both to social statics and dynamics; and looking at it from both points of view, it seems to me impossible to question its truth. In the intellectual order of phenomena, for instance, there is no accidental influence, nor any individual superiority, which can transfer to one period the discoveries reserved for a subsequent age, in the natural course of the human mind; nor can there be the reverse case of postponement. The history of the sciences settles the question of the close dependence of even the most eminent individual genius on the contemporary state of the human mind; and this is above all remarkable in regard to the improvement of methods of investigation, either in the way of reasoning or experiment. The same things happen in regard to the arts; and especially in whatever depends on mechanical means in substitution for human action. And there is not, in reality, any more room for doubt in the case of moral development, the character of which is certainly determined, in each period, by the corresponding state of the social evolution, whatever may be the modifications caused by education or individual organization. Each of the leading modes of social existence determines for itself a certain system of morals and manners, the common aspect of which is easily recognized in all individuals, in the midst of their characteristic differences; for instance, there is a state of human life in which the best individual natures contract a habit of ferocity, from which very inferior natures easily emancipate themselves, in a better state of society. The case is the same, in a political view, as our historical analysis will hereafter show. And in fact, if we were to review all the facts and reflections which establish the existence of the limits of variation, whose principle I have just laid down, we should find ourselves reproducing in succession all the proofs of the subjection of social phenomena to invariable laws; because the principle is neither more nor less than a strict application of the philosophical conception.

Order of modifying influences

We cannot enlarge upon the second head: that is, the classification of modifying influences according to their respective importance. If such a classification is not yet established in biology, it would be premature indeed to attempt it in social science. Thus, if the three chief causes of social variation appear to me to result from, first, race, secondly, climate, thirdly, political action in its whole scientific extent, it would answer none of our present purposes to inquire here whether this or some other is the real order of their importance. The political influences are the only ones really open to our intervention; and to that head general attention must be directed, though with great care to avoid the conclusion that that class of influences must be the most important because it is the most immediately interesting to us. It is owing to such an illusion as this that observers who believe themselves emancipated from old prejudices cannot obtain sociological knowledge, because they enormously exaggerate the power of political action. Because political operations, temporal or spiritual, can have no social efficacy but in as far as they are in accordance with the corresponding tendencies of the human mind, they are supposed to have produced what is in reality occasioned by a spontaneous evolution, which is less conspicuous, and easily overlooked. Such a mistake proceeds in neglect of numerous and marked cases in history, in which the most prodigious political authority has left no lasting traces of its well-sustained development, because it moved in a contrary direction to modern civilization; as in the instances of Julian, of Philip II., of Napoleon Bonaparte, etc. The inverse cases, unhappily too few, are still more decisive; those cases in which political action, sustained by an equally powerful authority, has nevertheless failed in the pursuit of ameliorations that were premature, though in accordance with the social movement of the time. Intellectual history, as well as political, furnishes examples of this kind in abundance. It has been sensibly remarked by Ferguson, that even the action of one nation upon another, whether by conquest or otherwise, though the most intense of all social forces, can effect merely such modifications as are in accordance with its existing tendencies; so that, in fact, the action merely accelerates or extends a development which would have taken place without it. In politics, as in science, *opportuneness* is always the main condition of all great and durable influence, whatever may be the personal value of the superior man to whom the multitude attribute social action of which he is merely the fortunate organ. The power of the individual over the race is subject to these general limits, even when the effects, for good or for evil, are as easy as possible to produce. In revolutionary times, for instance, those who are proud of having aroused anarchical passions in their contemporaries do not see that their miserable triumph is due to a spontaneous disposition, determined by the aggregate of the corresponding social state, which has produced a provisional and partial relaxation of the general harmony. As for the rest, it being ascertained that there are limits of variation among social phenomena, and modifications dependent on systematic political action; and as the scientific principle which is to describe such modifications is now known; the influence and scope of that principle must be determined in each case by the direct development of social science, applied to the appreciation of the corresponding state of circumstances. It is by such estimates, empirically attempted, that men of genius have been guided in all great and profound action upon humanity in any way whatever; and it is only thus that they have been able to rectify, in a rough way, the illusory suggestions of the irrational doctrines in which they were educated. Everywhere, as I have so often said, foresight is the true source of action.

The inaccurate intellectual habits which as yet prevail in political philosophy may induce an apprehension that, according to such considerations as those just presented, the new science of social physics may reduce us to mere observation of human events, excluding all continuous intervention. It is, however, certain that, while dissipating all ambitious illusions about the indefinite action of man on civilization, the principle of rational limits to political action establishes, in the most exact and unquestionable manner, the true point of contact between social theory and practice. It is by this principle only that political art can assume a systematic character, by its release from arbitrary principles mingled with empirical notions. It is thus only that political art can pass upwards as medical art has done; the two cases being strongly analogous. As political intervention can have no efficacy unless it rests on corresponding tendencies of the political organism or life, so as to aid its spontaneous development, it is absolutely necessary to understand the natural laws of harmony and succession which determine, in every period, and under every social aspect, what the human evolution is prepared to produce, pointing out, at the same time, the chief obstacles which may be got rid of. It would be exaggerating the scope of such an art to suppose it capable of obviating, in all cases, the violent disturbances which are occasioned by impediments to the natural evolution. In the highly complex social organism, maladies and crises are necessarily even more inevitable than in the individual organism. But, though science is powerless for the moment amidst wild disorder and extravagance, it may palliate and abridge the crises, by understanding their character and foreseeing their issue, and by more or less intervention, where any is possible. Here, as in other cases, and more than in other cases, the office of science is, not to govern, but to modify phenomena; and to do this, it is necessary to understand their laws.

Thus, then, we see what is the function of social science. Without extolling or condemning political facts, science regards them as subjects of observation: it contemplates each phenomenon in its harmony with co-existing phenomena, and in its connection with the foregoing and the following state of human development: it endeavours to discover, from both points of view, the general relations which connect all social phenomena: and each of them is *explained*, in the scientific sense of the word, when it has been connected with the whole of the existing situation, and the whole of the preceding movement. Favouring the social sentiment in the highest degree, this science fulfils the famous suggestion of Pascal, by representing the whole human race, past, present and future, as constituting a vast and eternal social unit, whose different organs, individual and national, concur, in their various modes and degrees, in the evolution of humanity. Leading us on, like every other science, with as much exactness as the extreme complexity of its phenomena allows, to a systematic prevision of the events which must result from either a given situation or a given aggregate of antecedents, political science enlightens political art, not only in regard to the tendencies which should be aided, but as to the chief means that should be employed, so as to avoid all useless or ephemeral and therefore dangerous action; in short, all waste of any kind of social force.

Means of investigation

This examination of the general spirit of political philosophy has been much more difficult than the same process in regard to any established science. The next step, now that this is accomplished, is to examine, according to my usual method, the means of investigation proper to social science. In virtue of a law before recognized, we may expect to find in sociology a more varied and developed system of resources than in any other, in proportion to the complexity of the phenomena, while yet, this extension of means does not compensate for the increased imperfection arising from the intricacy. The extension of the means is also more difficult to verify than in any prior case, from the novelty of the subject; and I can scarcely hope that such a sketch as I must present here will command such confidence as will arise when a complete survey of the science shall have confirmed what I now offer.

As social physics assumes a place in the hierarchy of sciences after all the rest, and therefore dependent on them, its means of investigation must be of two kinds: those which are peculiar to itself, and which may be called direct, and those which arise from the connection of sociology with the other sciences; and these last, though indirect, are as indispensable as the first. I shall review, first, the direct resources of the science.

Direct means

Here, as in all the other cases, there are three methods of proceeding: by observation, experiment and comparison.

Observation

Very imperfect and even vicious notions prevail at present as to what observation can be and can effect in social science. The chaotic state of doctrine of the last century has extended to method; and amidst our intellectual disorganization, difficulties have been magnified; precautionary methods, experimental and rational, have been broken up; and even the possibility of obtaining social knowledge by observation has been dogmatically denied; but if the sophisms put forth on this subject were true, they would destroy the certainty, not only of social science, but of all the simpler and more perfect ones that have gone before. The ground of doubt assigned is the uncertainty of human testimony; but all the sciences, up to the most simple, require proofs of testimony: that is, in the elaboration of the most positive theories, we have to admit observations which could not be directly made, nor even repeated, by those who use them, and the reality of which rests only on the faithful testimony of the original investigators; there being nothing in this to prevent the use of such proofs, in concurrence with immediate observations. In astronomy, such a method is obviously necessary; it is equally, though less obviously necessary even in mathematics; and, of course, much more evidently in the case of the more complex sciences. How could any science emerge from the nascent state, how could there be any organization of intellectual labour, even if research were restricted to the utmost, if every one rejected all observations but his own? The stoutest advocates of historical scepticism do not go so far as to advocate this. It is only in the case of social phenomena that the paradox is proposed; and it is made use of there because it is one of the weapons of the philosophical arsenal which the revolutionary metaphysical doctrine constructed for the intellectual overthrow of the ancient political system.

The next great hindrance to the use of observation is the empiricism which is introduced into it by those who, in the name of impartiality, would interdict the use of any theory whatever. No logical dogma could be more thoroughly irreconcilable with the spirit of the positive philosophy, or with its special character in regard to the study of social phenomena, than this. No real observation of any kind of phenomena is possible, except in as far as it is first directed, and finally interpreted, by some theory: and it was this logical need which, in the infancy of human reason, occasioned the rise of theological philosophy, as we shall see in the course of our historical survey. The positive philosophy does not dissolve this obligation, but, on the contrary, extends and fulfils it more and more, the further the relations of phenomena are multiplied and perfected by it. Hence it is clear that, scientifically speaking, all isolated, empirical observation is idle, and even radically uncertain; that science can use only those observations which are connected, at least hypothetically, with some law; that it is such a connection which makes the chief difference between scientific and popular observation, embracing the same facts, but contemplating them from different points of view: and that observations empirically conducted can at most supply provisional materials, which must usually undergo an ulterior revision. The rational method of observation becomes more necessary in proportion to the complexity of the phenomena, amidst which the observer would not know what he ought to look at in the facts before his eyes, but for the guidance of a preparatory theory; and thus it is that by the connection of foregoing facts we learn to see the facts that follow. This is undisputed with regard to astronomical, physical and chemical research, and in every branch of biological study, in which good observation of its highly complex phenomena is still very rare, precisely because its positive theories are very imperfect. Carrying on the analogy, it is evident that in the corresponding divisions, statical and dynamical, of social science, there is more need than anywhere else of theories which shall scientifically connect the facts that are happening with those that have happened: and the more we reflect, the more distinctly we shall see that in proportion as known facts are mutually connected we shall be better able, not only to estimate, but to perceive, those which are yet unexplored. I am not blind to the vast difficulty which this requisition imposes on the institution of positive sociology—obliging us to create at once, so to speak, observations and laws, on account of their indispensable connection, placing us in a sort of vicious circle, from which we can issue only by employing in the first instance materials which are badly elaborated, and doctrines which are ill-conceived. How I may succeed in a task so difficult and delicate, we shall see at its close; but, however that may be, it is clear that it is the absence of any positive theory which at present renders social observations so vague and incoherent. There can never be any lack of facts; for in this case even more than in others, it is the commonest sort of facts that are most important, whatever the collectors of secret anecdotes may think; but, though we are steeped to the lips in them, we can make no use of them, nor even be aware of them, for want of speculative guidance in examining them. The statical observation of a crowd of phenomena cannot take place without some notion, however elementary, of the laws of social interconnection: and dynamical facts could have no fixed direction if they were not attached, at least by a provisional hypothesis, to the laws of social development. The positive philosophy is very far from discouraging historical or any other erudition; but the precious night-watchings, now so lost in the laborious acquisition of a conscientious but barren learning, may be made available by it for the constitution of true social science, and the increased honour of the earnest minds that are devoted to it. The new philosophy will supply fresh and nobler subjects, unhoped-for insight, a loftier aim, and therefore a higher scientific dignity. It will discard none but aimless labours, without principle and without character; as in physics, there is no room for compilations of empirical observations; and at the same time, philosophy will render justice to the zeal of students of a past generation, who, destitute of the favourable guidance which we, of this day, enjoy, followed up their laborious historical researches with an instinctive perseverance, and in spite of the superficial disdain of the philosophers of the time. No doubt, the same danger attends research here as elsewhere: the danger that, from the continuous use of scientific theories, the observer may sometimes pervert facts, by erroneously supposing them to verify some ill-grounded speculative prejudices of his own. But we have the same guard here as elsewhere—in the further extension of the science: and the case would not be improved by a recurrence to empirical methods, which would be merely leaving theories that may be misapplied but can always be rectified, for imaginary notions which cannot be substantiated at all. Our feeble reason may often fail in the application of positive theories; but at least they transfer us from the domain of imagination to that of reality, and expose us infinitely less than any other kind of doctrine to the danger of seeing in facts that which is not.

It is now clear that social science requires, more than any other, the subordination of observation to the statical and dynamical laws of phenomena. No social fact can have any scientific meaning till it is connected with some other social fact; without which connection it remains a mere anecdote, involving no rational utility. This condition so far increases the immediate difficulty that good observers will be rare at first, though more abundant than ever as the science expands: and here we meet with another confirmation of what I said at the outset of this volume—that the formation of social theories should be confided only to the best organized minds, prepared by the most rational training. Explored by such minds, according to rational views of co-existence and succession, social phenomena no doubt admit of much more varied and extensive means of investigation than phenomena of less complexity. In this view, it is not only the immediate inspection or direct description of events that affords useful means of positive exploration; but the consideration of apparently insignificant customs, the appreciation of various kinds of monuments, the analysis and comparison of languages, and a multitude of other resources. In short, a mind suitably trained becomes able by exercise to convert almost all impressions from the events of life into sociological indications, when once the connection of all indications with the leading ideas of the science is understood. This is a facility afforded by the mutual relation of the various aspects of society, which may partly compensate for the difficulty caused by that mutual connection: if it renders observation more difficult, it affords more means for its prosecution.

Experiment

It might be supposed beforehand that the second method of investigation, experiment, must be wholly inapplicable in social science; but we shall find that the science is not entirely deprived of this resource, though it must be one of inferior value. We must remember (what was before explained) that there are two kinds of experimentation—the direct and the indirect: and that it is not necessary to the philosophical character of this method that the circumstances of the phenomenon in question should be, as is vulgarly supposed in the learned world, artificially instituted. Whether the case be natural or factitious, experimentation takes place whenever the regular course of the phenomenon is interfered with in any determinate manner. The spontaneous nature of the alteration has no effect on the scientific value of the case, if the elements are known. It is in this sense that experimentation is possible in sociology. If direct experimentation had become too difficult amidst the complexities of biology, it may well be considered impossible in social science. Any artificial disturbance of any social element must affect all the rest, according to the laws both of co-existence and succession; and the experiment would therefore, if it could be instituted at all, be deprived of all scientific value, through the impossibility of isolating either the conditions or the results of the phenomenon. But we saw, in our survey of biology, that pathological cases are the true scientific equivalent of pure experimentation, and why. The same reasons apply, with even more force, to sociological researches. In them, pathological analysis consists in the examination of cases, unhappily too common, in which the natural laws, either of harmony or of succession, are disturbed by any causes, special or general, accidental or transient; as in revolutionary times especially, and above all, in our own. These disturbances are, in the social body, exactly analogous to diseases in the individual organism: and I have no doubt whatever that the analogy will be more evident (allowance being made for the unequal complexity of the organisms) the deeper the investigation goes. In both cases it is, as I said once before, a noble use to make of our reason, to disclose the real laws of our nature, individual or social, by the analysis of its sufferings. But if the method is imperfectly instituted in regard to biological questions, much more faulty must it be in regard to the phenomena of social science, for want even of the rational conceptions to which they are to be referred. We see the most disastrous political experiments for ever renewed, with only some insignificant and irrational modifications, though their first operation should have fully satisfied us of the uselessness and danger of the expedients proposed. Without forgetting how much is ascribable to the influence of human passions, we must remember that the deficiency of an authoritative rational analysis is one of the main causes of the barrenness imputed to social experiments, the course of which would become much more instructive if it were better observed. The great natural laws exist and act in all conditions of the organism; for, as we saw in the case of biology, it is an error to suppose that they are violated or suspended in the case of disease: and we are therefore justified in drawing our conclusions, with due caution, from the scientific analysis of disturbance to the positive theory of normal existence. This is the nature and character of the indirect experimentation which discloses the real economy of the social body in a more marked manner than simple observation could do. It is applicable to all orders of sociological research, whether relating to existence or to movement, and regarded under any aspect whatever, physical, intellectual, moral, or political; and to all degrees of the social evolution, from which, unhappily, disturbances have never been absent. As for its present extension, no one can venture to offer any statement of it, because it has never been duly applied in any investigation in political philosophy; and it can become customary only by the institution of the new science which I am endeavouring to establish. But I could not omit this notice of it, as one of the means of investigation proper to social science.

Comparison

As for the third of those methods, comparison, the reader must bear in mind the explanations offered, in our survey of biological philosophy, of the reasons why the comparative method must prevail in all studies of which the living organism is the subject; and the more remarkably, in proportion to the rank of the organism. The same considerations apply in the present case, in a more conspicuous degree; and I may leave it to the reader to make the application, merely pointing out the chief differences which distinguish the use of the comparative method in sociological inquiries.

Comparison with inferior animals

It is a very irrational disdain which makes us object to all comparison between human society and the social state of the lower animals. This unphilosophical pride arose out of the protracted influence of the theologico-metaphysical philosophy; and it will be corrected by the positive philosophy, when we better understand and can estimate the social state of the higher orders of mammifers, for instance. We have seen how important is the study of individual life, in regard to intellectual and moral phenomena—of which social phenomena are the natural result and complement. There was once the same blindness to the importance of the procedure in this case as now in the other; and, as it has given way in the one case, so it will in the other. The chief defect in the kind of sociological comparison that we want is that it is limited to statical consideration; whereas the dynamical are, at the present time, the preponderant and direct subject of science. The restriction results from the social state of animals being, though not so stationary as we are apt to suppose, yet susceptible only of extremely small variations, in no way comparable to the continued progression of humanity in its feeblest days. But there is no doubt of the scientific utility of such a comparison, in the statical province, where it characterizes the elementary laws of social interconnection, by exhibiting their action in the most imperfect state of society, so as even to suggest useful inductions in regard to human society. There cannot be a stronger evidence of the natural character of the chief social relations, which some people fancy that they can transform at pleasure. Such sophists will cease to regard the great ties of the human family as factitious and arbitrary when they find them existing, with the same essential characteristics, among the animals, and more conspicuously, the nearer the organisms approach to the human type. In brief, in all that part of sociology which is almost one with intellectual and moral biology, or with the natural history of man; in all that relates to the first germs of the social relations, and the first institutions which were founded by the unity of the family or the tribe, there is not only great scientific advantage, but real philosophical necessity for employing the rational comparison of human with other animal societies. Perhaps it might even be desirable not to confine the comparison to societies which present a character of voluntary co-operation, in analogy to the human. They must always rank first in importance: but the scientific spirit, extending the process to its final logical term, might find some advantage in examining those strange associations, proper to the inferior animals, in which an involuntary co-operation results from an indissoluble organic union, either by simple adhesion or real continuity. If the science gained nothing by this extension, the method would. And there is nothing that can compare with such an habitual scientific comparison for the great service of casting out the absolute spirit which is the chief vice of political philosophy. It appears to me, moreover, that, in a practical view, the insolent pride which induces some ranks of society to suppose themselves as, in a manner, of another species than the rest of mankind, is in close affinity with the irrational disdain that repudiates all comparison between human and other animal nature. However all this may be, these considerations apply only to a methodical and special treatment of social philosophy. Here, where I can offer only the first conception of the science, in which dynamical considerations must prevail, it is evident that I can make little use of the kind of comparison; and this makes it all the more necessary to point it out, lest its omission should occasion such scientific inconveniences as I have just indicated. The commonest logical procedures are generally so characterized by their very application, that nothing more of a preliminary nature is needed than the simplest examination of their fundamental properties.

Comparison of co-existing states of society

To indicate the order of importance of the forms of society which are to be studied by the comparative method, I begin with the chief method, which consists in a comparison of the different co-existing states of human society on the various parts of the earth's surface—those states being completely independent of each other. By this method, the different stages of evolution may all be observed at once. Though the progression is single and uniform, in regard to the whole race, some very considerable and very various populations have, from causes which are little understood, attained extremely unequal degrees of development, so that the former states of the most civilized nations are now to be seen, amidst some partial differences, among contemporary populations inhabiting different parts of the globe. In its relation to observation, this kind of comparison offers the advantage of being applicable both to statical and dynamical inquiries, verifying the laws of both, and even furnishing occasionally valuable direct inductions in regard to both. In the second place, it exhibits all possible degrees of social evolution to our immediate observation. From the wretched inhabitants of Tierra del Fuego to the most advanced nations of western Europe, there is no social grade which is not extant in some points of the globe, and usually in localities which are clearly apart. In the historical part of this volume, we shall find that some interesting secondary phases of social development, of which the history of civilization leaves no perceptible traces, can be known only by this comparative method of study; and these are not, as might be supposed, the lowest degrees of evolution, which every one admits can be investigated in no other way. And between the great historical aspects, there are numerous intermediate states which must be observed thus, if at all. This second part of the comparative method verifies the indications afforded by historical analysis, and fills up the gaps it leaves: and nothing can be more rational than the method, as it rests upon the established principle that the development of the human mind is uniform in the midst of all diversities of climate, and even of race; such diversities having no effect upon anything more than the rate of progress. But we must beware of the scientific dangers attending the process of comparison by this method. For instance, it can give us no idea of the order of succession, as it presents all the states of development as co-existing: so that, if the order of development were not established by other methods, this one would infallibly mislead us. And again, if we were not misled as to the order, there is nothing in this method which discloses the filiation of the different systems of society; a matter in which the most distinguished philosophers have been mistaken in various ways and degrees. Again, there is the danger of mistaking modifications for primary phases; as when social differences have been ascribed to the political influence of climate, instead of that inequality of evolution which is the real cause. Sometimes, but more rarely, the mistake is the other way. Indeed, there is nothing in the matter that can show which of two cases presents the diversity that is observed. We are in danger of the same mistake in regard to races; for, as the sociological comparison is instituted between peoples of different races, we are liable to confound the effects of race and of the social period. Again, climate comes in to offer a third source of interpretation of comparative phenomena, sometimes agreeing with, and sometimes contradicting the two others; thus multiplying the chances of error, and rendering the analysis which looked so promising almost impracticable. Here, again, we see the indispensable necessity of keeping in view the positive conception of human development as a whole. By this alone can we be preserved from such errors as I have referred to, and enriched by any genuine results of analysis. We see how absurd in theory and dangerous in practice are the notions and declamations of the empirical school, and of the enemies of all social speculation: for it is precisely in proportion to their elevation and generality that the ideas of positive social philosophy become real and effective—all illusion and uselessness belonging to conceptions which are too narrow and too special, in the departments either of science or of reasoning. But it is a consequence from these last considerations that this first sketch of sociological science, with the means of investigation that belong to it, rests immediately upon the primary use of a new method of observation, which is so appropriate to the nature of the phenomena as to be exempt from the dangers inherent in the others. This last portion of the comparative method is the historical method, properly so called; and it is the only basis on which the system of political logic can rest.

Comparison of consecutive states

The historical comparison of the consecutive states of humanity is not only the chief scientific device of the new political philosophy. Its rational development constitutes the substratum of the science, in whatever is essential to it. It is this which distinguishes it thoroughly from biological science, as we shall presently see. The positive principle of this separation results from the necessary influence of human generations upon the generations that follow, accumulating continuously till it constitutes the preponderating consideration in the direct study of social development. As long as this preponderance is not directly recognized, the positive study of humanity must appear a simple prolongation of the natural history of man: but this scientific character, suitable enough to the earlier generations, disappears in the course of the social evolution, and assumes at length a wholly new aspect, proper to sociological science, in which historical considerations are of immediate importance. And this preponderant use of the historical method gives its philosophical character to sociology in a logical, as well as a scientific sense. By the creation of this new department of the comparative method, sociology confers a benefit on the whole of natural philosophy; because the positive method is thus completed and perfected, in a manner which, for scientific importance, is almost beyond our estimate. What we can now comprehend is that the historical method verifies and applies, in the largest way, that chief quality of sociological science—its proceeding from the whole to the parts. Without this permanent condition of social study, all historical labour would degenerate into being a mere compilation of provisional materials. As it is in their development especially that the various social elements are interconnected and inseparable, it is clear that any partial filiation must be essentially untrue. Where, for instance, is the use of any exclusive history of any one science or art, unless meaning is given to it by first connecting it with the study of human progress generally? It is the same in every direction, and especially with regard to political history, as it is called—as if any history could be other than political, more or less! The prevailing tendency to speciality in study would reduce history to a mere accumulation of unconnected delineations, in which all idea of the true filiation of events would be lost amidst the mass of confused descriptions. If the historical comparisons of the different periods of civilization are to have any scientific character, they must be referred to the general social evolution: and it is only thus that we can obtain the guiding ideas by which the special studies themselves must be directed.

In a practical view, it is evident that the preponderance of the historical method tends to develop the social sentiment, by giving us an immediate interest in even the earliest experiences of our race, through the influence that they exercised over the evolution of our own civilization. As Condorcet observed, no enlightened man can think of the battles of Marathon and Salamis without perceiving the importance of their consequences to the race at large. This kind of feeling should, when we are treating of science, be carefully distinguished from the sympathetic interest which is awakened by all delineations of human life—in fiction as well as in history. The sentiment I refer to is deeper, because in some sort personal; and more reflective, because it results from scientific conviction. It cannot be excited by popular history, in a descriptive form; but only by positive history, regarded as a true science, and exhibiting the events of human experience in co-ordinated series which manifest their own graduated connection. This new form of the social sentiment must at first be the privilege of the choice few; but it will be extended, somewhat weakened in force, to the whole of society, in proportion as the general results of social physics become sufficiently popular. It will fulfil the most obvious and elementary idea of the habitual connection between individuals and contemporary nations, by showing that the successive generations of men concur in a final end, which requires the determinate participation of each and all. This rational disposition to regard men of all times as fellow-workers is as yet visible in the case of only the most advanced sciences. By the philosophical preponderance of the historical method, it will be extended to all the aspects of human life, so as to sustain, in a reflective temper, that respect for our ancestors which is indispensable to a sound state of society and so deeply disturbed at present by the metaphysical philosophy.

As for the course to be pursued by this method, it appears to me that its spirit consists in the rational use of social series; that is, in a successive estimate of the different states of humanity which shall show the growth of each disposition, physical, intellectual, moral or political, combined with the decline of the opposite disposition, whence we may obtain a scientific prevision of the final ascendancy of the one and extinction of the other, care being taken to frame our conclusions according to the laws of human development. A considerable accuracy of prevision may thus be obtained, for any determinate period, and with any particular views; as historical analysis will indicate the direction of modifications, even in the most disturbed times. And it is worth noticing that the prevision will be nearest the truth in proportion as the phenomena in question are more important and more general, because then continuous causes are predominant in the social movement, and disturbances have less power. From these first general aspects, the same rational certainty may extend to secondary and special aspects, through their statical relations with the first; and thus we may obtain conclusions sufficiently accurate for the application of principles.

If we desire to familiarize ourselves with this historical method, we must employ it first upon the past, by endeavouring to deduce every well-known historical situation from the whole series of its antecedents. In every science we must have learned to predict the past, so to speak, before we can predict the future; because the first use of the observed relations among fulfilled facts is to teach us by the anterior succession what the future succession will be. No examination of facts can explain our existing state to us, if we have not ascertained, by historical study, the value of the elements at work; and thus it is in vain that statesmen insist on the necessity of political observation, while they look no further than the present, or a very recent past. The present is, by itself, purely misleading, because it is impossible to avoid confounding principal with secondary facts, exalting conspicuous transient manifestations over fundamental tendencies, which are generally very quiet; and above all, supposing those powers, institutions and doctrines, to be in the ascendent, which are, in fact, in their decline. It is clear that the only adequate corrective of all this is a philosophical understanding of the past; that the comparison cannot be decisive unless it embraces the whole of the past; and that the sooner we stop, in travelling up the vista of time, the more serious will be the mistakes we fall into. Before our very eyes, we see statesmen going no further back than the last century, to obtain an explanation of the confusion in which we are living: the most abstract of politicians may take in the preceding century, but the philosophers themselves hardly venture beyond the sixteenth; so that those who are striving to find the issue of the revolutionary period have actually no conception of it as a whole, though that whole is itself only a transient phrase of the general social movement.

The most perfect methods may, however, be rendered deceptive by misuse: and this we must bear in mind. We have seen that mathematical analysis itself may betray us into substituting signs for ideas, and that it conceals inanity of conception under an imposing verbiage. The difficulty in the case of the historical method in sociology is in applying it, on account of the extreme complexity of the materials we have to deal with. But for this, the method would be entirely safe. The chief danger is of our supposing a continuous decrease to indicate a final extinction, or the reverse; as in mathematics it is a common sophism to confound continuous variations, more or less, with unlimited variations. To take a strange and very marked example: if we consider that part of social development which relates to human food, we cannot but observe that men take less food as they advance in civilization. If we compare savage with more civilized peoples, in the Homeric poems or in the narratives of travellers, or compare country with town life, or any generation with the one that went before, we shall find this curious result, the sociological law of which we shall examine hereafter. The laws of individual human nature aid in the result by making intellectual and moral action more preponderant as man become more civilized. The fact is thus established, both by the experimental and the logical way. Yet nobody supposes that men will ultimately cease to eat. In this case, the absurdity saves us from a false conclusion; but in other cases, the complexity disguises much error in the experiment and the reasoning. In the above instance, we must resort to the laws of our nature for that verification which, taken all together, they afford to our sociological analysis. As the social phenomenon, taken as a whole, is simply a development of humanity, without any real creation of faculties, all social manifestations must be to be found, if only in their germ, in the primitive type which biology constructed by anticipation for sociology. Thus every law of social succession disclosed by the historical method must be unquestionably connected, directly or indirectly, with the positive theory of human nature; and all inductions which cannot stand this test will prove to be illusory, through some sort of insufficiency in the observations on which they are grounded. The main scientific strength of sociological demonstrations must ever lie in the accordance between the conclusions of historical analysis and the preparatory conceptions of the biological theory. And thus we find, look where we will, a confirmation of that chief intellectual character of the new science —the philosophical preponderance of the spirit of the whole over the spirit of detail.

This method ranks, in sociological science, with that of zoological comparison in the study of individual life; and we shall see, as we proceed, that the succession of social states exactly corresponds, in a scientific sense, with the gradation of organisms in biology; and the social series, once clearly established, must be as real and as useful as the animal series.

Promise of a fourth method

When the method has been used long enough to disclose its properties, I am disposed to think that it will be regarded as so very marked a modification of positive research as to deserve a separate place; so that, in addition to observation, properly so called, experiment, and comparison, we shall have the historical method, as a fourth and final mode of the art of observing. It will be derived, according to the usual course, from the mode which immediately precedes it: and it will be applied to the analysis of the most complex phenomena.

I must be allowed to point out that the new political philosophy, sanctioning the old leadings of popular reason, restores to history all its scientific rights as a basis of wise social speculation, after the metaphysical philosophy had striven to induce us to discard all large considerations of the past. In the foregoing departments of natural philosophy we have seen that the positive spirit, instead of being disturbing in its tendencies, is remarkable for confirming, in the essential parts of every science, the inestimable intuitions of popular good sense; of which indeed science is merely a systematic prolongation, and which a barren metaphysical philosophy alone could despise. In this case, so far from restricting the influence

which human reason has ever attributed to history in political combinations, the new social philosophy increases it, radically and
eminently. It asks from history something more than counsel and
instruction to perfect conceptions which are derived from another
source: it seeks its own general direction, through the whole
system of historical conclusions.

3   *Social Statics*

Social Statics, or, Theory of the Spontaneous Order of Human Society*

Though the dynamical part of social science is the most interesting, the most easily intelligible, and the fittest to disclose the laws of interconnection, still the statical part must not be entirely passed over. We must briefly review in this place the conditions and laws of harmony of human society, and complete our statical conceptions, as far as the nascent state of the science allows, when we afterwards survey the historical development of humanity.

Three aspects

Every sociological analysis supposes three classes of considerations, each more complex than the preceding: viz., the conditions of social existence of the individual, the family and society; the last comprehending, in a scientific sense, the whole of the human species, and chiefly, the whole of the white race.

The individual

Gall's cerebral theory has destroyed for ever the metaphysical fancies of the last century about the origin of man's social tendencies, which are now proved to be inherent in his nature, and not the result of utilitarian considerations. The true theory has exploded the mistakes through which the false doctrine arose—the fanciful supposition that intellectual combinations govern the general conduct of human life, and the exaggerated notion of the degree in which wants can create faculties. Independently of the guidance afforded by Gall's theory, there is a conclusive evidence against the utilitarian origin of society in the fact that the utility did not, and could not, manifest itself till after a long preparatory development of the society which it was supposed to have created . . .

The family

So much for the first statical division, the individual. Next, we must consider the family.

As every system must be composed of elements of the same nature with itself, the scientific spirit forbids us to regard society as composed of individuals. The true social unit is certainly the family—reduced, if necessary, to the elementary couple which forms its basis. This consideration implies more than the physiological truth that families become tribes and tribes become nations,

* *Pos. Phil.*, vol. 2, pp. 275–98.

so that the whole human race might be conceived of as the gradual development of a single family, if local diversities did not forbid such a supposition. There is a political point of view from which also we must consider this elementary idea, inasmuch as the family presents the true germ of the various characteristics of the social organism. Such a conception is intermediate between the idea of the individual and that of the species, or society. There would be as many scientific inconveniences in passing it over in a speculative sense as there are dangers in practice in pretending to treat of social life without the inevitable preparation of the domestic life. Whichever way we look at it, this necessary transition always presents itself, whether in regard to elementary notions of fundamental harmony, or for the spontaneous rise of social sentiment. It is by this avenue that man comes forth from his mere personality, and learns to live in another, while obeying his most powerful instincts. No other association can be so intimate as this primary combination, which causes a complete fusion of two natures in one. Owing to the radical imperfection of the human character, individual divergencies are too marked to admit of so close an association in any other case. The common experience of human life teaches us only too well that men must not live too familiarly together, if they are to bear, in mutual peace, the infirmities of our nature—whether of the intellect or the affections. Even religious communities, united as they are by a special bond, were, as we know, perpetually tormented by internal dissensions, such as it is impossible to avoid if we atempt to reconcile qualities so incompatible as the intimacy and the extension of human relations. Even in the family, the intimacy is owing to the strong spontaneousness of the common end, combined with the equally natural institution of an indispensable subordination. Whatever talk there may be, in modern times, of social equality, even the most restricted society supposes, not only diversities, but inequalities; for there can be no association without a permanent concurrence in a general operation, pursued by distinct means, mutually subordinated. Now, the most entire realization, possible of these elementary conditions is inherent in the family alone, where nature has supplied all the requisites of the institution. Thus, notwithstanding the temporary abuse of the family spirit in the way of excess, which has occasionally brought reproach on the institution, it is, and will ever be, the basis of the social spirit, through all the gradual modifications which it may have to undergo in the course of the human evolution . . .

The constitution of the human family has undergone modifications of a progressive kind which appear to me to disclose, at each epoch of development, the exact importance of the change wrought in the corresponding social state. Thus, the polygamy of less advanced nations must give a character to the family wholly different from that which it has among nations which are capable of that monogamy to which our nature tends. In the same way, the ancient family, which consisted partly of slaves, must be very unlike the modern, which is mainly reduced to the kindred of the couple, and in which the authority of the head is comparatively small. But the estimate of these modifications will find its right place in my historical review. Our object now is to consider the elementary scientific aspect of the family; that aspect which is made common to all social cases by regarding the domestic as the basis of all social life. In this view, the sociological theory of the family is reducible to the investigation of two orders of relations, viz., the subordination of the sexes, which institutes the family, and that of ages, which maintains it. A certain amount of voluntary association takes place from that degree of the biological scale at which sex begins; and it is always occasioned by the sexual union first, and then by the rearing of progeny. If the sociological comparison must stop at the two great classes of superior animals, birds and mammifers, it is because none below them present a sufficiently complete realization of this double elementary character . . .

Society

The third head of our statical analysis brings us to the consideration of society, as composed of families and not of individuals, and from a point of view which commands all times and places.

The main cause of the superiority of the social to the individual organism is, according to an established law, the more marked speciality of the various functions fulfilled by organs more and more distinct, but interconnected; so that unity of aim is more and more combined with diversity of means. We cannot, of course, fully appreciate a phenomenon which is for ever proceeding before our eyes, and in which we bear a part; but if we withdraw ourselves in thought from the social system, and contemplate it as from afar, can we conceive of a more marvellous spectacle, in the whole range of natural phenomena, than the regular and constant convergence of an innumerable multitude of human beings, each possessing a distinct and, in a certain degree, independent existence, and yet incessantly disposed, amidst all their discordance of talent and character, to concur in many ways in the same general development, without concert, and even consciousness on the part of most of them, who believe that they are merely following their personal impulses? This is the scientific picture of the phenomenon: and no temporary disturbances can prevent its being, under all circumstances, essentially true. This reconciliation of the individuality of labour with co-operation of endeavours, which becomes more remarkable as society grows more complex and extended, constitutes the radical character of human operations when we rise from the domestic to the social point of view. The degree of association that we observe among the superior animals has something voluntary in it, but there is no organization which can make it resemble the human: and the first individual specializing of common functions is seen in our simple domestic life, which is thus a type of the social organization. The division of labour can never, however, be very marked in the family, because the members are few; and yet more because such a division would soon show itself to be hostile to the spirit of the institution; for domestic training, being founded on imitation, must dispose the children to follow parental employments, instead of undertaking new ones: and again, any very marked separation in the employments of the members must impair the domestic unity which is the aim of the association. The more we look into the subject, the more we shall see that the appropriation of employments, which is the elementary principle of general society, cannot hold anything like so important a place in the family. In fact, the domestic relations do not constitute an association, but a *union*, in the full force of the term; and, on account of this close intimacy, the domestic connection is of a totally different nature from the social . . .

Distribution of employments

We must include in our view the division of employments something much more extensive than the material arrangements which the expression is usually understood to convey. We must include under it all human operations whatever, regarding not only individuals and classes, but also, in many ways, different nations, as participating, in a special mode and degree, in a vast common work, the gradual development of which connects the fellow-labourers with the whole series of their predecessors, and even with their successors. This is what is meant when we speak of the race being bound up together by the very distribution of their occupations; and it is this distribution which causes the extent and growing complexity of the social organism, which thus appears as comprising the whole of the human race. Man can hardly exist in a solitary state: the family can exist in isolation, because it can divide its employments and provide for its wants in a rough kind of way: a spontaneous approximation of families is incessantly exposed to temporary rupture, occasioned by the most trifling incidents. But when a regular division of employments has spread through any society, the social state begins to acquire a consistency and stability which place it out of danger from particular divergencies. The habit of partial co-operation convinces each family of its close dependence on the rest, and, at the same time, of its own importance, each one being then justified in regarding itself as fulfilling a real public function, more or less indispensable to the general economy, but inseparable from the system as a whole. In this view the social organization tends more and more to rest on an exact estimate of individual diversities, by so distributing employments as to appoint each one to the destination he is most fit for, from his own nature (which however is seldom very distinctly marked), from his education and his position, and, in short, from all his qualifications; so that all individual organizations, even the most vicious and imperfect (short of monstrosity), may be finally made use of for the general good. Such is, at least, the social type which we conceive of as the limit of the existing social order, and to which we may be for ever approximating, though without the hope of ever attaining it; and it is, in fact, a reproduction, with a large extension, of the domestic organism, with less power, in proportion to its extent, of appointing a due destination to every member; so that the social discipline must always be more artificial, and therefore more imperfect, than the domestic, which nature herself ordains and administers.

The necessities of this co-operation and distribution of special offices, cause inconvenience which I am compelled to advert to; for it is in the investigation of these that we find the scientific germ of the relation between the idea of society and that of government.

Inconveniences

Some economists have pointed out, but in a very inadequate way, the evils of an exaggerated division of material labour; and I have indicated, in regard to the more important field of scientific labour, the mischievous intellectual consequences of the spirit of speciality which at present prevails. It is necessary to estimate directly the principle of such an influence, in order to understand the object of the spontaneous system of requisites for the continuous preservation of society. In decomposing, we always disperse; and the distribution of human labours must occasion individual divergencies, both intellectual and moral, which require a permanent discipline to keep them within bounds. If the separation of social functions develops a useful spirit of detail, on the one hand, it tends, on the other, to extinguish or to restrict what we may call the aggregate or general spirit. In the same way, in moral relations, while each individual is in close dependence on the mass, he is drawn away from it by the expansion of his special activity, constantly recalling him to his private interest, which he but very dimly perceives to be related to the public. On both grounds the inconveniences of the division of functions increase with its characteristic advantages, without their being in the same relation, throughout the spontaneous course of the social evolution. The growing speciality of habitual ideas and familiar relations must tend to restrict the understanding more and more, while sharpening it in a certain direction, and to sever more and more the private interest from a public interest which is for ever becoming more vague and indirect; while, at the same time, the social affections, gradually concentrated among individuals of the same profession, become more and more alienated from all other classes, for want of a sufficient analogy of ways and ideas. Thus it is that the principle by which alone general society could be developed and extended, threatens, in another view, to decompose it into a multitude of unconnected corporations, which almost seem not to belong to the same species; and hence it is that the gradual expansion of human ability seems destined to produce such minds as are very common among civilized peoples, and prodigiously admired by them— minds which are very able in some one respect and monstrously incapable in all others. If we have been accustomed to deplore the spectacle, among the artisan class of a workman occupied during his whole life in nothing else but making knife-handles or pins' heads, we may find something quite as lamentable in the intellectual class, in the exclusive employment of a human brain in resolving some equations, or in classifying insects. The moral effect is, unhappily, analogous in the two cases. It occasions a miserable indifference about the general course of human affairs, as long as there are equations to resolve and pins to manufacture. This is an extreme case of human automatism; but the frequency, and the growing frequency, of the evil gives a real scientific importance to the case, as indicating the general tendency, and warning us to restrain it. Thus it appears to me that the social destination of government is to guard against and restrain the fundamental dispersion of ideas, sentiments and interests, which is the inevitable result of the very principle of human development, and which, if left to itself, would put a stop to social progression in all important respects.

Basis of the true theory of government

Here we have, in my opinion, the basis of the elementary and abstract theory of government, regarded in its complete scientific extension; that is, as characterized by the universal necessary reaction—first spontaneous and then regulated—of the whole upon the parts. It is clear that the only way of preventing such a dispersion is by setting up this reaction as a new special function, which shall intervene in the performance of all the various functions of the social economy, to keep up the idea of the whole, and the feeling of the common interconnection: and the more energetically, the more individual activity tends to dissolve them. Not itself affecting any determinate social progress, it contributes to all that society can achieve, in any direction whatever, and which society could not achieve without its concentrating and protective care. The very nature of its action indicates that it cannot be merely material, but also, and much more, intellectual and moral; so as to show the double necessity of what has been called the temporal and spiritual government, the rational subordination of which was the best feature of the social organization that was happily effected in its day, under the influence of the prevalent Catholicism. Moreover, this ruling function must become more, instead of less necessary, as human development proceeds, because its essential principle is inseparable from that of the development itself. Thus, it is the habitual predominance of the spirit of the whole which constitutes government, in whatever way it is regarded. The next consideration is, how such an action arises, independently of all systematic combination, in the natural course of the social economy ...

My sketch has perhaps been so abstract and condensed that the conceptions of this chapter may appear obscure at present; but light will fall upon them as we proceed. We may already see, however, the practical advantage which arises from the scientific evolution of human relations. The individual life, ruled by personal instincts; the domestic, by sympathetic instincts; and the social, by the special development of intellectual influences, prepare for the states of human existence which are to follow: and that which ensues is, first, personal morality, which subjects the preservation of the individual to a wise discipline; next, domestic morality, which subordinates selfishness to sympathy; and lastly, social morality, which directs all individual tendencies by enlightened reason, always having the general economy in view, so as to bring into concurrence all the faculties of human nature, according to their appropriate laws.

Positive Theory of the Social Forces*

I therefore proceed to the positive theory of the various social forces, for without this all sociological reasoning would be incomplete.

All social force results from co-operation

Every true social force, is the product of a co-operation, on a larger or smaller scale, concentrated in some individual organ. This co-operation may be subjective or objective; it is almost always both at the same time, in proportions varying with the degree that time or space enters into the subject. The only form of force truly individual is physical force in its strictest sense; and even then it is only individual, when it makes no use of weapons, for these suppose some kind of co-operation, either in the past or the present. Now force of this kind is easily overcome by the smallest combination of others. As to intellectual force, vanity itself has to admit, how much it owes to predecessors and contemporaries. Besides, by itself, it is unable to generate any real force such as can issue in immediate act. The efficiency of intellectual power is always indirect, and requires voluntary assent, either on the part of any who yield to its influence, or at least in those who form that public opinion which induces them to yield. The influence itself tends to promote co-operation, but cannot dispense with it. We must say the same thing of moral power, properly so called; its influence is deeper but not more direct; it depends entirely on co-operation.

Concentrated in a personal organ

But whilst insisting on the necessity of co-operation as the basis of every social force, we must not forget the second half of the preceding definition, the need of an individual representative. Although all social functions are essentially collective, their exercise always requires a person as their organ, more or less conscious. Co-operation, which was not so concentrated, would remain perfectly sterile; indeed, until it has an organ, the co-operation is only seeming. For it means the grouping of several individuals for a

* *Pos. Pol.*, vol. 2, pp. 223–49.

greater or less period of time, around one pre-eminent individuality. When this influence from the centre anticipates the readiness of the parts towards combination, co-operation is systematic, for it results from the action of the chief over the followers. The co-operation is spontaneous on the other hand, when the tendency to combine shows itself before a common centre is found. But in the latter case, hitherto the more common, the co-operation, and consequently the force, does not really arise until the concentration is complete.

Double character of every human association

This essential condition of concentration in a person, is the point in which the positive theory of the social forces differs so strikingly from the various metaphysical theories. The vague, and therefore subversive ideas, which still prevail respecting political power, spring in truth from forgetfulness of the need of condensation in a person, as the leading feature of all social co-operation. In its ordinary form, this first principle gives rise to the cardinal axiom: society without a government is no less impossible, than a government without society. In the smallest as in the largest associations, the positive theory of a polity never leaves sight of these two correlative ideas, without which theories would lead us astray, and society would end in anarchy. The constant presence of both in combination points to the double character of the true human organism, that it is collective in its nature and individual in its functions, each of its individual elements being naturally independent.

All force is centralized co-operation

Since in sociology, every force results from a centralized co-operation, the statical theory of these forces is mainly concerned with determining the general laws of this co-operation.

The first principle is that a true social combination must take in all the essential sides of every human life, however unequally these may share in it; for such is the tendency of personality to preponderate that the co-operation will be either sterile or precarious, if any one of the principal cerebral regions is left out. The neglected instinct will either embarrass or dissolve the combination. In sociology therefore, we must treat every real force as being at once, material, intellectual and moral; that is to say, at the same time as concerned with action, speculation and affection. These three essential elements, however, may be very unequally distributed, and the leading element alone gives its name to the combination, though we must never forget the inevitable presence of the others . . .

In this classification of the three great elementary forces of the social organism, we have a new instance of the general principle of classification so often applied. Decrease in generality and intensity, corresponding to increase of complexity and dignity, is very marked in the passage from material to intellectual power, and from the latter to moral power. Thus the positive synthesis co-ordinates our social opinions and our philosophical conceptions, giving consistence to the former, and practical value to the latter. My general law of classification just mentioned, had originally a merely subjective purpose, as a logical instrument for the true co-ordination of thought; but I have invariably pointed out, that it had also a necessary correspondence with the objective order of phenomena. It has now been applied to the classification of real existences and their various properties. The 'Positive Philosophy' gave several illustrations of this principle; and in this work they are far more numerous and marked, and it may be applied to the collective organism of man.

Again, this fundamental arrangement of the social forces is to be recognized in the growth of the individual, which in successive periods reproduces the movement of social progress as revealed by history. In childhood we perceive, and long over-estimate, the ascendancy of material force; experience then proves to us the reality of intellectual power; and it is only in our maturity that we are convinced of the worth of moral greatness. It is true that the education of the future, will hasten the recognition of all three forms of power, and also diminish the effect of personal differences; but thoughtful minds will never have any difficulty in tracing the necessary course through which humanity must pass. Nor will language fail to bear witness to the same fact; for it reserves the word *force* for material power, and applies it only with qualifications or by metaphor to the two modifying influences, intellectual and moral power.

Force, in sociology, answers to tissue in biology

This classification of the social forces really sums up the abstract theory of the collective organism. It takes the same place that the doctrine of the elementary tissues holds in the study of individual organization. In both we have first, a primary tissue, the seat of the life of nutrition; in biology, it is the cellular tissue, in sociology, material force. We have next, in the individual, as in the social organism, two orders of tissue, of lower energy but of higher dignity, the one passive, the other active, their respective functions being rightly to understand and fitly to modify the environment. All thinkers able to follow it out will see in this analogy a new proof of the soundness of my statical theory, both of the individual and of society.

Force, either dispersed or concentrated, is indeed the natural basis of the social organism: intelligence, artistic or scientific, modifies it in conformity to its environment; whilst the heart, in its masculine or feminine form, inspires that organism with suitable springs of action. Thus the positive theory of the social organism may be drawn deductively from the grand principle, laid down twenty-two centuries ago, by the true founder of provisional sociology, which explained order apart from progress. The incomparable Aristotle laid down the true principle of every collective organism, when he described it as the distribution of functions, and the combination of labour. Strangely enough, our modern economists claim the discovery of this luminous conception, whilst narrowing it, with metaphysical empiricism, to a mere law of industry . . .

Political influence of territorial property

So marked is the political influence of territorial property that in place of insisting on it, there might be more need to combat the exaggerations respecting it, into which our Physiocrats fell in the last century. But the reader will hardly need to be told that, though the soil is an indispensable instrument for the creation of wealth, it is certainly not the true source of it; for all temporal power, we have seen, comes from human life as a whole. In the succeeding volume we shall see how essential is territorial property to the entire course of human activity, not only for the industrial life, on which we are entering, but for the military life, through which we have passed. The 'Positive Philosophy' gave many illustrations of the importance of settled societies in developing the ancient system of conquest.

The whole of the social forces are thus connected with nature

We have thus the whole of human life, both in the family and in the national group, associated with its earthly habitation, thus completing the statical theory already stated for property, family and language. Having analysed the social forces into the three forms, material, intellectual and moral, I had only to connect them, as I have just done, with the general laws of external nature, which ever govern them.

We have thus established a true correspondence between the statical analysis of the social organism in sociology, and that of the individual organism in biology. But this analogy must not be pushed too far; for the former is capable of being resolved into its component parts, whilst the latter is not. The elements of social life are not destroyed by being separated: those of individual life are. And thus, if we insisted on an exact similarity between the two, we should get fanciful comparisons instead of useful suggestions. Biology has hitherto been the guide and preparation for sociology; but, as shown in the first volume, sociology will in the future be rather the type for the ultimate systematization of biology. Throughout philosophy the direct study of the true 'great being', the only being which attains to its perfect development, will form the groundwork of our knowledge of the smaller organisms, and that for purposes of science as well as of logic. The subjective method, the sole source of any real synthesis, implies this passage from the higher to the lower study. And this is the principle of all true classification, which ought to follow the order, of which society exhibits the universal type, that is to say, the higher organization determines the lower. The public and private life of the individual is, as it has ever been, subordinate to the social organism of which he is a part. And this is the point of view from which we must conceive the relations of every other unit to its system, whether in thought or in expression, whether in the real or in the ideal world.

Analogies of biology and sociology

There is therefore no justification in trying to find servile analogies in analysing the social and the individual organism, imperfect as our conception of the latter is in the hands of our academic specialists. At the same time there is a real correspondence in the main analyses of the two sciences. If we take the best ascertained points in biology, we may decompose structure anatomically into *elements*, *tissues* and *organs*. We have the same things in the social organism; and may even use the same names. I have already shown how in society the three forms of social power correspond to the *tissue*, the most marked and most important constituent of all. As to the *element*, this is supplied by the family, which is more completely the germ of society than the cell or the fibre of the body. We have only to find in sociology what it is that corresponds with the *organ* in biology.

This may readily be found by following out what has already been said as to the relation of the organism with its environment. The Fatherland establishes a relation between the soil and social order; and thus the *organs* of the 'great being' can only be *cities*, the root of the word being the nucleus of the term *civilization*. Cities are, in truth, themselves beings; so organically complete that, as each is capable of separate life, it instinctively aspires to become the centre of the vast organism of humanity. In this tendency the social organ differs radically from the organ in biology, which has no such separate completeness. Nor can our analysis of society be carried further than this notion of *organs*, or we shall be led into fanciful or passing distinctions. The smallest *city* contains all the *elements* and *tissues*, required for the life of the great being, in the families, and in the classes or castes, within it. The greatest human associations always began really in a mere town, which gradually incorporated others by its attraction or by arms. The eternal instance of this truth is the great name of Rome.

Between the city, uniting man and his dwelling-place, and the full development of the great being around a fitting centre, a number of intermediate forms of association may be found, under the general name of *states*. But all these forms, differing only in extent and in permanence, may be neglected as undefined. In social statics, we must keep in view the existence of humanity in its completeness, however distant may be its actual advent; and we may therefore rest in that form of association which has a complete and distinct career of its own. When property, family and language, have found a suitable territory, and have reached the point at which they combine any given population under the same, at least the same spiritual, government, there a possible nucleus of the great being has been formed. Such a community, or city, be it ultimately large or small, is a true *organ* of humanity. When the supreme being has its full development, we shall see how these essential organs will be combined into *apparatus*, such as we have in biology. But to attempt this now would be premature as well as useless; and we see how indistinct and arbitrary are all the definitions of the intermediate states, such as are called provinces, nations, etc.

Nevertheless, we shall not run any risk of forcing our analogies, if we extend to the analysis of society the other two anatomical conceptions of biology. Besides cells, tissues and organs, every individual organism gives us a more elaborate degree of vital structure which we call *apparatus*. There is, further, now recognized an intermediate form of organization between tissues and organs, which is called *system*. Statical biology therefore gives us five stages of organic life: cell, tissue, system, organ, apparatus. We may find five similar stages in sociology, though all are not essential. They will however serve to combine the different nuclei of the great being, whilst these remain various and separate as they long must be. Although the advent of humanity in its entirety is yet distant, it has long been familiar to the loftier spirits and minds. As was stated in the first chapter of this volume, the greater statesmen long dreamed of a universal family of man, so soon as the Roman Empire was complete. But this idea gained force and extent, when the separation of the spiritual community from the temporal society in the Middle Ages pointed out the natural mode of the ultimate unity of man. When the Catholic bond of union was destroyed, the various relations, industrial, scientific and artistic, continued to keep all minds in the West fixed on the hope of a complete assimilation of the human race. Until this hope has found its satisfaction, we may properly think of the different groups, out of which the great being is to arise, in such a way as will point to their ultimate combination. Thus, the *cities* which form the social *organs* may be imagined as grouped into *nations*, so as to correspond with the *apparatus* of biology. We may further go on to group the social *tissues*, that is the *classes*, so as to correspond with the *systems* in anatomy. It will serve to give precision to our ideas of the common functions of these tissues in the organ. We thus get, in sociology as in biology, the five statical types arranged in both sciences in an analogous series. In the ultimate realization of humanity these two provisional terms of *apparatus* and *system* will not be needed to carry on an exact parallelism, so far as regards the social organism. The notions they express will be modified in a way I need not dwell upon here. We may notice their existence, without attaching too much importance to them in the general analysis of society.

Whatever use may ultimately be made of the five divisions, I shall confine my attention in this work on sociology to the three modes of analysing social life, the same three which will prove of the main importance in biology. And I shall treat the social organism as definitely composed of the families which are the true elements or cells, next of the classes or castes which are its proper tissues, and lastly of the cities and communes which are its real organs.

Theory of social organization

This conception, which has a scientific as well as a logical value, enables us by the light of the reasoning above to determine the positive theory of social order, by means of the great principle of Aristotle previously alluded to.

This principle, in fact, lays down as the two general conditions, independence and co-operation, the task of any collective organization being to establish due relations between the two.

Distribution of function, the test of political society

On the one hand, without separation of function, there would be no true association between a number of families; they would only form an agglomeration, even in a settled community. Distribution of function is the point which marks off the political society, the basis of which is co-operation, from the domestic union, the basis of which is sympathy. This is a striking proof of the utterly anarchical character of the modern revolutionary theories, which end by exalting mere individualism, for they bring all down to a common level.

We thus get the essential character of the great organism as made up of beings capable of separate life, but joining more or less voluntarily in a common end. The classes formed by the various combinations of the three elements of every social force differ from each other; but their respective functions are only completely called out by an increasing diversity of occupation.

This, the source of the differences and even of the inequalities between men, is also the chief agent in the gradual extension of the great being, until this reaches the natural limits of its abode on the planet. Directly that a settled society brings out the social importance of this fundamental principle, the distribution of functions, fresh fields are at once opened for the growth of the spirit of solidarity with contemporaries, and of continuity with our predecessors. A valuable reaction upon the moral nature follows along with it, owing to the stimulus it affords to the instinct of general benevolence. Each family, when confined to a labour which directly produces only what will satisfy a small portion of its own wants, is forced to recognize the importance of other families to itself as well as its own usefulness to them. When the feelings and the thoughts are brought into harmonious relations with such a position, human existence at once develops its true nature 'to live for others'.

Combination of efforts

On the other hand, the noble part played by this distribution of functions would be abortive, unless it were completed by a combination of efforts, either spontaneous or disciplined. Nay, the division of occupation is very apt to give rise to serious struggles, intensifying as it does differences in habit, opinion and propensity, between different families. The desire for co-operation, which cannot be separated from the desire for independence, must also be regularly satisfied; it finds satisfaction in that primary social institution, founded to secure joint action. A power to amalgamate men is the more needed that the combative and self-regarding instincts are more energetic than those which prompt us to union. This is the part of that cohesive force in society, everywhere called *government*, the business of which is at once to combine and to direct. The admirable conception of Aristotle respecting the distribution of functions and the combination of effort happily correlates the two necessary elements of every political idea, society and government.

It must also be remembered, that by reason of the distribution of functions, every human life has its double side: the one special, the other general. Every family has first duly to fulfil the common task assigned to it by the great organism, of which it is a member. But to do so, it needs constantly to rest upon the sense of that general harmony, towards which it contributes its note. Now, every true citizen is thus penetrated with a sense of order; and he grows earnest to cause it to be respected by others. The same disposition, moreover, fosters the growth of the three social instincts within each man, particularly the widest of these instincts, general benevolence. Such is the compound process which disposes men to submit to government; so soon as a suitable governing power succeeds in availing itself of the disposition ready to its hand.

Origin of government

This last condition of order, a governing power, springs spontaneously out of the inequalities between men, upon the separation of social functions . . .

How, and how naturally, such a power arises, we may best see, by looking not to the general function whereby all citizens conspire to maintain and complete the state, but to the different special functions of the citizens. This general function of all citizens is not at first sufficiently defined to have an organ at all. The particular functions of each citizen being clearly marked, throws up in each group a special government of its own, which controls and directs it on a small scale, as occasion arises. This is the germ of the wider government of society, which is the product of the smaller combinations when their common ends are duly made general. Military activity, the only one fully organized at present, has a direct tendency to form lasting combinations; for it can gain no success without union.

The ultimate form of life, the industrial, has also the same political value, though its action is long restricted to private life. When undisturbed it throws up its permanent chiefs, men whose importance is continually on the increase, as we may see in history in the succeeding volume. As the ancient world had in war its school of discipline and of government, the modern world finds these in industry. The habit of regarding all citizens as public functionaries, so as to determine their duties, has more than a purpose of social morality. It is just as necessary for theory, to explain the origin of political government. Thus government springs from agreement between the natural chiefs of the various types of industry, who gather round their best representative. The habits of command and of obedience already formed in industry have only to extend to public spheres, to found a power in the state capable of controlling the divergencies, and regulating the convergencies, of the individuals within it.

Government rests on force

Thus the principle of co-operation, the basis of political society, calls out the government required for its maintenance and growth. It is a power essentially material, arising as it does from rank or wealth. It is important to note that social order can have no other direct base. The famous maxim of Hobbes, that government is the natural result of force, is the principal step which till now the positive theory of power made since Aristotle. It is true that in the Middle Age the admirable discovery of the division of the temporal and spiritual powers had been made: but the occasion was in its favour, and it was due to feeling rather than reason; nor had it ever been regularly justified on principle before my own early essays. What caused the bitterness that Hobbes' view encountered was the metaphysical nature of its origin, and the want of distinction between the statical and the historical character of government. Had his critics been more wise or less angry, this should only have shown them the merit of this great law, of which the positive philosophy alone saw the importance.

As was shown above, force is essential as the basis of every human society. We have only to suppose it absent, as happens in times of anarchy. Those who are so indignant with Hobbes' principle would be rather perplexed, if they were told that political government must be based on weakness, if it be not based on force. But this would be the real consequence of their theories, if we follow out the analysis of the three constituents of social force. For, through want of a real material force, the basis of power would have to be found in the intellect or the heart, and they are far too feeble for such a purpose. Their sole business is to modify an already existing system of control, and till material force has succeeded in forming this, neither the intellect nor the heart can have much effect on society. Whenever force as a fundamental base for politics is absent, they will seek as far as they can to restore it, without attempting to supply its place. Social science would remain for ever in the cloud-land of metaphysics, if we hesitated to adopt the principle of force as the basis of government. Combining this doctrine with that of Aristotle, that society consists in the combinations of efforts and the distribution of functions, we get the axioms of a sound political philosophy . . .

Force requires further powers

But though force is the indispensable foundation of every organization of society, we must remember that by itself it is wholly insufficient. Force always requires a double complement in the intellect and the heart, and further a proper controlling influence, to make it the durable base of political authority.

Intellectual

Material order being secured, a proper organ is at once ready to take the general direction of the social combination. The government of the society is only an extension of the special government of each smaller group; and these lower forms of authority are wanting in the breadth of view required for this purpose. At least, capacity of the kind would be very exceptional, and would only succeed in primitive forms of society. The point of view required for governing a state in all its relations, so that its authority should be felt and respected by all, implies an intellectual training as to the past and future of civilization, which is rarely to be met with in the average heads of private undertakings. It was rare enough, even in old times, that military ability was found to imply political skill, and it would be hopeless to expect it in mere industrial ability, which is necessarily special even in vast modern works.

Thus governing power requires its intellectual complement to enable it to fulfil its duty of simply maintaining order; and certainly it needs it for that of directing movement.

Moral

In the second place, moral weight is no less indispensable to government, to secure it that respect, without which it cannot govern, or even exist. And we must remember that political power always results directly or indirectly from a co-operation voluntary or involuntary, active or passive; and this may always be withdrawn the moment the desire for union is weakened. Thus without the aid of any spirit of insurrection, power which is always suspected and always envied, is liable even in stable states to be overturned, when it reaches a given point of unpopularity. However natural may be its authority, a moral sanction for government is just as indispensable as an intellectual guidance.

Social control

After the moral and intellectual supports of power, we come to that which it is so difficult for society to supply for it, and yet without which it cannot be permanent, a regulating influence. All force is liable to abuse; especially is this true of that political or material force, which on the mental and moral side is so meagrely qualified for rule. The truth is, that every power from the first tends to find its own regulating influence by exercise, according as it is accepted by the public which it affects. And in this unconscious way power always found its own means of regulating itself, during the early ages, when the development of man's capacities was of more importance than the discipline of them. The authorities of former times, military or theological, were too absolute in their nature to admit of any really systematic discipline. This belongs only to the last phase of the transitional epoch, which prepares the way for the final system; and it is but a foreshadowing of that, as I showed in the historical sketch which closed the first chapter of this volume. But the social organism, it is clear, will be in a most imperfect condition, so long as the political power, which is to control the various activities of the state, is itself without any check to control its dangerous tendencies. The abuse of a kind of force, which is itself the product of personal ascendancy, may do more than check the progress of society. In an organism so complex and so extensive, the abuse of power might menace it with actual destruction.

Political power needs all three besides its basis in force

Close study, therefore, shows us that there are three things necessary for all political power, besides its basis of material force: an
intellectual guidance, a moral sanction and lastly a social control.
Without all three, political order will never be stable, even with all
the support it receives from the domestic order . . .

Limits of Social Variation*

The second source of social variations, that of vital conditions, is
therefore in general of a higher rank than that of the material conditions. At the same time, we need not be surprised if it be even less
understood, because it is closely dependent upon the first class of
variations; and these have been so imperfectly studied down to the
present time. In fact, the most marked and the most permanent of
these vital differences, from which we get the irrational notion of
races, appear to be due to local influences, slowly accumulated by
inheritance, in such a way as to produce the maximum amount of
organic variation. At least, this happy suggestion of Blainville is
the best hypothesis we can frame, and consequently is the one
which sound philosophy would have us use, so long as it is not
opposed by plain and constant observations. We thus perceive that
the principal influences which life exerts over society are themselves due to the reaction which material variations exercise over
life. To study them regularly, therefore, we depend directly upon
the study of the biologic environment; and this is not yet reduced
to system. But, besides these alterations rising from the world
without, the vital order, like every other sphere, is subject to
spontaneous alterations of its own; and lastly to others arising out
of the order succeeding it in the series. Now, both of these, in their
turn, react upon sociality, itself dependent upon vitality; and thus
they modify society in permanent ways with reference to places,
and in a gradual way with reference to times.

Common exaggeration respecting it

This outline will show the extreme complexity, and the greater
difficulty of the theory of biologic influences, which is still less
understood than the theory of material influences. Its effect is felt
in a confused way in the vague principle of races, just as the former

* *Pos. Pol.*, vol. 2, pp. 367–82.

theory was once represented by the theory of climates. But both ideas alike are without any truly positive character. The so-called philosophers who pretend to be authorities in sociology, whilst ignorant of arithmetic, now parade their views about race, as their predecessors used to parade theirs upon climate, and they thus get a cheap reputation for scientific profundity. The very men who criticize so sharply the irrational exaggeration of Montesquieu, as to the effect of material conditions in modifying society, themselves confidently lay down principles no less fallacious as to the influence of vital conditions. Both of these kindred schools forget to apply that principle of positive logic: *that every examination of any kind of variations, must be a corollary of fundamental laws found in the normal type.* Their error lies in converting simple differences of intensity and of rate of speed into radical divergences, each having laws of its own; and they thus destroy anything like general conceptions, and made sound explanation impossible. When we see what deplorable confusion now reigns in the two theories, as to the effect on society of material or vital conditions, it must strike all how urgent, and yet how difficult, is any really systematic handling of this subject.

Direct reaction: sociologic influences

We now proceed to those influences which directly modify society, that is to say, those which result from its own proper movement. We must note a fundamental distinction between them, or we shall be involved in a fruitless repetition running through our whole system of sociology.

General social evolution is the subject of historical sociology

In fact, the ordered evolution of human life is continually modifying our normal existence, in the very act of giving it incessant development. We shall study this progressive reaction systematically in its proper place, in the third volume treating of social dynamics. In fact, there is no necessity for any special treatment of these direct influences of variation; for they are an integral part of social science, and their place in it is the most familiar side, the philosophy of history. The variations which society itself throws up, forming the dynamic existence, whilst it develops the statical existence, may be put aside for our present purpose, by reason in fact of their immense importance. Unless we reserve them for their proper place in the philosophy of history, the science of sociology would be exposed to inextricable confusion. But at the same time we have still left, the third class of social variations, mentioned above.

Reaction of the various societies upon each singly

For, we ought to reserve the name of modifying powers for the merely accessory influences; and under this head will come a second form of collective reaction: that of the sum of all societies upon each singly.

In abstract sociology we conceive humanity as formed and as developed from a single nucleus. In fact, the laws of existence and the laws of evolution, must be in essentials the same for all possible centres of this immense aggregate. Whatever be the nucleus that finally preponderates, and whatever be the mode in which the others agglomerate around it, the fundamental conceptions of sociology are in no way affected thereby; and my eminent predecessor Condorcet felt the logical necessity for this law. It will no doubt be an important service of social science to determine both of these ultimate results; but they have no bearing on the formation of the science itself. Even if the separate groups of humanity were always to remain so numerous as to make the unity of humanity on earth impossible in fact, sociology, whether statical or dynamical, would not be very seriously affected. At the same time, when Condorcet, with an admirable instinct in logic, threw out his hypothesis of framing history as for a single people, he was well aware that this abstract conception, if indispensable as a starting point for historical science, involved the subsequently returning to consider the influence of nations on each other. We may fairly compare this procedure in social science, with the working out of problems in mechanics by using the artifice of *inertia*, as was done from the commencement of positive philosophy. It was then found necessary, in order to pass from the abstract to the concrete, to reintroduce forces which had been previously eliminated. We know how difficult geometers have found this process, and it has been the principal cause of their practical failures when attempting to give too great precision to the solution of some special problem. The same is true in a higher degree, when we attempt in sociology to state the abstract condition in terms of the concrete condition with an approximation closer than is needed for any practical purpose.

Important in concrete and exceptional cases

The laws of existence and the laws of evolution, have always and everywhere the same essential character; but, if their force together determines the main movement of each group of humanity, they still leave any group exposed to the reaction of the rest. Directly we attempt, in statics or in dynamics, to push our explanations beyond a given degree of precision, we find ourselves forced to consider these mutual influences of each group over others. For the ordinary purposes of sociologic theory we can fortunately neglect this kind of reaction; but it is at times indispensable for the treatment of exceptional cases. In the third volume I shall note some striking examples of this, especially in respect to the Middle Age. At the opening of this great transitional period the progress of the West was signally affected by political changes of very distant origin; so that we find the general state of Europe depending on that of Asia, even of its most eastern side. At the same time, these influences, though essentially discontinuous in visible result, have in reality nothing accidental about them. They could always have been foreseen by sufficient knowledge of the entire situation of mankind.

Reaction of each group upon the rest

The third class of social variation is, therefore, produced by the inevitable but intermittent reaction of the various groups, one upon another. The judicious Ferguson was the first to hit upon the true principle of this latter source of normal variations. It is in fact implied in the law of Broussais; inasmuch as it would represent modifications as being nothing but varieties in intensity or in speed, according to our general law of modifiability. These secondary influences over society are often so much exaggerated that they make any sound social theory impossible; for when they are looked upon as governing forces, their number and their inconsistency are such that no regular scheme of human phenomena can be framed. Ferguson has however skilfully proved, that even in the case of conquest, the action of a foreign people over the conquered gives rise simply to modifications which would have developed of themselves a little sooner or a little later, the minor changes excepted . . .

Influence of individuals on society

I have now only to explain the fourth class of variations in sociology: those which are due to individual action. This is the last indirect modifying force of the collective order, although in a sense the inverse of the more general modifying forces. If we consider separately each group of mankind, this kind of influence may often be found more important than any other; and thus it attracted the principal attention of the public and even of philosophers, down to the foundation of sociology. This puerile blunder, which took individual forces of the sovereign arbiter of human progress, often gave rise to violent and dangerous extravagancies; for it fanned the pride of the great men and surrounded them with the illusions of the public. Nevertheless, the practical instinct of true statesmen usually taught them, by rude experience, the limits fixed to their power; and showed them how completely it depended on the general conditions of society . . .

Series of intermediate stages between the extreme limits

If we press to its consequences the admirable axiom of Broussais, we see that it destroys the old absolute distinction between health and disease. Between the extreme limits of the two, we may always find a multitude of intermediate stages, not merely imaginary, but perfectly real, and together forming an almost insensible chain of delicate gradations. I may give an instance of this necessity for an unbroken series of change, in the alterations to be met with in cerebral existence; where the biologic point of view may be easily kept subordinate to the sociologic law. I shall also have further occasion for the observation which I proceed to state.

Illustrated by mental health or disease

If the reader recalls what I have already said on the nature of all human conceptions, as at once objective and subjective, he will admit that the opposite states of reason and madness differ only in the respective activity of the two elements in every state of mind. In any act of thought, the objective and the subjective process both enter in varying proportions. Should the balance of these proportions be seriously disturbed, either may be exaggerated at the expense of the other; until it prepares the way for, and if persisted in, produces actual insanity. Excessive surrender of the mind to the external world, with no due effort of the mind within, leads to pure idiocy. Madness, on the contrary, is an excessive activity of the mind within, apart from special hallucination. It arises from the apparatus of meditation failing to correct the suggestions afforded by the apparatus of observation.

Borderland between unsound logic and insanity

This morbid state may be better studied in the incomparable work of Cervantes than in any treatise on biology. We might even trace from it the great principle of Broussais; and might then apply it to society, as I have now done for the first time. In fact, the law of continuity runs through the whole current of *Don Quixote*, in the sound instinct with which it marks the intermediate stages between reason and madness. Cervantes indirectly expounds the primary principle of positive logic: *that directness of mind consists in choosing the simplest hypothesis which fits the case.* It would follow from this, that the habit of resorting to complicated reasons to explain facts is, in reality, a step towards madness; in that it unduly stimulates the subjective action of the mind. A vigorous brain once started on this course will know no bounds to the extravagance of its arbitrary creations. Every time that facts from the world without refute its hypotheses, such a mind manages to evade conviction by still more elaborate devices to explain them away.

Personal unsoundness of mind is relative to the time and place

The admirable picture of folly drawn by Cervantes also points to the way in which the due proportions of objectivity and subjectivity in each mind must vary in accordance with the state of society around it. The regular proportion of the two elements ought to follow the course of human civilization. We shall state in the third volume the general law of these continuous variations: *that the subjective element of thought constantly decreases, and the objective element constantly increases.* If we compare states of mind in striking antagonism, either in widely different times or widely different places, we find that opinions and desires which are properly called *madness*, in one age or one place, are a perfectly normal state of mind in other ages, or other hemispheres. This is a signal proof of the nicety required in judging individual cases of madness; and it is a grave danger that in our day they are handed over to an ignorant, and often an immoral, materialism. The truth is, that whatever the disturbance of reason, the positive laws of cerebral life, whether in mind or feeling, may be always traced by philosophic intelligence. And the great Cervantes instinctively portrays them, amid all the eccentricities of his hero.

Revolutions are simple cases of degree in change

This identity in the elements of health and disease, the key of the entire law of variability, holds good as much for the collective order as for the individual order. It is indeed more easily recognized in the former case, inasmuch as it is really less involved in complication. If they saw the whole bearing of this scientific truth, statesmen would not be so ready to believe that the normal laws of society cease to have any application in times of revolution. The truth however is that in revolutions the disturbance of society is always, as in every other case, a simple question of degree, either in the intensity of some fixed element, or in the rapidity of movement. I shall often have occasion to give specific instances of this, in describing the anarchy of modern times, in spite of the activity which distinguishes it, resulting from the profound breach in the sense of continuity with the past.

Chronic unsoundness of the West due to a loss of any sense of continuity

If we analyse the cerebral condition of the West we find it in a morbid state, amounting in reality to chronic unsoundness; chiefly, it is true, intellectual, but continually complicated by moral disturbance, and often attended with material agitation. The note of unsoundness, consisting in the fact that meditation is unable to correct the errors of observation, is only too conspicuous in our modern life, especially when we look to the law of subjective continuity, the main source of collective order. Never was there a time when the term *mental alienation*, in its etymological sense, could be more truly applied than to this melancholy spectacle, of the entire race of the living stolidly rebelling against the beneficent rule of the past, even in the act of dreaming about the future. Now, however grave such a disturbance of society may be, we are never at a loss to detect in it the laws of the normal state; and some of them appear to me more striking than they do in situations of a more regular kind. But when we see what different opinions are current on this subject, we may learn how completely relative all such judgments are; for they depend on the notion we form of the normal type . . .

Law of development in the four classes of social variation

This general theory of social variations will now be complete, when I have added one more essential principle, that of the continuous development traceable in the relative force of these four kinds of modifying influences. Since no one of these four can be always and equally intense as human existence advances, we have still to describe the common law of these inevitable changes. We may find the solution in the growing regularity of the human order, due mainly to the reaction of human society over the original imperfections of the order of nature, an influence which man exerts at first instinctively, and then more and more in systematic ways.

Growing regularity in social existence, by internal effort

At first sight it might appear that such a law contradicts the growing complication in social phenomena, due to the gradual extension both of solidarity and continuity throughout mankind. But through all the hierarchy of nature, the law of *inevitable increase in complication in proportion with the decrease of generality*, gives rise to two inverse consequences. And these tend to balance each other ever more and more; because *as liability to imperfection increases, capacity for improvement increases*. If we consider material order, and even vital order alone, notwithstanding this principle it is true that the real harmony of the system would become less perfect, in proportion as it becomes more complex; and the same rule would hold good for the human order if it were ever delivered over blindly to the natural consequences of its greater complication. Such a hypothesis, however, is fortunately out of the question; or at least it can only be realized for a season, at a moment when man's subjective experience from the past is confounded or neutralized, by the anarchy of the objective present. In the general view, I showed how the inevitable conflict waged by human providence against the fatality of nature, gave our existence a regularity far beyond that which would otherwise belong to so complex an organization as man's. I shall now reduce this suggestion to a complete law; that is to say I shall show a continuous progress in this conflict, whilst I treated it before as an unvarying phenomenon.

Law, that the normal type steadily tends to overcome the variations

If we take the general sources of variation just described, we may easily see in each of them the general law: *that man's activity is continually giving fresh ascendency to the normal state over the different modifications of it.*

Civilization diminishes the effects of climate

In the first place this is obvious with regard to climate; the active care of the great being, even in the beginning of civilization, gradually reduces all the influences of climate which are open to man's intervention, and it preserves us in a growing degree from all those which are beyond his resources. Thus it is that man's planet tends to become uniformly habitable, if we except certain spots of extremely unpromising conditions. The permanent expedients of civilization sometimes succeed in freeing the vital conditions from their natural dependence upon material order. For instance, the artificial warmth of towns in Russia often causes menstruation to take place as early as it does in India. The extravagance of those who dogmatize about climate is, therefore, the more singular, inasmuch as its effects are in a very great measure neutralized by civilization.

The influence of race grows ever of less importance

The same is true of race, though this second modifying influence of society is more important than the former. The pretentious philosophers, who are ever ready with this fantastic explanation of social movement, are hardly aware that they are forcing the theory, at the very time when this kind of influence is being more and more confined to minor variations. Differences of race at no time did more than affect the rate of our social evolution, and they never changed its character or the course which it took; but the truth is, that the reaction of race upon society was formerly much greater than at present. In the first place, the continually increasing mixture of races, has a direct tendency to do away with this source of variety; but furthermore, the progress of mankind in the mass, is gradually undermining the consequences of race differences, even more completely than it overcomes the effects of climate. And beside, as cosmic influences are lessened in effect, this tends to diminish the varieties of vital conditions; for the latter were originally produced by the environment . . .

As we saw that the indirect and involuntary modifications of society are at once diminished and made regular by the expansion of civilization, so also, the direct and more or less voluntary modifications are yet more subject to the same law of change . . .

The influence of individuals over society grows less

Lastly in the fourth class of social modifications, we may trace yet more evidently than in the other three, the common law: that they are becoming weaker and more regular. Both of these results are yet more distinctly than before, due to the growing dominion of the dead over the living, a truth which is at the bottom of all sound explanations in Sociology, as it is at the bottom of all harmony in

Practical life. In face of this irresistible pressure of our ancestors, the agitations of our contemporaries grow more and more idle; even in situations where they have the greatest scope. The history of the past, supplies us with many decisive instances of this. However deplorable, for instance, was the retrograde tyranny of Bonaparte, it has had less influence over Europe than the domination of Attila, which indeed was of a nobler kind. And in like manner conversely, the excellent personal influence of Frederick was certainly less than that not merely of Alexander, but also of Cæsar, and even of Charlemagne.

Human order grows ever more regular

The short analysis just given, amounts therefore to this: that it gives us fresh assurance of that consolatory law, which a synthetic view of civilization suggested at the outset. *Human order exhibits a course of increasing regularity*, by virtue of man's ever growing power to affect the sum of his destinies. Although all the forces modifying society grow less and less intense, the reaction of the great being over the fatality upon which it depends, grows ever more and more complete. We thus dispose of that serious difficulty which threatened us, when the conclusion of social statics seemed to point to a constantly increasing complication of society. A complete answer is given by means of the universal law that explains all variations in nature. Phenomena of all kinds, whilst they are growing more and more complex, at the same time are growing more and more capable of modification. Where development takes place, in like manner complication is multiplied as evolution is effected. But at the same time, the highest class of phenomena, which are also the most complex, tend to exhibit an order more and more regular, which almost recalls in its symmetry the higher types of celestial movement. This balance in favour of regularity is due to the wisdom and energy of the grand agent of progress. For humanity is ever at work to assert its own high freedom of action, and thus triumphs over the blind fatality encompassing its life . . .

Growing assimilation of languages

The impressive truth to which this chapter has brought us may be illustrated in a very striking way, if we apply it to the institution of language, the most social of all institutions, and yet the one best fitted to develop personal qualities. Under the increasing pressure exerted by subjective influences, human language is perpetually tending to full and ultimate symmetry, in the degree that man's solidarity and continuity broaden; notwithstanding the objective varieties in it due to climate, to race, and to nationalities or individualities.

Theory of Social Existence*

Mental phenomena are subordinate to general laws

Each class of phenomena has doubtless its own laws not derived from the rest of the economy of nature. But they are always subordinate to the laws of all the less complex and more general phenomena. If the intelligence were freed from this external influence, its aberrations would not be free from all limit. In the first place, it would be still under the force of the affective instincts, and consequently, of the reaction over them of the organs of vegetative life. Hence, to observe directly the laws of the understanding, we must get rid of this internal regulation. We shall, therefore, only get indirect ways of observing these laws, by means of their constant association with our chief ideas; and the reaction upon these of the affections is very variable, and disappears at once in the progress of the race collectively.

Mind is dependent on environment

But this essential basis for our study of the laws of mind leaves in full force, and even brings out more clearly, the second invariable element of the great dualism, the external stimulus of mind. The relative shares of the two are not fixed. Two observations, the converse of each other, serve to prove to us day by day the general dependence of the understanding on the order of nature. Under very unfavourable surrounding conditions, the mind is incapable of any regular work. Again, the vagueness and incoherence of our ideas when we shut out eyes, without sleeping, is an evidence of this dependence of mind on fact; although the objects we see are not those upon which the mind directly dwells. It is therefore impossible to dispute the natural tendency of our intelligence to yield itself up to the spectacle of the world without, so as ultimately to reproduce it to us in a systematic way. Still, this natural disposition is very late in becoming habitual, either in consequence of the difficulties of adequately explaining the external order, or by reason of the vagaries of the mind, springing from inexperience and maintained by our personal instincts. It is no exaggeration to say, that this harmony between the world and mind, the chief

* *Pos. Pol.*, vol. 2, pp. 312–14.

product of our long civilization, is hardly yet established even in the better understandings; and even then it is too often overthrown by the least burst of passion.

As to the other constitutional influence to which the intellect is subjected, that of the vital organs, it is no less indisputable henceforth in spite of the foolish assumptions of metaphysicians to the contrary. Since Cabanis and Gall wrote, there is little need to prove that thought is not an isolated function of our nature, having no part in the general consensus of vital phenomena. But the subordination of thought to social influences is not so well accepted as its connection with organic conditions. Nevertheless, the former is just as certain as the power over thought of the world without, when we regard it from the point of view needed for systematic estimate. That is to say, the laws of thought can only be understood by the aid of sociology, as certainly as they are connected with the laws of biology. And all of them are governed by the more general laws of cosmology.

The entire bearing of this work relieves me from the need of any explanation in detail of this connection, which was also fully treated in my philosophical work. The direct proof of it may be found in the acknowledged influence which language exerts over all other intellectual operations. For no one can doubt how much language depends on the development of society, whether we regard it in the present or in the past; nor can we assign language to any individual origin, as metaphysicians crudely pretend. Viewed more directly, the same is true of all other intellectual functions. It is plain that the growth of any single mind is subject to the place and time of its development. The progress of science would admit of no consistency unless society thus acted upon intellect; and the same is true of the fine arts, which, less distinctly than science, reflect the changing points of view of the society in which they spring.

All mental action depends on social support

For observation as for reflection, each mind constantly depends on others to furnish it with materials or to verify its results. In the morbid effect which the insane exert over the physicians devoting themselves to their care, we may see how the mind is shaken by earnestness of conviction, even when we know it to be mistaken. The boldest innovator rarely has full belief in his own discoveries, until they have won some amount of willing acceptance. And he cannot forego the sanction this gives him unless he feels a similar support in the general progress of humanity. In a word, the order of individual life depends on the order of society as much in its details as in its entirety. But in these details, the superior influence of the past as against that of the present is more than ever conspicuous. Thus in the philosophic history of the sciences we may map out the field of discovery proper to each phase of progress, more precisely than specialists imagine.

4 Social Dynamics

Social Dynamics; or, Theory of the Natural Progress of Human Society*

Scientific view of human progression

If we regard the course of human development from the highest scientific point of view, we shall perceive that it consists in educing, more and more, the characteristic faculties of humanity, in comparison with those of animality; and especially with those which man has in common with the whole organic kingdom. It is in this philosophical sense that the most eminent civilization must be pronounced to be fully accordant with nature, since it is, in fact, only a more marked manifestation of the chief properties of our species; properties which, latent at first, can come into play only in that advanced state of social life for which they are exclusively destined. The whole system of biological philosophy indicates the natural progression. We have seen how, in the brute kingdom, the superiority of each race is determined by the degree of preponderance of the animal life over the organic. In like manner, we see that our social evolution is only the final term of a progression which has continued from the simplest vegetables and most insignificant animals, up through the higher reptiles, to the birds and the mammifers, and still on to the carnivorous animals and monkeys, the organic characteristics retiring, and the animal prevailing more and more, till the intellectual and moral tend towards the ascendancy which can never be fully obtained, even in the highest state of human perfection that we can conceive of. This comparative estimate affords us the scientific view of human progression, connected, as we see it is, with the whole course of animal advancement, of which it is itself the highest degree. The analysis of our social progress proves indeed that, while the radical dispositions of our nature are necessarily invariable, the highest of them are in a continuous state of relative development, by which they rise to be preponderant powers of human existence, though the inversion of the primitive economy can never be absolutely complete. We have seen that this is the essential character of the social organism in a statical view: but it becomes much more marked when we study its variations in their gradual succession.

Course of man's social development

Civilization develops, to an enormous degree, the action of man upon his environment: and thus, it may seem, at first, to concen-

* *Pos. Phil.,* vol. 2, pp. 299–333.

trate our attention upon the cares of material existence, the support and improvement of which appear to be the chief object of most social occupations. A closer examination will show, however, that this development gives the advantage to the highest human faculties, both by the security which sets free our attention from physical wants, and by the direct and steady excitement which it administers to the intellectual functions, and even the social feelings. In man's social infancy, the instincts of subsistence are so preponderant, that the sexual instinct itself, notwithstanding its primitive strength, is at first controlled by them: the domestic affections are then much less pronounced; and the social affections are restricted to an almost imperceptible fraction of humanity, beyond which everything is foreign, and even hostile: and the malignant passions are certainly, next to the animal appetites, the mainspring of human existence. It is unquestionable that civilization leads us on to a further and further development of our noblest dispositions and our most generous feelings, which are the only possible basis of human association, and which receive, by means of that association, a more and more special culture. As for the intellectual faculties, we see, by the habitual improvidence which characterizes savage life, how little influence reason has over men in that stage of existence. Those faculties are then undeveloped, or show some activity only in the lowest order, which relate to the exercise of the senses: the faculties of abstraction and combination are almost wholly inert, except under some transient stimulus: the rude curiosity which the spectacle of nature involuntarily inspires is quite satisfied with the weakest attempts at theological explanation; and amusements, chiefly distinguished by violent muscular activity, rising at best to a manifestation of merely physical address, are as little favourable to the development of intelligence as of social qualities. The influence of civilization in perpetually improving the intellectual faculties is even more unquestionable than its effect on moral relations. The development of the individual exhibits to us in little, both as to time and degree, the chief phases of social development. In both cases, the end is to subordinate the satisfaction of the personal instincts to the habitual exercise of the social faculties, subjecting, at the same time, all our passions to rules imposed by an ever-strengthening intelligence, with the view of identifying the individual more and more with the species. In the anatomical view, we should say that the process is to give an influence by exercise to the organs of the cerebral systems, increasing in proportion to their distance from the vertebral column, and their nearness to the frontal region. Such is the ideal type which exhibits the course of human development, in the individual, and, in a higher degree, in the species. This view enables us to discriminate the natural from the artificial part of the process of development; that part being natural which raises the human to a superiority over the animal attributes; and that part being artificial by which any faculty is made to preponderate in proportion to its original weakness: and here we find the scientific explanation of that eternal struggle between our humanity and our animality which has been recognized by all who have made man their study, from the earliest days of civilization till now, and embodied in many forms before its true character was fixed by the positive philosophy.

Rate of progress

This, then, is the direction of the human evolution. The next consideration is the rate at which it proceeds, apart from any differences which may result from climate, race or other modifying causes. Taking into the account only universal causes, it is clear that the speed must be in proportion to the combined influence of the chief natural conditions relating to the human organism first, and next to its medium. The invariableness, the evident impossibility of suspending these fundamental conditions, must ever prevent our estimating their respective importance, though we may have a general conviction that our spontaneous development must be hastened or retarded by any change in these elementary influences, organic or inorganic; supposing, for instance, our cerebral system to be slightly inferior, in the frontal region; or our planet to become larger or more habitable. Sociological analysis can, by its nature, reach only to accessory conditions, which are rendered susceptible of estimate by their variations.

Among these secondary but permanent influences, which affect the rate of human development, *ennui* is the first which presents itself. Man, like other animals, cannot be happy without a sufficient exercise of all his faculties, intense and persistent in proportion to the intrinsic activity of each faculty. The greater difficulty experienced by man in obtaining a development compatible with the special superiority of his nature renders him more subject than the other animals to that remarkable state of irksome languor which indicates at once the existence of the faculties and their insufficient activity, and which would become equally irreconcilable with a radical debility incapable of any urgent tendency, and with an ideal vigour, spontaneously susceptible of indefatigable exercise. A disposition at once intellectual and moral, which we daily see at work in natures endowed with any energy, must have powerfully accelerated the human expansion, in the infancy of humanity, by the uneasy excitement it occasioned either in the eager search for new sources of emotion, or in the more intense development of direct human activity. This secondary influence is not very marked till the social state is sufficiently advanced to make men feel a growing need to exercise the highest faculties, which are, as we have seen, the least energetic. The strongest faculties, which are the lowest, are so easily exercised that in ordinary circumstances they can hardly generate the *ennui* which would produce a favourable cerebral reaction. Savages, like children, are not subject to much *ennui* while their physical activity, which alone is of any importance to them, is not interfered with. An easy and protracted sleep prevents them, as if they were mere animals, from feeling their intellectual torpor in any irksome way. This brief notice of the influence of *ennui* was necessary, to show what its operation really amounts to in accelerating the speed of our social evolution.

Duration of human life

But perhaps the most important of all accelerating influences is the ordinary duration of human life, which I mention in the second place. There is no denying that our social progression rests upon death. I mean, the successive steps suppose the steady renewal of the agents of the general movement, which is almost imperceptible in the course of any single life, and becomes marked only on the succession of a new generation. Here again the social resembles the individual organism, being under the same necessity to throw off its constituent parts as they become, by the vital action itself, unfit for further use, and must be replaced by new elements. To illustrate this, we need not go so far as to suppose an indefinite duration of human life, which would presently put a stop to all progression whatever . . .

Increase of population

Another cause which affects the rate of progress is the natural increase of population, which contributes more than any other influence to accelerate the speed. This increase has always been regarded as the clearest symptom of the gradual amelioration of the human condition; and nothing can be more unquestionable when we take the whole race into the account; or at least, all the nations which have any mutual interest: but this is not the view with which my argument is concerned. I have to consider only the progressive condensation of our species as a last general element concurring in the regulation of our rate of social progress. It is clear that by this condensation, and especially in its early stages, such a division of employments is favoured as could not take place among smaller numbers: and again, that the faculties of individuals are stimulated to find subsistence by more refined methods; and again, that society is obliged to react with a firmer and better concerted energy against the expansion of individual divergences. In view of these considerations, I speak, not of the increase of the numbers of mankind, but of their concentration upon a given space, according to the special expression which I have made use of, and which is particularly applicable to the great centres of population, whence, in all ages, human progression has started. By creating new wants and new difficulties, this gradual concentration develops new means, not only of progress but of order, by neutralizing physical inequalities, and affording a growing ascendency to those intellectual and moral forces which are suppressed among a scanty population. If we go on to inquire into the effect of a quicker or slower concentration, we shall perceive that the social movement is further accelerated by the disturbance given to the old antagonism between the conservative and the innovating instincts—the last being strongly reinforced. In this sense the sociological influence of a more rapid increase of population is in analogy with that which we have just been considering in regard to the duration of life; for it is of little consequence whether the more frequent renewal of individuals is caused by the short life of some, or the speedier multiplication of others; and what was said in the former case will suffice for the latter. It must be observed, however, that if the condensation and rapidity were to pass beyond a certain degree, they would not favour, but impede this acceleration. The condensation, if carried too far, would render the support of human life too difficult; and the rapidity, if extreme, would so affect the stability of social enterprises as to be equivalent to a considerable shortening of our life. As yet, however, the increase of population has never nearly reached the natural limits at which such inconveniences will begin; and we have really no experience of them, unless in a few exceptional cases of disturbance caused by migrations, ill-managed as to their extent of numbers and of time. In an extremely distant future, our posterity will have to consider the question, and with much anxiety; because, from the smallness of the globe, and the necessary limitation of human resources, the tendency to increase will become extremely important, when the human race will be ten times as numerous as at present, and as much condensed every-where as it now is in the west of Europe. Whenever that time comes, the more complete development of human nature, and the more exact knowledge of the laws of human evolution, will no doubt supply new means of resistance to the danger; means of which we can form no clear conception, and about which it is not for us to decide whether they will, on the whole, afford a sufficient compensation.

These are not all the accelerating influences which could be mentioned; but they are the chief; and they are enough for us, in our abstract view of our subject. I have now only to exhibit the main subordination which the different aspects of human develop-ment must mutually present.

The order of evolution

Though the elements of our social evolution are connected, and always acting on each other, one must be preponderant, in order to give an impulse to the rest, though they may, in their turn, so act upon it as to cause its further expansion. We must find out this superior element, leaving the lower degrees of subordination to disclose themselves as we proceed: and we have not to search far for this element, as we cannot err in taking that which can be best conceived of apart from the rest, notwithstanding their necessary connection, while the consideration of it would enter into the study of the others. This double characteristic points out the intel-lectual evolution as the preponderant principle. If the intellectual point of view was the chief in our statical study of the organism, much more must it be so in the dynamical case. If our reason required at the outset the awakening and stimulating influence or the appetites, the passions, and the sentiments, not the less has human progression gone forward under its direction. It is only through the more and more marked influence of the reason over the general conduct of man and of society, that the gradual march of our race has attained that regularity and persevering continuity which distinguish it so radically from the desultory and barren ex-pansion of even the highest of the animal orders, which share, and with enhanced strength, the appetites, the passions, and even the primary sentiments of man. If the statical analysis of our social organism shows it resting at length upon a certain system of funda-mental opinions, the gradual changes of that system must affect the successive modifications of the life of humanity: and this is why, since the birth of philosophy, the history of society has been regarded as governed by the history of the human mind. As it is necessary, in a scientific sense, to refer our historical analysis to the preponderant evolution, whatever it may be, we must in this case choose, or rather preserve, the general history of the human mind as the natural guide to all historical study of humanity. One consequence of the same principle—a consequence as rigorous but less understood—is that we must choose for consideration in this intellectual history, the most general and abstract conceptions, which require the exercise of our highest faculties. Thus it is the study of the fundamental system of human opinions with regard to the whole of phenomena—in short, the history of philosophy, whatever may be its character, theological, metaphysical or positive—which must regulate our historical analysis. No other department of intellectual history, not even the history of the fine arts, including poetry, could, however important in itself, be employed for this object; because the faculties of expression, which lie nearer to the affective faculties, have always, in their palmiest days, been subordinated, in the economy of social progress, to the faculties of direct conception. The danger (which is inherent in every choice, and which is least in the choice that I have made) of losing sight of the interconnection of all the parts of human development, may be partly guarded against by frequently comparing them, to see if the variations in any one corresponds with equivalent variations in the others. I believe we shall find that this confirmation is eminently obtainable by my method of historical analysis. This will be proved at once if we find that the development of the highest part of human interests is in accordance with that of the lowest—the intellectual with the material. If there is an accordance between the two extremes, there must be also between all the intermediate terms.

We have indicated the general direction of the human evolution, its rate of progress, and its necessary order. We may now proceed at once to investigate the natural laws by which the advance of the human mind proceeds. The scientific principle of the theory appears to me to consist in the great philosophical law of the succession of the three states (the primitive theological state, the transient metaphysical and the final positive state) through which the human mind has to pass, in every kind of speculation. This seems to be the place in which we should attempt the direct estimate of this fundamental law, taking it as the basis of my historic analysis, which must itself have for its chief object to explain and expand the general notion of this law by a more and more extended and exact application of it in the review of the entire past of human history. I hope that the frequent statement and application of this law throughout the preceding part of my work will enable me to condense my demonstration of it here, without impairing its distinctness, or injuring its efficacy in such ulterior use as we shall have to make of it.

Law of the three periods

The reader is by this time abundantly familiar with the interpretation and destination of the law. All thoughtful persons can verify for themselves its operation in individual development, from infancy to manhood, as I pointed out at the beginning of this work. We can test it, as we have tested other laws, by observation, experiment and comparison. I have done so through many years of meditation; and I do not hesitate to say that all these methods of investigation will be found to concur in the complete establishment of this historical proposition, which I maintain to be as fully demonstrated as any other law admitted into any other department of natural philosophy . . .

The theological period

The necessity of the intellectual evolution I assert lies in the primary tendency of man to transfer the sense of his own nature into the radical explanation of all phenomena whatever. Philosophers tell us of the fundamental difficulty of knowing ourselves; but this is a remark which could not have been made till human reason had achieved a considerable advance. The mind must have attained to a refined state of meditation before it could be astonished at its own acts—reflecting upon itself a speculative activity which must be at first incited by the external world. If, on the one hand, man must begin by supposing himself the centre of all things, he must, on the other hand, next set himself up as a universal type. The only way that he can explain any phenomena is by likening them, as much as possible, to his own acts—the only ones whose mode of production he can suppose himself, by the accompanying sensations, to understand. We may therefore set up a converse statement, and say that man knows nothing but himself; and thus, his philosophy, in his earliest stage, consists principally in transferring this spontaneous unity, more or less fortunately, into all subjects which may present themselves to his nascent attention. It is the highest proof of his philosophical maturity when he can, at length, apply the study of external nature to his own. When I laid this down as the basis of biological philosophy, I intimated the extreme rarity of such an attainment. At the outset, under the inverse process, the universe is always subordinated to man, in speculative as well as in active respects. We shall not have attained a truly rational position till we can reconcile these two great philosophical views, at present antagonistic, but admitting of being made mutually complementary, and, in my opinion, prepared for being so, from this time forward. Such a harmony is even now barely conceivable in the brightest insight of philosophical genius, and there could have been no choice between the two courses in the earliest days of human development. The starting-point must have been that which alone was naturally possible. This was the spontaneous origin of the theological philosophy, the elementary spirit of which consists in explaining the intimate nature of phenomena, and their mode of production, and in likening them, as much as possible, to the acts of human will, through our primary tendency to regard all beings as living a life analogous to our own, and often superior, from their greater habitual energy. This procedure is so eminently exclusive, that men are unable to emancipate themselves from it, even in the most advanced stages of evolution, except by abandoning altogether these inaccessible researches, and restricting themselves to the study of the laws of phenomena, apart from their causes. Whenever, at this day, the human mind attempts to pass these inevitable limits, it involuntary falls again into the primary errors, even in regard to the simplest phenomena, because it recurs to an aim and point of view essentially analogous, in attributing the production of phenomena to special volitions, internal, or more or less external.

Social influences of the theological philosophy

There are two views which must be considered, in relation to the high social office of the theological philosophy: first, its function in organizing society; and next, its provision for the permanent existence of a speculative class. As to the first, we must perceive that the formation of any society, worthy to be so called, supposes a system of common opinions, such as may restrain individual eccentricity; and such an influence, if needful now, when men are connected together by such a concurrence of obligations as high civilization introduces, must be absolutely indispensable in the infancy of society, when families adhere to each other so feebly, by means of relations as precarious as they are defective.

Institution of a speculative class

Another way in which the theological philosophy was politically indispensable to human progress was by instituting, in the midst of society, a special class regularly devoted to speculative activity.

In this view, the social supremacy of the theological philosophy has lasted to our own time. It is scarcely possible for us to form any but an indirect idea of the difficulty of establishing, in the earliest period of society, any permanent division between theory and practice, such as is effected by the existence of a class regularly occupied with speculation. Even now, amidst all the refinement of our mental habits, we find extreme difficulty in duly estimating any new operation which has no immediate practical bearing: and by this we may imperfectly understand how impossible it was, in the remotest ages, to institute among populations of warriors and slaves a corporation that should be disengaged from military and industrial employments, and whose activity should be mainly of an intellectual kind. Such a class could, in those times, have been neither established nor tolerated if it had not been introduced in the natural course of social movement, and invested with authority beforehand by the influence of the theological philosophy. The political function of that philosophy thus was to establish a speculative body whose social existence not only admitted of no preparatory discussion, but was itself an indispensable preparation for the regular organization of all other classes. Whatever might have been the confusion of intellectual labour, and the inanity of the leading investigations of the sacerdotal orders, it is not the less true that the human mind owes to them the first effectual separation between theory and practice, which could take place in no other manner. Mental progress, by which all other progress is directed, would certainly have been destroyed at its birth, if society had continued to be composed of families engaged in the cares of material existence, or, as the only alternative, in the excitement of a brutal military activity. Any spiritual expansion supposes the existence of a privileged class, enjoying the leisure indispensable to intellectual culture, and at the same time urged, by its social position, to develop to the utmost the kind of speculative activity compatible with the primitive state of humanity, and this description is answered by the sacerdotal institution, established by the theological philosophy. Though, in the decrepitude of the old philosophy, we see the theological class sunk in mental lethargy, we must not forget that but for their activity in the days of its prime, human society would have remained in a condition much like that of a company of superior monkeys. By forming this speculative class, then, the theological philosophy fulfilled the political conditions of a further progression of the human mind.

The positive stage

If this starting-point of human development has been placed beyond dispute, the final, or positive stage, does not admit of it. We have seen enough of the establishment of the positive philosophy in other departments to be satisfied of its destined prevalence in sociology. For the same reasons which explain and justify the early supremacy of the theological philosophy, we see that it must be a provisional state, for its supremacy was owing to its aptitude to meet the needs of a primitive state of humanity; and those needs are not the same, nor requiring the same philosophy to satisfy them, as those which arise in a more advanced stage of the human evolution. After having awakened human reason, and super-intended its progress, in the absence of a more real philosophy, theology began to repress the human mind from the first moment of its coming into direct antagonism with the positive philosophy . . .

Attempted union of the two philosophies

The general, like the individual human mind, is governed by imagination first, and then, after a sufficient exercise of the faculties at large, more and more by reason. The same grounds on which the process takes place in the individual case determine that of the whole species; and with the more certainty and power on account of the greater complexity and perpetuity of the social organism. Supreme as the theological philosophy once was, it is certain that such a method of philosophizing was resorted to only because no other was possible. Wherever there has been a choice, in regard to any subject whatever, man has always preferred the study of the laws of phenomena to that of their primary causes, though prior training, which there has been no rational education adapted to counteract, has often occasioned lapse into his old illusions. Theological philosophy has, however, never been absolutely universal. That is, the simplest and commonest facts in all classes of phenomena have always been supposed subject to natural laws, and not to the arbitrary will of supernatural agents. Adam Smith made the remark that there never was, in any age or country, a god of weight. In more complex cases, if only the relations of phenomena are seen to be invariable, the most superficial observer recognizes the presence of law. Even among moral and social phenomena, where the entrance of positive philosophy has been interdicted, we are all obliged to act daily on the supposition of natural laws, in order to conduct the common affairs of life, for all forecast would be impossible if we supposed every incident to be ascribable to supernatural agency, and no other resource therefore possible than prayer, for influencing the course of human actions. It is even noticeable that the principle of the theological philosophy itself lies in the transference to the phenomena of external nature of the first beginnings of the laws of human action; and thus the germ of the positive philosophy is at least as primitive as that of the theological philosophy itself, though it could not expand till a much later time. This idea is very important to the perfect rationality of our sociological theory; because, as human life can never present any real creation, but only a gradual evolution, the final spread of the positive spirit would be scientifically incomprehensible, if we could not trace its rudiments from the very beginning. From that scarcely appreciable presence at the beginning, the rise of the positive spirit has been recognizable, in proportion to the extension and generalization of our observations, and the theological philosophy has been slowly but steadily driven back within the narrowing limits of phenomena whose natural laws were still unknown. Thus was the function of the old philosophy clearly a provisional one—to maintain our mental activity by the only exercise open to it, till the positive philosophy should usher it into the wide field of universal knowledge, made accessible to the whole race. This destination has only recently exhibited itself in an unquestionable way since the disclosure of natural laws in phenomena so numerous and so various as to suggest the necessary existence of analogous laws in all other departments, however remote their actual discovery may be . . .

The metaphysical period

We have now only to take a cursory survey of the intermediate state. I have pointed out more than once before, that any intermediate state can be judged of only after a precise analysis of the two extremes. The present case is a remarkable illustration of this necessity; for, if it is once admitted that the human mind must set out from the theological state, and arrive certainly at the positive, we may easily understand how it must pass through the metaphysical, which has no other destination than to afford a transition from the one to the other. The bastard and mobile character of the metaphysical philosophy fits it for this office, as it reconciles, for a time, the radical opposition of the other two, adapting itself to the gradual decline of the one and the preparatory rise of the other, so as to spare our dislike of abrupt change, and to afford us a transition almost imperceptible. The metaphysical philosophy takes possession of the speculative field after the theological has relinquished it, and before the positive is ready for it: so that in each particular case, the dispute about the supremacy of any of the three philosophies is reduced to the mere question of opportuneness, judged by a rational examination of the development of the human mind. The method of modification consists in substituting gradually the entity for a deity when religious conceptions become so generalized as to diminish perpetually the number of supernatural agents, as well as their active intervention, and at length arrive, professedly if not really, at rigorous unity. When supernatural action loses its original speciality, it consigns the immediate direction of the phenomenon to a mysterious entity, at first emanating from itself, but to which daily custom trains the human mind to refer more and more exclusively the production of each event. This strange process has favoured the withdrawal of supernatural causes, and the exclusive consideration of phenomena; that is, the decline of the theological and the rise of the positive spirit . . .

Co-existence of the three periods

During the whole of our survey of the sciences, I have endeavoured to keep in view the great fact that all the three states, theological, metaphysical and positive, may and do exist at the same time in the same mind in regard to different sciences. I must once more recall this consideration, and insist upon it; because in the forgetfulness of it lies the only real objection that can be brought against the grand law of the three states. It must be steadily kept in view that the same mind may be in the positive state with regard to the most simple and general sciences; in the metaphysical with regard to the more complex and special; and in the theological with regard to social science, which is so complex and special as to have hitherto taken no scientific form at all. Any apparent contradiction must certainly arise, even if it could be shown to exist, from the imperfection of our hierarchical arrangement, and not from the law of evolution itself. This once fully understood, the law itself becomes our guide in further investigation, as every proved theory does, by showing us by anticipation, what phenomena to look for, and how to use those which arise: and it supplies the place of direct exploration, when we have not the necessary means of investigation. We shall find that by this law alone can the history of the human mind be rendered intelligible. Having convinced ourselves of its efficacy in regard to all other sciences, and in interpreting all that has yet come to pass in human history, we must adhere to it steadily in analysing the present, and in forming such anticipation of the future as sociology, being a real science, enables us to rely upon.

To complete my long and difficult demonstration, I have only now to show that material development, as a whole, must follow a course, not only analogous, but perfectly correspondent with that of intellectual development, which, as we have seen, governs every other.

Corresponding material development

All political investigation of a rational kind proves the primitive tendency of mankind, in a general way, to a military life; and to its final issue in an industrial life. No enlightened mind disputes the continuous decline of the military spirit, and the gradual ascendancy of the industrial. We see now, under various forms, and more and more indisputably, even in the very heart of armies, the repugnance of modern society to a military life. We see that compulsory recruiting becomes more and more necessary, and that there is less and less voluntary persistence in that mode of life. Notwithstanding the immense exceptional development of military activity which was occasioned by anomalous circumstances at the beginning of the present century, our industrial and pacific instincts have returned to their regular course of expansion, so as to render us secure of the radical tranquillity of the civilized world, though the peace of Europe must often appear to be endangered through the provisional deficiency of any systematic organization of international relations; a cause which, though insufficient to produce war, keeps us in a state of frequent uneasiness. We need not then go over again the proof of the first and last terms of the evolution; which will be abundantly illustrated by the historical analysis that I shall offer. We have only to refer the facts of human experience to the essential laws of human nature, and the necessary conditions of social development: a scientific procedure which has never yet been attempted.

Primitive military life

As long as primitive man was averse to all regular toil, the military life alone furnished a field for his sustained activity. Apart from cannibalism, it offered the simplest means of subsistence. However deplorable the necessity, its universal prevalence and continuous development, even after subsistence might have been obtained by other means, proves that the military regime must have had some indispensable, though provisional office to fulfil in the progression of the race. It was indeed the only one under which human industry could make a beginning; in the same way that the scientific spirit could not have arisen without the protection of the religious. The industrial spirit supposed the existence of a considerable social development, such as could not have taken place till isolated families had been connected by the pursuits of war. The social, and yet more the political properties of military activity are, in their early stages, perfectly clear and decisive, and, in short, fully appropriate to the high civilizing function which they had to fulfil. It was thus that habits of regularity and discipline were instituted, and the families of men were brought into association for warlike expeditions or for their common defence. The objects of association could not possibly be more obvious or urgent, nor the elementary conditions of concurrence more irresistible. In no other school could a primitive society learn order; as we may see at this day in the case of those types of ancient humanity—the exceptional individuals who cannot now be made amenable to industrial discipline. This ascendancy of the military spirit was indispensable, not only to the original consolidation of political society, but yet more to its continuous extension, which could not otherwise have taken place but with excessive slowness; and such extension was, to a certain degree, indispensable to the final development of human industry. Thus, then, we find humanity involved in the same kind of vicious circle with regard to its temporal as we saw it to be with its spiritual progress; and in both cases an issue was afforded by the fortunate expansion of a preliminary tendency.

Primitive slavery

In fact, the necessary basis of the military regime has everywhere been the individual slavery of the producing class, by which warriors were allowed the full and free development of their activity. We shall see hereafter that the great social operation which was to be accomplished, in due time, by the continuous progression of a military system, powerfully instituted and wisely carried out, must have failed in its earliest stages. We shall also see how this ancient slavery was the necessary preparation for the final prevalence of the industrial life, by imposing on the majority of the race, irresistibly and exclusively, that toil to which man is constitutionally averse, though an ultimate condition of laborious perseverance was in store for all. To view the case without prejudice, we must transport ourselves to those primitive times, and not regard the slavery of that age with the just horror with which we view that of modern times—the colonial slavery of our day, which is truly a social monstrosity, existing as it does in the heart of an industrial period, subjecting the labourer to the capitalist in a manner equally degrading to both. The ancient slavery was of the producer to the warrior; and it tended to develop their respective energies, so as to occasion their final concurrence in the same social progression.

The military regime provisional

Necessary as this military regime was, it was not the less merely provisional. While industrial activity has the fine quality of bearing the most energetic extension among all individuals and nations without making the rise of the one irreconcilable with that of the other, it is evident that the exaltation of the military life among any considerable portion of the race must occasion the restriction of all the rest; this being, in fact, the proper function of the regime in regard to the whole field of civilization. Thus, while the industrial period comprehends the whole term of human progress under natural laws—that is, the whole future that we can conceive of— the military period could last no longer than the formation of those preparatory conditions which it was its function to create. This end was attained when the chief part of the civilized world was at length united under the same rule; that is, in regard to Europe, when Rome had completed its conquests. From that time forward, military activity had neither object nor ailment; and from that time forward, therefore, it declined, so as no longer to disguise that gradual rise of the industrial spirit, which had been preparing during the interval. But, notwithstanding this connection, the industrial state was so radically different from the military as to require an intermediate term; and in the same way that, in the spiritual evolution, an intermediate term was required between the theological and the positive spirit. In both cases, the middle phase was fluctuating and equivocal. We shall see hereafter that, in the temporal case, it consisted, first, in a substitution of a defensive for an offensive military organization, and afterwards in an involuntary general subordination, more and more marked, of the military spirit to the instinct of production. This transitory phase being the one in which we live, its proper nature, vague as it is, can be estimated by indirect intuition.

Such is the temporal evolution, briefly surveyed in its three periods. No philosophical mind can help being struck by the analogy between this indisputable progression and our primary law of succession of the three states of the human mind. But our sociological demonstration requires that we should establish the connection between them by exhibiting the natural affinity which has always existed, first between the theological and the military spirit, and afterwards between the scientific and industrial; and, consequently, between the two transient functions of the meta-physicians and the legists. This elucidation will impart the last degree of precision and consistency to my demonstration, and will thus establish it as the rational basis of the entire historical analysis which will follow.

Affinity between the theological and military regime

The occasional rivalry between the theological power and the military, which history presents, has sometimes disguised their radical affinity, even in the eyes of philosophers. But, if we con-sider, there can be no real rivalry but among the different elements of the same political system, in consequence of that spontaneous emulation which, in all cases of human concurrence, must become more earnest and extensive as the end is more important and indirect, and therefore the means more distinct and independent, without the participation, voluntary or instinctive, being thereby prevented. When two powers, equally energetic, rise, increase, and decline together, notwithstanding the difference of their natures, we may be assured that they belong to the same regime, whatever may be their habitual conflicts. Conflict indicates radical incom-patibility only when it takes place between two elements employed in analogous functions, and when the gradual growth of the one coincides with the continuous decline of the other. As to the present case, it is evident that, in any political system, there must be an incessant rivalry between the speculative and the active powers, which, through the imperfection of our nature, must often be inclined to ignore their necessary co-ordination, and to disdain the general limits of their reciprocal attributes. Notwithstanding the social affinity between science and industry, we must look for similar conflict between them hereafter, in proportion to the political ascendancy which they will obtain together. We see signs of it already in the intellectual and moral antipathy of science to the natural inferiority of these labours of industry which yet are the means of wealth, and in the instinctive repugnance of industry to the abstraction which characterizes science, and to the just pride by which it is animated.

Having dispatched these objections, we may now contemplate

the strong bond which unites the theological and military powers, and which has in all ages been felt and honoured by all enlightened men who have borne a part in either, notwithstanding the passions of political rivalry. It is plain that no military system could arise and endure without the countenance of the theological spirit, which must secure for it the complete and permanent subordination essential to its existence. Each period imposes equal exigencies of this sort in its special manner . . .

We shall see again that the theological spirit is as hostile to the expansion of industry as the military. Thus the two elements of the primitive political system have not only a radical affinity, but common antipathies and sympathies, as well as general interests; and it must be needless to enlarge further in this place on the sociological principle of the concurrence of these powers, which my historical analysis will present as constantly engaged in consolidating and correcting each other.

Affinity between the positive and industrial spirit

The latest case of political dualism is even more unquestionable than the earliest, and we are favourably circumstanced for observing it, the two elements not having yet attained their definite ascendency, though their social development is sufficiently marked. When the time arrives for their political rivalry, it may be more difficult than now to exhibit that resemblance in origin and destination, and that conformity of principles and interests, which could not be seriously disputed as long as their common struggle against the old political system acts as a restraint upon their divergencies. The most remarkable feature that we have to contemplate in their case is the aid which each renders to the political triumph of the other, by seconding its own efforts against its chief antagonist. I have already noticed, in another connection, the secret incompatibility between the scientific spirit and the military. There is the same hostility between the industrial spirit, when sufficiently developed, and the theological. The most zealous advocates of the old regime are very far removed from the old religious point of view; but we can transport ourselves to it for a moment, and see how the voluntary modification of phenomena by the rules of human wisdom must thence appear as impious as the rational prevision of them, as both suppose invariable laws, finally irreconcilable with all arbitrary will. According to the rigorous though barbarous logic of the least civilized nations, all human intervention to improve the economy of nature is an injurious attack upon providential government. There is no doubt, in fact, that a strong preponderance of the religious spirit benumbs the industrial, by the exaggerated feelings of a stupid optimism, as has been abundantly clear on many decisive occasions. That this disastrous effect has not been more fatal is owing to priestly sagacity, which has so managed this dangerous power as to educe its civilizing influence, while neutralizing its injurious action by constant and vigilant effort, in a way which I shall presently exhibit. We cannot then overlook the political influence by which the gradual expansion of human industry must aid the progressive ascendency of the scientific spirit, in its antagonism to the religious; to say nothing of the daily stimulus which industry and science impart to each other, when once strong enough for mutual action. Thus far their office has chiefly been to substitute themselves for the ancient political powers which are yielding up their social influence; and our attention is necessarily drawn chiefly to the aid they have afforded to each other in this operation. But it is easy to perceive what force and what efficacy must reside in their connection, when it shall have assumed the organic character, in which it is at present deficient, and shall proceed to the final reorganization of modern society.

Intermediate regime

Now that we have examined the two extreme states, the intermediate dualism requires little notice. The interconnection of the convergent powers, spiritual and temporal, which constitutes the transitory regime, is a necessary consequence of all that we have been observing. Indeed, we need but look at the labours of metaphysicians and legists to see what their affinity is, amidst their rivalries; an affinity which stakes the philosophical ascendency of the one class on the political preponderance of the other. We may, then, regard as now complete the necessary explanation required by our fundamental law of human evolution, in order to see its direct application to the study of this great phenomenon. That study will be guided by the consideration of the three dualisms which I have established as the only basis of sound historical philosophy. It is worth noticing the conformity of this law of succession, at once intellectual and material, social and political, with the historical order which popular reason has instinctively established, by distinguishing the ancient and the modern world, separated and reunited by the Middle Ages. The sociological law which I have propounded may be found to have for its destination to take up a vague empirical notion, hitherto barren, and render it rational and prolific. I hail this spontaneous coincidence, as giving a sanction to my speculative labours; and I claim this confirmation, in virtue of that great aphorism of positive philosophy which I have quoted so often, which enjoins upon all sound scientific theories to start from a point sufficiently accordant with the spontaneous indications of popular reason, of which true science is simply a special prolongation.

The series of views of social dynamics sketched out in this chapter has established the fundamental law of human development, and therefore the bases of historical philosophy. We had before ascertained the spirit and method of that philosophy; and we may now therefore proceed to apply this great sociological conception to the analysis of the history of mankind.

Preparation of the Historical Question*

The best way of proving that my principle of social development will ultimately regenerate social science, is to show that it affords a perfect interpretation of the past of human society—at least in its principal phases. If, by this method, any conception of its scope and proper application can be obtained, future philosophers can extend the theory to new analyses, and more and more special aspects of human progression. The application which I propose now to enter upon must, however, in order to be brief, be restricted; and the first part of my task is to show what the restrictions must be.

Limitations of the analysis

The most important of these restrictions, and the one which comprehends all the rest, is, that we must confine our analysis to a single social series; that is, we must study exclusively the development of the most advanced nations, not allowing our attention to be drawn off to other centres of any independent civilization which has, from any cause whatever, been arrested, and left in an imperfect state. It is the selectest part, the vanguard of the human race, that we have to study: the greater part of the white race, or the European nations—even restricting ourselves, at least in regard to modern times, to the nations of western Europe . . .

Our first limit then is that we are to concentrate our sociological analysis on the historical estimate of the most advanced social development.

For this object we want only the best-known facts; and they are

* *Pos. Phil.*, vol. 3, pp. 1–6.

so perfectly co-ordinated by the law of the three periods, that the largest phases of social life form a ready and complete elucidation of the law; and when we have to contemplate the more special aspects of society, we have only to apply in a secondary way the corresponding sub-divisions of the law to the intermediate social states. Social physiology being thus directly founded, its leading conception will be more and more precisely wrought out by our successors by its application to shorter and shorter intervals, the last perfection of which would be, if it could be reached, that the true filiation of every kind of progress should be traced from generation to generation.

In this department of science, as in every other, the commonest facts are the most important. In our search for the laws of society, we shall find that exceptional events and minute details must be discarded as essentially insignificant, while science lays hold of the most general phenomena which everybody is familiar with, as constituting the basis of ordinary social life. It is true, popular prejudice is against this method of study; in the same way that physics were till lately studied in thunder and volcanoes, and biology in monstrosities: and there is no doubt that a reformation in our ignorant intellectual habits is even more necessary in sociology than in regard to any of the other sciences.

Abstract treatment of history

The restrictions that I have proposed are not new, or peculiar to the latest department of study. They appear in all the rest under the form of the distinction between abstract and concrete science . . .

In the same way we must avoid confounding the abstract research into the laws of social existence with the concrete histories of human societies, the explanation of which can result only from a very advanced knowledge of the whole of these laws. Our employment of history in this inquiry, then, must be essentially abstract. It would, in fact, be history without the names of men, or even of nations, if it were not necessary to avoid all such puerile affectation as there would be in depriving ourselves of the use of names which may elucidate our exposition, or consolidate our thought . . .

Co-existence of successive states

One more preliminary consideration remains. We must determine more precisely than I have yet done the regular mode of definition of the successive periods which we are about to examine. The law of evolution, no doubt, connects the chief historical phases with the corresponding one of the three periods: but there is an uncertainty of a secondary kind for which I must provide a solution. It arises out of the unequal progression of the different orders of ideas, which occasions the coexistence, for instance, of the metaphysical state of some intellectual category with the theological state of a later category, less general and less advanced—or with the positive state of a former category, less complex and more advanced. The apparent confusion thus produced must occasion perplexing doubts in minds which are not in possession of the explanation about the true philosophical character of the corresponding times: but the hesitation may be obviated or relieved by its being settled what intellectual category is to decide the speculative state of any period. On all accounts, the decision must be grounded on the most complex and special; that is, the category of moral and social ideas, not only on account of their eminent importance, but from their position at the extremity of the encyclopedical scale. The intellectual character of each period is governed by that order of speculations; and it is not till any new mental regime has reached that category that the corresponding evolution can be regarded as realized, beyond all danger of a return to the prior state.

Three Interconnected Laws of Development*

The first law consists in the succession of the three states, fictitious, abstract and positive, through which every understanding passes in all its conceptions without exception, but with a velocity proportioned to the generality of the particular phenomena in question. The second is a recognition of an analogous progression in human activity, which in its first stage is conquest, then defence; lastly industry. The third law shows that man's social nature follows the same course; that it finds satisfaction, first, in the family, then in the state, lastly in the race, in conformity with the peculiar nature of each of the three sympathetic instincts. These two last laws have no immediate connection with the intelligence, but are not the less indispensable to any clear conception of its movements. For they preside over the necessary and persistent relations which exist between our scientific conceptions and our practical operations on the one hand, our moral impulses on the other, the former being the object, the latter the source of the said conceptions.

* *Pos. Pol.,* vol. 4, p. 157.

5   *Socialism and Communism*

Comte's discussion of socialism and communism needs to be read with the clear understanding that he is referring to what Marx called 'utopian socialism', and in view of this it will be apparent that he is making many of the same criticisms of it that Marx made when he attempted to provide a scientific basis for a social and political movement to bring about a new and better system of human relations. Most of Marx's efforts were published too late for Comte to have taken account of them, but many of the points that Comte singles out as good in the socialism and communism of his day were upheld by Marx, especially the emphasis on property as being social in its nature and in need of control. Where they differed fundamentally was over solutions, for Comte insisted on separating the spiritual (moral) from the temporal (political) power. Linked to this was another criticism which Comte made of communism: the 'dangerous tendency to suppress individuality'.

Some other criticisms of communist theory and spirit that Comte made, such as its 'anti-historic spirit', now seem incongruous in the light of Marx's work. There can be no doubt that Comte would have approved of the change, and there are many fundamental similarities of scope and method in the systems of Comte and Marx. But there was little if any direct influence of the one on the other. Comte was ignorant of Marx's work, and Marx in turn had not read anything by Comte before 1866 and when he did his main response was to compare him unfavourably with Hegel.[1]

NOTES AND REFERENCES

1. Cf. T. B. Bottomore and M. Rubel (eds.), *Karl Marx: Selected Writings in Sociology and Social Philosophy*, Harmondsworth: Penguin (1963), pp. 28–30.

Socialism and Communism*

All three conditions of public opinion exist, but have not yet been combined

Our theory of public opinion shows us at once how far we have already gone in organizing this great regulator of modern society; how far we still fall short of what is wanted. The doctrine has at last arisen: there is no doubt of the existence of the power; and even the organ is not wanting. But they do not as yet stand in their right relation to each other. The effective impulse towards social regeneration depends, then, on one ultimate condition; the formation of a firm alliance between philosophers and proletaries.

Of this powerful coalition I have already spoken. I have now to explain the advantages which it offers to the people in the way of obtaining sufficient recognition of all legitimate claims.

Of these advantages, the principal, and that by which the rest will speedily be developed and secured, is the important social function which is hereby conferred upon them. They become auxiliaries of the new spiritual power; auxiliaries indispensable to its action. This vast proletary class, which ever since its rise in the Middle Ages has been shut out from the political system, will now assume the position for which by nature it is best adapted, and which is most conducive to the general well-being of society. Its members, independently of their special vocation, will at last take a regular and more important part in public life, a part which will compensate for the hardships inseparable from their social position. Their combined action, far from disturbing the established order of things, will be its most solid guarantee, from the fact of being moral, not political. And here we see definitely the alteration which positivism introduces in the revolutionary conception of the action of the working classes upon society. For stormy discussions about rights, it substitutes peaceable definition of duties. It supersedes useless disputes for the possession of power, by inquiring into the rules that should regulate its wise employment.

Spontaneous tendencies of the people in a right direction

A superficial observer of the present state of things might imagine our working classes to be as yet very far from this frame of mind. But he who looks deeper into the question will see that the very

* *Pos. Pol.,* vol. 1, pp. 119–29.

experiment which they are now trying, of extending their political rights, will soon have the effect of showing them the hollowness of a remedy which has so slight a bearing upon the objects really important to them. Without making any formal abdication of rights, which might seem inconsistent with their social dignity, there is little doubt that their instinctive sagacity will lead them to the still more efficacious plan of indifference. Positivism will readily convince them that whereas spiritual power, in order to do its work, must ramify in every direction, it is essential to public order that political power should be as a rule concentrated. And this conviction will grow upon them, as they see more clearly that the primary social problems which are very properly absorbing their attention are essentially moral rather than political.

One step in this direction they have already taken of their own accord, though its importance has not been duly appreciated. The well-known scheme of communism, which has found such rapid acceptance with them, serves, in the absence of sounder doctrine, to express the way in which they are now looking at the great social problem. The experience of the first part of the revolution has not yet wholly disabused them of political illusions, but it has at least brought them to feel that property is of more importance than power in the ordinary sense of the word. So far communism has given a wider meaning to the great social problem, and has thereby rendered an essential service, which is not neutralized by the temporary dangers involved in the metaphysical forms in which it comes before us. Communism should therefore be carefully distinguished from the numerous extravagant schemes brought forward in this time of spiritual anarchy; a time which stimulates incompetent and ill-trained minds to the most difficult subjects of thought. The foolish schemes referred to have so few definite features, that we have to distinguish them by the names of their authors. But communism bears the name of no single author, and is something more than an accidental product of anomalous circumstances. We should look upon it as the natural progress in the right direction of the revolutionary spirit; progress of a moral rather than intellectual kind. It is a proof that revolutionary tendencies are now concentrating themselves upon moral questions, leaving all purely political questions in the background. It is quite true that the solution of the problem which Communists are now putting forward, is still as essentially political as that of their predecessors; since the only mode by which they propose to regulate the employment of property, is by a change in the mode of its tenure. Still it is owing to them that the question of property is at last brought forward for discussion: and it is a question which so evidently needs a moral solution, the solution of it by political means is at once so inadequate and so destructive, that it cannot long continue to be debated without leading to the more satisfactory result offered by positivism. Men will see that it forms a part of the final regeneration of opinion and of life, which positivism is now inaugurating.

To do justice to communism, we must look at the generous sympathies by which it is inspired, not at the shallow theories in which those sympathies find expression provisionally, until circumstances enable them to take some other shape. The workmen connected with the communist utopia, caring but very little for metaphysical principles, do not attach nearly the same importance to these theories as is done by men of literary education. As soon as they see a better way of bringing forward the points on which they have such legitimate claims, they will very soon adopt the clear and practical conceptions of positivism, which can be carried out peaceably and permanently, in preference to these vague and confused chimeras, which, as they will instinctively feel, lead only to anarchy. Till then they will naturally abide by communism, as the only method of bringing forward the most fundamental of social problems in a way which there shall be no evading. The very alarm aroused by those proposed solutions of the problem helps to stir public attention and fix it on this great subject. But for this constant appeal to their fears, the metaphysical delusions and aristocratic self-seeking of the governing classes would shelve the question altogether, or pass it by with indifference. And even when the mistakes of communists have been rectified, it does not follow that they should give up the name, which is a simple assertion of the paramount importance of social feeling. However, now that we have happily passed from monarchy to republicanism, the name of *communist* is no longer indispensable; the word *republican* expresses the meaning as well, and without the same danger. Positivism, then, has nothing to fear from communism; on the contrary, it will probably be accepted by most of the communist workmen, especially in France, where abstractions have but little influence on minds thoroughly emancipated from theology. The people will gradually find that the solution of the great social problem which positivism offers is better than the communistic solution.

Its new title of socialism

A tendency in this direction has already shown itself since the first edition of this work was published. French workmen have now adopted a new expression, *socialism*, thus indicating that they accept the problem of the communists while rejecting their solution. Indeed that solution would seem to be finally disposed of by the voluntary exile of their leader. Yet, if the socialists at present keep clear of communism, it is only because their position is one of criticism or inaction. If they were to succeed to power, with principles so far below the level of their sympathies, they would inevitably fall in the same errors and extravagances which they now instinctively feel to be wrong. Consequently the rapid spread of socialism very naturally alarms the upper classes; and their resistance, blind though it be, is at present the only legal guarantee for material order. In fact, the problem brought forward by the communists admits of no solution but their own, so long as the revolutionary confusion of temporal and spiritual power continues. Therefore the universal blame that is lavished on these utopian schemes cannot fail to lead men towards positivism, as the only doctrine which can preserve western Europe from some serious attempt to bring communism into practical operation. Positivists standard forward now as the party of construction, with a definite basis for political action; namely, systematic prosecution of the wise attempt of medieval statesmen to separate the two social powers. On this basis they are enabled to satisfy the poor, and at the same time to restore the confidence of the rich. It is a final solution of our difficulties which will make the titles of which we have been speaking unnecessary. Stripping the old word *republican* of any false meaning at present attached to it, we may retain it as the best expression of the social sympathies on which the regeneration of society depends. For the opinions, manners, and even institutions of future society, *positivist* is the only word suitable.

Property is in its nature social, and needs control

The peculiar reality of positivism, and its invariable tendency to concentrate our intellectual powers upon social questions, form a two-fold reason for its presentation in a systematic form of the spontaneous principle of communism; namely, that property is in its nature social, and that it needs control.

Property has been erroneously represented by most modern jurists as conferring an absolute right upon the possessor, irrespectively of the good or bad use made of it. The instinctive objection of workmen to this view is shared by all true philosophers. It is an anti-social theory, due historically to exaggerated reaction against previous legislation of a peculiarly oppressive kind, but it has no real foundation either in justice or in fact. Property can neither be created, nor even transmitted by the sole agency of its possessor. Since the co-operation of the public is always necessary, whether in the assertion of the general principle or in its special application, the tenure of property cannot be regarded as purely individual. In every age and in every country the state has intervened, to a greater or less degree, making property subservient to social requirements. Taxation evidently gives the public an interest in the private fortune of each individual: an interest which, instead of diminishing with the progress of civilization, has been always on the increase, especially in modern times, now that the connection of each member of society with the whole is becoming more apparent. The practice of confiscation, which also is in universal use, shows that in certain extreme cases the community considers itself authorized to assume entire possession of private property. Confiscation has, it is true, been abolished for a time in France. But this isolated exception is due only to the abuses which recently accompanied the exercise of what was in itself an undoubted right; and it will hardly survive when the causes which led to it are forgotten, and the power which introduced it has passed away. In their abstract view of property, then, Communists are perfectly able to maintain their ground against the jurists.

They are right, again, in dissenting as deeply as they do from the economists, who lay it down as an absolute principle that the application of wealth should be entirely unrestricted in society. This error, like the one just spoken of, is attributable to instances of unjustifiable interference. But it is utterly opposed to all sound philosophical teaching, although it has a certain appearance of truth, in so far as it recognizes the subordination of social phenomena to natural laws. But the economists seem to have adopted this important principle only to show how incapable they are of comprehending it. Before they applied the conception of law to the higher phenomena of nature, they ought to have made themselves well acquainted with its meaning, as applied to the lower and more simple phenomena. Not having done so, they have been utterly blind to the fact that the order of nature becomes more and more modifiable as it grows more complicated. This conception lies at the very root of our whole practical life; therefore nothing can excuse the metaphysical school of economists for systematically resisting the intervention of human wisdom in the various departments of social action. That the movement of society is subject to natural laws is certain; but this truth, instead of inducing us to abandon all efforts to modify society, should rather lead to a wiser application of such efforts, since they are at once more efficacious and more necessary in social phenomena than in any other.

So far, therefore, the fundamental principle of communism is one which the positivist school must obviously adopt. Positivism not only confirms this principle, but widens its scope, by showing its application to other departments of human life; by insisting that, not wealth only, but that all our powers shall be devoted in the true republican spirit to the continuous service of the community. The long period of revolution which has elapsed since the Middle Ages has encouraged individualism in the moral world, as in the intellectual it has fostered the specializing tendency. But both are equally inconsistent with the final order of modern society. In all healthy conditions of humanity, the citizen, whatever his position, has been regarded as a public functionary, whose duties and claims were determined more or less distinctly by his faculties. The case of property is certainly no exception to this general principle. Proprietorship is regarded by the positivist as an important social function; the function, namely, of creating and administering that capital by means of which each generation lays the foundation for the operations of its successor. This is the only tenable view of property; and wisely interpreted, it is one which, while ennobling to its possessor, does not exclude a due measure of freedom. It will in fact place his position on a firmer basis than ever.

Property to be controlled by moral not legal agencies

But the agreement here pointed out between sociological science and the spontaneous inspirations of popular judgment, goes no farther. Positivists accept, and indeed very much enlarge, the programme of communism; but we reject its practical solution on the ground that it is at once inadequate and subversive. The chief difference between our own solution and theirs is that we substitute moral agencies for political. Thus we come again to our leading principle of separating spiritual from temporal power; a principle which, disregarded as it has hitherto been in the system of modern renovators, will be found in every one of the important problems of our time to be the sole possible issue. In the present case, while throwing such light on the fallacy of communism, it should lead us to excuse the fallacy, by reminding us that politicians of every accredited school are equally guilty of it. At a time when there are so very few, even of cultivated minds, who have a clear conception of this the primary principle of modern politics, it would be harsh to blame the people for still accepting a result of revolutionary empiricism, which is so universally adopted by other classes.

I need not enter here into any detailed criticism of the utopian scheme of Plato. It was conclusively refuted twenty-two centuries ago, by the great Aristotle, who thus exemplified the organic character, by which, even in its earliest manifestations, the positive spirit is distinguished. In modern communism, moreover, there is one fatal inconsistency, which while it proves the utter weakness of the system, testifies at the same time to the honourable character of the motives from which it arose. Modern communism differs from the ancient, as expounded by Plato, in not making women and children common as well as property; a result to which the principle itself obviously leads. Yet this, the only consistent view of communism is adopted by none but a very few literary men, whose affections, in themselves too feeble, have been perverted by vicious intellectual training. Our untaught proletaries, who are the only communists worthy of our consideration, are nobly inconsistent in this respect. Indivisible as their erroneous system is, they adopt that side of it which touches on their social requirements, energetically repudiating the other aspect as offensive to all their highest instincts.

Without discussing these chimerical schemes in detail, it will be well to expose the errors inherent in the method of reasoning which leads to them, because they are common to all the other progressive schools, the positivist school excepted. The mistake consists in the first place, in disregarding or even denying the natural laws which regulate social phenomena; and secondly, in resorting to political agencies where moral agency is the real thing needed. The inadequacy and the danger of the various utopian systems which are now setting up their rival claims to bring about the regeneration of society, are all attributable in reality to these two closely-connected errors. For the sake of clearness, I shall continue to refer specially to communism as the most prominent of these systems. But it will be easy to extend the bearing of my remarks to all the rest.

Individualization of functions as necessary as co-operation

The ignorance of the true laws of social life under which communists labour is evident in their dangerous tendency to suppress individuality. Not only do they ignore the inherent preponderance in our nature of the personal instincts; but they forget that, in the collective organism, the separation of functions is a feature no less essential than the co-operation of functions. Suppose for a moment that the connection between men could be made such that they were physically inseparable, as has been actually the case with twins in certain cases of monstrosity; society would obviously be impossible. Extravagant as this supposition is, it may illustrate the fact that in social life individuality cannot be dispensed with. It is necessary in order to admit of that variety of simultaneous efforts which constitutes the immense superiority of the social organism over every individual life. The great problem for man is to harmonize, as far as possible, the freedom resulting from isolation, with the equally urgent necessity for convergence. To dwell exclusively upon the necessity of convergence would tend to undermine not merely our practical energy, but our true dignity; since it would do away with the sense of personal responsibility. In exceptional cases where life is spent in forced subjection to domestic authority, the comforts of home are often not enough to prevent existence from becoming an intolerable burden, simply from the want of sufficient independence. What would it be, then, if everybody stood in a similar position of dependence towards a community that was indifferent to his happiness? Yet no less a danger than this would be the result of adopting any of those utopian schemes which sacrifice true liberty to uncontrolled equality, or even to an exaggerated sense of fraternity. Wide as the divergence between positivism and the economic schools is, positivists adopt substantially the strictures which they have passed upon communism; especially those of Dunoyer, their most advanced writer.

Industry requires its captains as well as war

There is another point in which communism is equally inconsistent with the laws of sociology. Acting under false views of the constitution of our modern industrial system, it proposes to remove its directors, who form so essential a part of it. An army can no more exist without officers than without soldiers; and this elementary truth holds good of industry as well as of war. The organization of modern industry has not been found practicable as yet; but the germ of such organization lies unquestionably in the division which has arisen spontaneously between capitalist and workman. No great works could be undertaken if each worker were also to be a director, or if the management, instead of being fixed, were entrusted to a passive and irresponsible body. It is evident that under the present system of industry there is a tendency to a constant enlargement of undertakings: each fresh step leads at once to still further extension. Now this tendency, so far from being opposed to the interests of the working classes, is a condition which will most seriously facilitate the real organization of our material existence, as soon as we have a moral authority competent to control it. For it is only the larger employers that the spiritual power can hope to penetrate with a strong and habitual sense of duty to their subordinates. Without a sufficient concentration of material power, the means of satisfying the claims of morality would be found wanting, except at such exorbitant sacrifices, as would be soon found incompatible with all industrial progress. This is the weak point of every plan of reform which limits itself to the mode of acquiring power, whether public power or private, instead of aiming at controlling its use in whosoever hands it may be placed. It leads to a waste of those forces which, when rightly used, form our principal resource in dealing with grave social difficulties.

Communism is deficient in the historical spirit

The motives, therefore, from which modern communism has arisen, however estimable, lead at present, in the want of proper scientific teaching, to a very wrong view both of the nature of the disease and of its remedy. A heavier reproach against it is that in one point it shows a manifest insufficiency of social instinct. Communists boast of their spirit of social union: but they limit it to the union of the present generation, stopping short of historical continuity, which yet is the principal characteristic of humanity. When they have matured their moral growth, and have followed out in time that connection which at present they only recognize in space, they will at once see the necessity of these general conditions which at present they would reject. They will understand the importance of inheritance, as the natural means by which each generation transmits to its successor the result of its own labours and the means of improving them. The necessity of inheritance, as far as the community is concerned, is evident, and its extension to the individual is an obvious consequence. But whatever reproaches communists may deserve in this respect are equally applicable to all the other progressive sects. They are all pervaded by an anti-historic spirit, which leads them to conceive of society as though it had no ancestors; and this, although their own ideas for the most part can have no bearing except upon posterity.

As a system, it is worthless

Serious as these errors are, a philosophic mind will treat the communism of our day, so far as it is adopted in good faith with indulgence, whether he look at the motives from which it arose, or at the practical results which will follow from it. It is hardly fair to criticize the intrinsic merits of a doctrine the whole meaning and value of which are relative to the peculiar phase of society in which it is proposed. Communism has in its own way discharged an important function. It has brought prominently forward the greatest of social problems; and, if we except the recent positivist explanation, its mode of stating it has never been surpassed. And let no one suppose that it would have been enough simply to state the problem, without any such dangerous solution as is here offered. Those who think so do not understand the exigencies of man's feeble intellect. In far easier subjects than this, it is impossible to give prolonged attention to questions which are simply asked, without any attempt to answer them. Suppose, for instance, that Gall and Broussais had limited themselves to a simple statement of their great problems without venturing on any solution; their principles, however incontestable, would have been barren of result, for want of the renovating impulse which nothing can give but a systematic solution of some kind or other, hazardous as the attempt must be at first. Now it is hardly likely that we should be able to evade this condition of our mental faculties in subjects which are not only of the highest difficulty, but also more exposed than any others to the influence of passion. Besides, when we compare the errors of communism with those of other social doctrines which have recently received official sanction, we shall feel more disposed to palliate them. Are they, for instance, more shallow and more really dangerous than the absurd and chimerical notion which was accepted in France for a whole generation, and is still upheld by so many political teachers; the notion that the great Revolution has found its final issue in the constitutional system of government, a system peculiar to England during her stage of transition? Moreover, our so-called conservatives only escape the errors of communism by evading or ignoring its problems, though they are becoming every day more urgent. Whenever they are induced to deal with them, they render themselves liable to exactly the same dangers, dangers common to all schools which reject the division of the two powers, and which consequently are for ever trying to make legislation to the work of morality.

6   *Sociology and Inequality of the Sexes:*
     The Comte-Mill Correspondence

In contrast with the lack of contact between Comte and Marx, the contacts between Comte and another great contemporary, John Stuart Mill, were very close for several years. In fact, the correspondence between them has been described by the French sociologist Lucien Levy-Bruhl as a 'precious document', and he added: 'In the evolution of the ideas of the nineteenth century there is perhaps no episode more instructive than the coming together and separation of these two philosophers.'[1]

The following translated extracts from that correspondence focus on only one specific issue, but one which is still topical: the question of inequality of the sexes, whether it is innate and desirable or determined by culture and an undesirable situation from which women should be liberated. The correspondence discloses how, despite their mutual admiration and agreement about the nature and methods of sociology, Comte and Mill found that what they had originally thought of as a difference over a secondary matter had much wider ramifications. Their discussion of this issue reveals some of the deeper problems about social statics, the relative contributions of 'nature' and 'nurture' in creating social differences, and the relation of sociology to other disciplines such as phychology and biology.

The two problems which were treated in sufficient depth for Comte and Mill to decide that they could no longer continue to collaborate as they had originally planned, and which caused them to terminate their lengthy and intimate correspondence, were first, their disagreement about psychology, and second, the question of whether inequality of the sexes was due mainly to innate attributes or to social factors.

It became clear that the two problems were closely interrelated. According to Mill, psychology had as its aim the discovery of 'laws of the mind' and its special method was 'introspective analysis'. Comte denied the possibility of such a science and he divided what we call psychology into the physiologist's study of the functioning of the brain, the sociologist's study of the historical development of human thought, and the study of the individual by a still to be developed moral science. On the second question, Mill claimed to have proved that inequality of the sexes, though generally accepted, was in fact no more than a prejudice. Comte could not accept this; he believed that the findings of physiologists and common experience combined to prove that women were naturally inferior to men in intelligence and superior to them in feeling. His social statics enshrined this doctrine of the natural inequality of the sexes and their separate but complementary social functions.

It was Mill who drew out the relation between the two problems. Although he admitted to knowing less about biological findings than Comte, he insisted that mental differences between men and women were not proven from an anatomical or physiological point of view. Furthermore, he maintained that the social scientist should not settle for explaining differences by reference to innate characteristics as natural or inevitable until he had tried every other possible mode of explanation. Inequality could be secondary or acquired; it could be the result of conditions in which women had lived from time immemorial. It might be altered by changing conditions.

On these particular questions subsequent developments suggest that Mill had more to offer than Comte. However, the first two letters printed below show just how much Mill owed to Comte for providing him with an education in sociology. It is perhaps also significant that after the break up of the collaboration with Comte, Mill found it impossible to give scientific form to his 'ethological meditations' (the study of individual and collective character formation)[2] which he believed to be the main deficiency in Comte's sociology. It was then that, somewhat despairingly, he returned to the narrower specialism of political economy. No doubt sociology's loss was economics' gain, but to leave sociology for economics was to renounce all hope of reconciliation, for Comte had long insisted that the interdependence of social phenomena was such that any attempt to constitute a separate discipline of economics prior to the development of sociology and independent of it must necessarily fail.

The correspondence between Comte and Mill reveals some of the real aspirations, achievements and disappointments of the first generation who contributed to the making of sociology.

NOTES AND REFERENCES

1. Introduction to *Lettres Inédites de John Stuart Mill à Auguste Comte avec les Responses de Comte*, Paris: Alcan (1899), pp. xxxvi–xxxvii.
2. Cf. A. Bain, *J. S. Mill: A Criticism, with Personal Recollections*, London (1882), p. 78.

Mill to Comte, London, 8 November 1841*

It was in 1828, Sir, that I first read your small *Traité de Politique Positive*, and the experience of reading it gave my ideas a serious jolt which, together with other causes, though of far greater importance than them, finally determined me to break with the Benthamite section of the revolutionary school in which I was brought up, and into which I can almost say I was born. Although there is no doubt that Benthamism has remained very far from the true spirit of the positive method, this doctrine still seems to me to be the best preparation that exists today for a really positive approach to social doctrines, whether as a result of its rigorous logic and the care it has always taken to understand itself, or of its systematic opposition to any attempt to explain phenomena in terms of ridiculous metaphysical entities, the essential vacuity of which it taught me to see from an early age.

Since the time when I became aware of the first outlines of your sociological ideas, I believe I can say that the seeds sown by that small work have not lain idle in my mind. It was, however, only in 1837 that I became acquainted with the first two volumes of your *Cours*, which, fortunately, I was in quite a good position to appreciate, having had at least some contact with all of the basic sciences, in each of which, moreover, I had sought above all the methodological ideas that it could provide. Since that happy moment when I came to know those two volumes, I have awaited each new volume with real intellectual passion. I had in fact already adopted a position which was quite similar to your own, above all as a result of the inspiration given me by your earlier work; but there were still many things of great importance that I still had to learn from you, and I hope at some time to give you evidence of the fact that I have learnt them well. There remain several points of secondary importance on which my opinions differ from yours; perhaps one day those differences will be resolved: at least I don't think I flatter myself in believing that there is no ill-founded opinion of mine which might be so entrenched as to remain impervious to serious discussion of the kind which it might undergo if you were to allow me to submit my ideas to you occasionally and to ask you for further enlightenment on your own.

Sir, you know that religious ideas still have a surer hold in this country than in any other in Europe, although here as elsewhere they long ago lost their civilizing influence. And it is, I believe, to be regretted that the revolutionary philosophy which twelve years ago

* Extracts from *Lettres Inédites*, pp. 2–10 and 230–65.

was flourishing should today have waned without having accomplished its task. It is all the more urgent for us that we should replace it by devoting ourselves whole-heartedly to positive philosophy; and it is with great pleasure that I am able to tell you, despite the openly anti-religious spirit of your work, that that great monument to the true modern philosophy has begun to make itself felt here, though less among political theorists than among the various classes of scientists. It is, however, possible to note for the first time in this country that for some time now there has been a quite marked tendency among practitioners of the physical sciences towards scientific generalities which seems to me a very good omen and which leads me to believe that we can expect more from them than from the politicians, either in terms of speculation or of action. The latter, indeed, have fallen into a state of chaos similar to that which has shown itself so clearly in France since 1830—one where everyone can see that it is only possible to do new things with the help of a new doctrine; only the majority do not believe such a doctrine will appear and thus remain in a state of scepticism which becomes increasingly debilitating and discouraging.

Sir, I hope you will be so good as to forgive me this somewhat presumptuous effort to establish direct intellectual contact with one of the great minds of our time—the one for whom I have the greatest esteem and admiration—and that you will believe me when I say that the fulfilment of my desire in this would be of enormous value to me.

Comte to Mill, Paris, 20 November 1841

Both by preference and necessity I live extremely isolated from everyday life, even intellectual life, and have no other regular diversion than that of attending the Italian opera during our musical season. For more than three years I have systematically increased this isolation by scrupulously refusing to read any newspapers, even monthly or quarterly ones; and I find that this cerebral hygiene suits me too well for me to change it now, given the ease with which it enables me to achieve and maintain myself without effort at the level of a more general perspective, as well as that of purer and more impartial thoughts. But, in spite of this regime, which I believe to be necessary for the full development of my philosophical existence, I am far from being indifferent to the effect of my work on our intellectual milieu, although I never have either the time or the means to take account of it. From an early age I had the good fortune never to possess any serious illusions about the degree of popularity that such work would achieve in these days, and I never aimed to have an immediate effect except on about a hundred thinkers, scattered here and there throughout Europe. All the same, as a result of this same limitation, you can imagine how much importance I attach to receiving from time to time spontaneous demonstrations of interest as valuable, as decisive and as encouraging as that with which you have honoured me and which gives me a direct sense that the most highly developed minds are essentially thinking in unison with me. Without such rewards, themselves of necessity extremely rare, I would perhaps find it extremely difficult to maintain the indefatigable effort required by the long and arduous task which I have undertaken since my youth. In this respect I am particularly grateful to the English thinkers, among whom, it seems to me, my work has been much better received than anywhere else, even in France. The only complementary review which has ever (at least to my knowledge) appeared on the subject was that in the *Edinburgh Review* of July 1838 which your gracious fellow-countryman, Grote, was kind enough to bring to my attention despite my rigorous abstention from such reading matter: although this judgment only applies to the first two volumes its complete spontaneity showed me with what devotion and high-mindedness your critics understand their mission. I now attach even more value to such encouragements in so far as I already find myself, by the very nature of my philosophical development, engaged in an inevitable and unceasing struggle with all theological and above all metaphysical spirits and am therefore led in the sixth and last volume, which will appear next spring, to attack, albeit in another guise, but in a manner which for that very reason will probably appear all the less excusable, the rudiments of the positive spirit which are already officially established among us—that is the professional learned bodies whose empiricism and egoism may well constitute, and in particular in France, the most dangerous obstacle to the final revolution, opposing themselves blindly to any generalization as a result of the deplorable extension of the provisional regime of fragmented specialisms which has for a long time dominated the first developments of modern science. Sir, you can imagine how delightful it is for me in the midst of so many kinds of natural enemies to feel myself, however distantly, in spontaneous harmony with a few eminent thinkers. Although your scrupulous modesty leads you to exaggerate the part which my writings may have played in your philosophical development I am immediately reminded that among minds of real worth, such an influence can only consist in stimulating at an opportune moment a development for which the main precondition is its essential spontaneity.

Benthamism, in which you were brought up, is a definitive proof of the natural conformity of our intellectual tendencies, independently of all contact; for that doctrine, the most illustrious product of what is called political economy, seems to me, as it does to you, to be, especially in England, an immediate preparation for sociological positivism; if I have myself avoided that phase, that is doubtless the result of the personal circumstances of my education which, having imbued me since childhood with the rudiments of the true positive method, allowed me to sense in time how imperfectly Bentham had understood this method, despite his obvious tendency to give it priority throughout his work.

These summary explanations will easily allow you to conceive, Sir, what great value I attach to the gracious overtures which you have deigned to make to me, and how glad I should be for any opportunity, whether in writing or better still in conversation, which allowed me to respond to them, either by answering your particular objections or by examining any communication of importance.

Your letter arrived precisely at the moment when I had just arrived at the notion of an important philosophical measure which I shall propose directly in my last volume and which would consist in the immediate establishment of a European committee with permanent responsibility for directing the general philosophical renewal once positivism has planted its flag or rather its light in the midst of the disorder and confusion of our century which will, I hope, be the natural result of the publication of my completed work. This permanent committee, composed, at least at first, of a maximum of about thirty members, would represent the various peoples of western Europe which, since the time of Charlemagne, have always to a greater or lesser extent marched in step, whether in the temporary development of the Catholic and feudal system and its later disintegration, or in the developments, whether in the realm of industry, aesthetics, science or philosophy, which form the basis of our modern society. I believe that all the rest of Europe and of the world should, for a long time to come, remain outside this association, which constitutes the elements of the great European republic of which we are both fellow-citizens. You will understand, Sir, what enormous pleasure your letter must have given me in the midst of these thoughts since it demonstrated to me in the most unequivocal way how England, despite its philosophical collapse, was already in a position to provide a worthy deputation to such a meeting of élites. I had previously learnt with great pleasure through a chance comment of M. Marrast that your intelligence and strength of mind had happily resisted the blind obsession of your friends with parliamentary life. Only an extremely powerful reason could have made you sense how infinitely much more useful your philosophical activity could be if it rejected the too mundane perspective of parliamentary criticism which tends directly to inhibit any systematic application of a general perspective at a time when general concepts are precisely what society needs most. However rational your decision, it is so contrary to the prevailing mode in which everything encourages immediate action, that it presupposes both a rightness of judgment and a courage for which I sincerely congratulate you while hoping that human evolution, so independent today of the empty utterings of our parliaments, will benefit greatly from it.

The organization of a great philosophical work, outside any political activity, now seems to me, in England as in France, to be the most important priority. The collapse of politics which one feels in both countries is the direct result of the proven inadequacy of the negative philosophy which has until now guided the great revolutionary movement and which can only result in the development of another philosophy, which will secure both order and progress and alone can effectively contain in these days the imminent outburst of metaphysical theories which will subvert the whole fabric of society by giving priority to the unswerving but measured examination of the *duties* of the various classes over the discussion—as empty as it is tempestuous—of individual *rights*. I find as you do, Sir, that purely negative philosophy has been suppressed in our time, above all in England, before having accomplished its task; but that was without doubt inevitable, because the need for reorganization has everywhere become obvious since society cannot live on mere negations. This spontaneous collapse must, moreover, become one more stimulus to the development of positive philosophy, whose rise can alone really bring the revolutionary operation to completion, although that in itself is no more than a secondary application of it, because this philosophy can alone succeed in completely eliminating from the political scene the last remains of the *ancien régime*, beginning with the theological order. I have always wanted there to be a direct confrontation between the frankly reactionary school, which is today represented by pure Catholicism, and our burgeoning positive school.

Although I have little hope of bringing the battle directly on to that precise and decisive terrain, I confess that I note with pleasure in the natural consequences of contemporary events all that might serve to bring us closer to such a position on this question through the gradual elimination of the intermediate metaphysical camp who are now, in my eyes, the main reason for the current continuing confusion of ideas and the indecisiveness of the debate.

Comte to Mill, 16 July 1843

Social statics, biology and sex

I am lacking the time needed to touch on the serious discussion of social statics which you involuntarily began in your last letter; but I am very happy that you have begun this kind of naïve confession of heresy, and I beg you to continue it in your own time. When your gradual exposition has acquired the character of a more determined dissent, its appraisal will be very useful to both of us in pushing me to anticipate in a summary fashion the doctrine which will be formally set out in the second volume of the great work which I shall begin next year. Without in any way being frightened by these differences between the only two real mouthpieces which the new philosophy today possesses, I am sure that our complete agreement on method and the fact that we share a fundamental doctrine of dynamics will soon result in the spontaneous ending of this disagreement in statics. It seems to me that this is now due only to the fact that you do not perhaps take the totality of biological studies, even present ones, into such intimate and familiar consideration as you do those of the inorganic notions whose various orders, as can be seen from your treatise, are deeply familiar to you and have been for a long time.

However imperfect biology is, it seems to me that it is already able to give a solid basis to the hierarchy of the sexes by showing both anatomically and physiologically that in almost the whole range of animal life and above all in our species, the female sex is constituted in a kind of state of radical infancy that makes it essentially inferior to the corresponding organic type. Looking at it from the sociological point of view, modern life, characterized by industrial activity and the positive spirit, should not, in the last analysis, develop these fundamental differences any the less, albeit in another way, than the military and the theological life of former populations, although the novelty of this situation has not yet provided a sufficient manifestation of these final differences, whereas the former seem to be disappearing. The idea of a queen, for example, even without her being a Popess, is now almost ridiculous, so heavily did it depend on the theological state; but only three centuries ago it was not yet like that. As for the inevitable imperfection of sympathies based on inequality, I agree with you; and on this subject I think that the fullness of human sympathies can only exist between two eminent men whose morality is sufficiently strong to contain all serious drive towards competition; this type of harmony seems to me to be far superior to that which can ever be obtained between the sexes. But obviously this could not be the normal type of the most elementary and communal relations, in which the natural hierarchy of the sexes and then of age constitutes the most powerful link.

The qualification of equality has been too sophisticated in our time to be properly employed to describe the principle of universal relationships; I would much prefer to use the formula of fraternity which all the modern populations have spontaneously devoted to this purpose, and which I have at this moment, for example, the satisfaction of finding so deeply, so recognizably, imprinted on the Spanish tongue, where it is continually allied with the expression of the most vigorous of hierarchical ideas.

Mill to Comte, 30 August 1843

Differences between the sexes

To return to our important sociological discussion, I think I know what you mean by comparing the organic constitution of the female sex to a prolonged childhood. I am not unaware of what has been said on the subject by many physiologists and I know that not only in terms of their muscular and cellular system, but also of their nervous system and probably their cerebral structure, women are less removed from the organic character of children than are men. But that is, however, far from being of definitive importance for me. For that to be so it would have to be proved that the inferiority of children in relation to men was the result of the anatomical differences between their brains, whereas it obviously depends to a great extent, if not entirely, on the mere lack of experience. If one could always keep the brain of a child while developing its functions through education and through careful and regular exercise one would definitely not remain a child, one would be a man and one could become a very superior man, while doubtless offering notable deviations from the ordinary human type. In the same way I do not deny that the type of feminine morality presents on average considerable differences from the masculine type. I do not claim to define exactly what these differences are and I do not know if the time has yet come for that, but I know that very eminent physiologists claim that the brain of women is less big, less strong as a result, but more active than that of men. As a consequence, women should be less capable of intellectual work of a continuous and prolonged nature but better at doing more in a short time than men, and in doing better than them, all that demands quickness of mind. They would thus be less well suited to science and better suited, at least by their constitution, to poetry and practical life. This seems to me to be in accordance with what we observe in life. Nevertheless we are in danger of exaggerating the degree of real difference if we do not take into account differences of education and social position; for whether or not women are inferior in their capacity for prolonged intellectual effort, there is no doubt that nothing in their education is arranged in such a way as to develop that capacity in them, whereas there is a definite tendency for men to study sciences and even dead languages. Moreover, for a great many men, particularly in the upper classes, their daily occupations demand, or at least permit, continuous intellectual work, whereas for the great majority of women the perpetual obsession with the everyday cares of domestic life, something which distracts the mind without occupying it, does not provide them with any intellectual work which demands either physical isolation or even sustained application. Among men themselves one does not find a great aptitude for intellectual work among those whose childhood was divorced from any study, and the necessities of their later life do not replace in this respect what was lacking in their early education. I also find that in the everyday things of life on which the intelligence of women is exercised as much as or even more than that of men, even mediocre women normally display greater aptitude than mediocre men. An ordinary man only ever displays intelligence in his own speciality whereas women display it in regard to the most general interests. You will tell me that emotions have a greater weight in women than the intellect, but you yourself would admit that that should only be understood as applying to the life of the heart. Pure egoism dominates men far more often than it does women; and if affection usually becomes in women an egoism embracing several people this is also true of all men, with the exception of those few who have so far had an education which has developed to a high degree a total perspective and the habit of foreseeing the most general results of some line of conduct. You know that that is what is most lacking in the education of women to the point where it is not even considered a virtue in their sex to give preference to the general interest above that of their family or their friends.

I do not for all that want to deny that women, like all those whose nervous excitability is greater than normal, do not resemble young men more than older men nor that they have more diffi- culty than men of the first rank in abstracting from immediate and individual interests; but I believe that this defect is spon- taneously compensated for by the absence of another defect which is peculiar in philosophers, who often abstract not only from im- mediate interests but from all real interests; whereas women, whose position means that they automatically take the practical point of view, rarely become speculative dreamers and rarely forget that they are dealing with real interests, either of their happiness or their sufferings.

Let us not forget that it is in no sense a question of making women govern society but of knowing whether it would not be better if it was governed by men and women rather than women alone. But it is perhaps natural that you and I should have different opinions in this respect. You are French and it has always been noted that the French character already possesses some of the de- fects as well as the good qualities which are usually found among young people and women. You might therefore well think that in giving women a larger part one would give more force to some- thing which already perhaps has too much; but the defects of the English character are rather of the opposite kind. Without going any further into this secondary discussion I will draw your atten- tion to this one thing that people have always recognized in the French up to a point: the constitution is regarded as feminine; but despite that, what people has produced greater philosophers and more distinguished men of state?

Comte to Mill, 5 October 1843

Differences between the sexes

The more I reflect on our serious sociological and biological dis- agreement on the condition and destiny of women, the more suited it is, it seems to me to stand as a symbol of the deplorable mental anarchy of our times in that it shows the difficulty of arriving at a sufficiently similar perspective even for the best minds (between whom there already exists, apart from a natural attraction, a logical fellowship as basic as ours), and who nevertheless disagree, at least for the moment, on one of the most fundamental questions which sociology can raise on what is, to tell the truth, the main elementary basis of all social hierarchies. Such a sight would even be enough to inspire a kind of philosophical despair—a belief that it is ultimately impossible, as religious minds claim, to create a real intellectual agreement on a purely rational basis if a deep and well-tried appreciation of our mental state, and even sufficient personal experience, did not tend to convince me that the present situation of your mind does not really constitute in this respect anything more than a necessarily transitory phase, the last indirect reflection of the great negative period.

All thinkers who seriously like women other than as delightful toys have, I think, in our times passed through an analogous position; I remember very well in my case the time when the strange work of Mary Wollstonecraft (before she married Godwin) made a great impression on me. It was above all in working directly to clarify for others the true elementary ideas of the domestic order that, about twenty years ago, I set my mind irrevocably against any such assault on my sympathies. I have no doubt that my particular appreciation of this fundamental principle in the work that I am about to begin will succeed in dissipating on this subject all your uncertainties if before then your own reflections have not already run ahead of this important proof about which we can talk in our brotherly encounter before then.

Taking up briefly, then, the points of your last letter, I hope that our spontaneous agreement is nearer than I had at first feared. While admitting the anatomical differences which separate the feminine organism even farther from the human type, I believe that you do not accord them a sufficiently powerful physiological influence, whereas you exaggerate perhaps the possible influence of exercise which above all necessarily supposes a suitable constitution. If, according to your hypothesis, our cerebral apparatus never achieved the adult state, no imaginable exercise would render it capable of the sophisticated operations which, in fact, it becomes able to perform; and it is this to which I attribute the collapse, alas too frequent these days, of so many unhappy children who are cruelly forced to perform operations which are beyond their age. Women fall into the same category.

In a systematic discussion I would have few important things to add to your judicious appraisal of the normal limits of their faculties; but I find that you do not attach enough importance to the real consequences of a natural inferiority. Their characteristic inaptitude for abstraction and argument, the almost complete impossibility of setting aside passionate inspiration in rational operations, even though their passions are, in general, more generous, must continue indefinitely to prevent them from undertaking any high level organization of human affairs, not only in science and philosophy, as you state, but also in aesthetic life, and even in practical life, whether industrial or military, where the consecutive mind surely represents the main condition of sustained success. I believe that women are as unsuited to direct any large industrial or commercial enterprise as they are any important military operation; and it is all the more the case that they are radically incapable of any government even in domestic affairs unless it be of a secondary nature. In no sphere are they suited either to direction or execution; they are essentially capable only of giving advice and modifying other people's plans—something in which their passive position enables them to use very well their characteristic wisdom and nature. I have often had the opportunity to observe the female organism at close quarters even in the case of several eminent exceptions: I could also on this subject cite the example of my own wife who, without having written anything, at least until now, possesses more mental energy, profundity and at the same time correct judgment than most of the members of her sex who most deserve to be praised. I have always found the essential characteristics of this type to be a very deficient capacity for generalization and for deduction as well as for making reason rule the passions.

All the cases of this type are, to my mind, too common and too pronounced for one to be able to impute to education in particular the differences between the results; for I find the same essential attributes where the whole spectrum of influences had certainly encouraged as far as possible the development of quite other dispositions. After all, moreover, is it not true to say that in many respects it is a final advantage rather than a real source of inconvenience for women that they are preserved from the disastrous education full of words and entities which has replaced the old military education during the great modern transition?

As for the fine arts, above all, it is surely obvious that for two or three centuries many women have been very well placed and educated for their practice without nevertheless having been able to produce anything of real eminence whether it was in music, in painting or in poetry. Taking a more profound appraisal of the whole picture one is, I think, led to recognize that this social order which has received so much criticism is, on the contrary, radically disposed to favour in essence the development best suited to feminine qualities. Destined, apart from their maternal functions, spontaneously to constitute the domestic auxiliaries of all spiritual powers by reinforcing with the feelings the practical influence of the intelligence in modifying at the moral level the natural reign of material force, women are more and more placed in the position best suited to fulfil this special mission by virtue of their very isolation from active specialities which enables them to exercise in a judicious fashion their gentle capacity for moderating intervention at the same time that their own interests are thus inevitably tied to the triumph of universal morality. If it were possible that their position changed in this respect and they became the equals of men instead of their companions, I think that the very qualities that you attribute to them would be far less developed: their small-scale instantaneous kind of wisdom would become, for example, almost sterile as soon as, ceasing to be passive themselves without being indifferent, they had to conceive and direct instead of looking on and advising without serious responsibility.

Moreover, for truly positive philosophers who know that in all things our systematic influence should limit itself to modifying intelligently the exercise of natural laws without ever thinking of radically changing their character and direction, the immense experience which has already been acquired in this respect by the whole of humanity must, it seems to me, be entirely decisive, for we know what is the philosophical worth of the theatrical declamations on the alleged abuse of force by the male. Even without our knowledge of anatomy, having satisfactorily sketched out the explicit proof of the organic superiority of our species over the rest of the animal kingdom—something which has in fact become possible only recently—our exploration of physiology would leave us in no doubt, given the single fact of the progressively greater ascendancy man has achieved. It is much the same with the question of the sexes even though to a much lesser degree: for how can we explain in any other way the constant social subordination of the female sex? The strange revolt organized in our time on behalf of women, though not by them, will doubtless only confirm this universal experience, although this serious example of our anarchy also produces deplorable temporary consequences, whether these are public or private. The great majority of our species has for a long time been plunged everywhere into a social condition which is inferior in a quite different way from that for which we today pity women; but the élite populations have, since the beginning of the Middle Ages, learnt how to extract themselves from it bit by bit because this collective subjection, a temporary condition of ancient society, was not attached to any real organic difference between the rulers and the ruled. But on the contrary, the subjection of women will necessarily be of indefinite duration although it will become more and more consistent with the universal moral type because it rests directly on a natural inferiority which nothing can destroy and which is even more pronounced in man than in the higher animals. In making women better and better suited to their proper destiny I am convinced that the modern process of regeneration will attach them more completely to their domestic life, from which the disorder inseparable from the great transition has I believe temporarily diverted them in respect of various secondary considerations. The natural movement of our industry certainly tends to make men pass gradually into those professions which for a long time were the province of women; and this spontaneous disposition is to my mind just one example of the growing tendency of our whole social organization to deny to women access to all the occupations which are not sufficiently reconcilable with their domestic destiny whose importance will become more and more dominant; this is, as you know, very far from denying to them a great and useful degree of indirect participation in the totality of the social movement which merely has never been directed by them even in respect of the rise of ideas and customs which particularly affect them. Any other way of conceiving of their position and as a result of their duties and ours would really be contrary at the very least to their own happiness and to the harmony of society as a whole. If, from the perspective of protectors of women, men become their rivals they would, I think, become extremely unhappy given the impossibility they would inevitably soon experience in sustaining such competition, which would be directly contrary to their conditions of existence. I believe, therefore, that those who really love them, who ardently desire the greatest possible development of the faculties and the functions which are best suited to them, should wish that these anarchic utopias are never put into effect.

Mill to Comte, 30 October 1843

Sex question treated as element of social statics

Our disagreement on the question, which you rightly characterize as the most fundamental which social speculation can raise, should certainly not give rise to any anxiety about the final possibility of a sufficient convergence of opinion among educated people on a purely rational basis. But this disagreement and the way of thinking which the discussion reveals throughout confirms me in the opinion that the intellectual basis of static sociology are not as yet sufficiently well laid.

The foundations of social dynamics are, to my mind, already fully constituted. But as for statics, given that history no longer holds prime of place in it and cannot serve except as some kind of secondary source of clarification (although I do not underestimate the importance of this secondary role), the passage of social statics to the truly positive state demands as a result, when compared to social dynamics, a much greater perfection of the science of individual man. It presupposes above all a very advanced state of the secondary science which I have called ethology, that is to say the theory of the influence of the various external circumstances either individual or social on the formation of the moral and intellectual character. This theory, the necessary basis of a rational education, seems to me now to be the least advanced of all the scientific speculations of some importance. A certain real, even empirical, knowledge of this order of natural relationships seems to me to be extremely rare, and sound observations even rarer, either as a result of the difficulty of the subject or of the tendency which is most dominant in this order of research to regard as inexplicable all that one has not succeeded in explaining. The kind of biological studies begun, albeit with much exaggeration, by Helvetius has found no successors and I cannot help thinking that the reaction of the nineteenth century against the philosophy of the eighteenth is responsible for the exaggeration we see today in the opposite direction which tends to give too large an influence to primitive differences and to cloak in several respects their real nature. I find it very natural that you should explain my opinion on this subject by reference to my insufficient knowledge of the physical theory of animal life and above all of cerebral physiology. I am doing, and will continue to do, all I can to abolish any such objection.

I have studied conscientiously on this subject: I have even read with scrupulous attention the six volumes of Gall. I found a large part of his polemic against the psychology of his critics well justified, though I had myself long ago abandoned their point of view. But you already know that the general principles, which alone, according to you, have until now been ascertained in the science of phrenology, do not seem to be proved by his book which, on the contrary, if it proves anything, would, it seems to me, rather tend, in accordance with the aims of the author, to determine the cerebral organ of certain special instincts whether these are animal or in particular mental. I admit the need to take into serious consideration all the relations which we can hope to establish between the anatomical structure and the intellectual and moral functions. I will be eager to seize any means of enlightening myself further on this subject. If you could indicate to this end a few new items I could read I will read them; but all that I have read and thought so far encourages me to think that nothing has really been established, that everything is still vague and uncertain in this area of speculation; it seems to me very difficult even for this situation to change as long as the ethological analysis of the influence of even general external circumstances is as backward as it is at present, since the variety of anatomical forms will only respond to residues (and here I make use of my logical terminology) after one has abstracted from the total phenomenon everything that constitutes another explanation of it. If, in our discussion of the characteristic tendencies of the two sexes, I have quoted an opinion that I knew to be that of several eminent physiologists and that would have us believe that women are less well suited than men to intellectual work of a protracted nature starting with the sciences and philosophy, that is not because that is my own opinion; I gave it as the only one among the theories of this kind which did not seem to me to be in flagrant contradiction with the facts; moreover, if one accepted it, it would not indicate that women had any lack of aptitude for science but only a lesser specialist vocation for it. Now whether or not this physiological theory is true is not something I claim to decide; the progress of science will probably decide that one day.

I will therefore leave on one side in our discussion the various anatomical considerations, holding myself ready to embrace any new pieces of information that you might give me or that might present itself from elsewhere. You think, moreover, that independently of these considerations an exact analysis of the general experience both everyday and historical will be sufficient to establish your conclusions.

As for everyday experience, I must admit that on this subject mine is not in accordance with yours. Do not think that I flatter myself in any way that I know women well; it is very difficult to know anyone really well; and the difficulty for any man of getting to know, I won't say women, but a woman, really well is almost insuperable. Those who know them best in some respects, don't know them at all in others. Nevertheless I believe that the English milieu is more favourable, taken all in all, for getting to know them than the French. From all that I have been able to learn, either from books or from my own observation or that of others, the education of young women is much more sexual, as you might say, in France than in England. I do not say this in the physical sense although in that respect too it is also true; I mean that the effect they wish to produce on the other sex is always present to them, without saying that it is always actually proposed to them as the principal aim of their conduct from infancy onwards. That is far less true here, it isn't even true at all in general, and this difference has immense consequences, not only for the development of their faculties but also for the possibility of men knowing them well, since in France they are always to be found in a permanent state of simulation; here, on the contrary, there is in general only dis-simulation, the effect of social pressure. Moreover this itself is involuntary, women themselves usually being completely unaware of it. They definitely regard themselves here (and men regard them too) much less as women than as human beings in general. Their education imposes on them as women certain special rules of con-duct but as general principles and without these relating to their position *vis-à-vis* men or towards a particular man. Their social dependence is a great hindrance to their development, but does not hinder it as much as in France.

Whatever the case, my own observations point to nothing which would justify the absolute judgment that you pass on women of being incapable of directing any kind of operation. First of all, in respect of domestic government, it is, I think, generally recognized that households are better run in England than anywhere else, at least insofar as discipline and obedience are concerned whether we are speaking of children or of servants. The latter in general (except in Scotland) are less intelligent than in France or in Italy but they perform their duties with much greater exactitude and material perfection which can only be the result of intelligent and con-tinuous direction. But domestic organization belongs here entirely to the province of women; the husband would think himself mad to involve himself in it: he often displays a sovereign ignorance of, and incapacity for, all these kinds of details.

In industrial management, women have never so far exercised control except in enterprises of a very modest scope in which how-ever it has not been noticed that they acquitted themselves any less well than men nor that they lacked the ability to follow things through. In fact when we are clear what we mean by that phrase, I do not find that that is at all what they lack. The sense of method which seems to you, with good reason, to be the main condition for enduring success in industrial enterprises of the first order, cannot be the same as the capacity to sustain a forceful intellectual argument for eight or ten hours each day; if that were the case, few men would succeed at it. The methodical approach is doubtless that of being able to persevere in a given project or a set plan until sufficient effort has been made. But I do not believe that we can dispute that women have this ability when compared to men. I do not think that caprice and the changeability of which they are accused (although we are far from accusing them of such in England) are noticeable in things which relate to their permanent interests. I think that nowhere do we find in matters of importance more patience and persistence than among them: moreover I find their caprice, even in the most pronounced cases, much more apparent than real although they know very well how to make use of it as a way of acting on those men who see them, to use your words, as delightful toys.

You consider them less able than men to rule passion with reason, that is, more given to following the present impulse of every powerful wish. I would say on the contrary that they are much less so, if you want me to judge this question on the basis of my everyday experience; for renunciation of the things they desire is for them the natural order of life, whereas among male heads of families these sacrifices are only made on great occasions and these men normally show themselves to be very impatient of such sacrifices in matters where they are unaccustomed to have to make them. But I don't want to base anything on this because I recognize that the patience of women like the impatience of men in matters which touch their inclinations is the natural effect of power on the one hand and impotence on the other. One must therefore decide this question on *a priori* grounds. But it seems to me that the power of reason over the passions is proportionate to the degree to which one is accustomed to examine oneself and to take stock of one's character and even one's faults. Someone who has not succeeded in gaining an exact knowledge of his own character will not be able to direct his conduct according to the dictates of reason. He will continue to follow his habits whether these are a matter of action, feeling or thought. I think that this examination of oneself, unfortunately too rarely found, is nevertheless in evidence as much among men as among women. A close knowledge of oneself, and the self control which this gives, are very exceptional in both, but if you asked the majority of Englishmen their opinion on this point you would find among them (whatever, moreover, their opinion on women) a quite different belief from the doctrine you are suggesting. Many of them would be inclined to believe that men were incapable of exercising on themselves the strength of moral restraint that they regard as typical of women. Without sharing this exaggerated idea I at least accept it as an indication that the evidence of experience is not all on the other side. Moreover general opinion normally invests women with a more scrupulous conscience than men: but what is conscience if not the subjection of the passions to reason?

I come now to the argument, based on the persistence right up to our own time, of the social inferiority of women compared to the gradual emancipation of the inferior classes in the most advanced nations although these classes began everywhere as slaves. This historical difference only appears explicable to you on the basis of an organic inferiority on the part of women. I believe however that there is an adequate answer to that argument. It is true that slaves in the élite populations have always succeeded in raising themselves to the level of freedom and sometimes of egality within society. But I do not believe that this has ever been the case with domestic slaves. These have not, I believe, ever emancipated themselves; they reached emancipation after the other slaves without having contributed to the process through their own efforts. This is because there is a continuous dependence that operates at every moment, something that dulls the soul and inhibits from the very beginning any drive towards independence. The serf is in a quite different position. He has more or less fixed duties to fulfil with regard to his master; once these duties are fulfilled he is more or less free. He has property of his own, he is forced to show foresight, he does not receive bread from others, he is responsible for his own survival; he even has power over others; he is master in his own home; he has a wife and children. He is responsible for them, he enjoys the position of commander, he learns to think that he is something. All this was already true to a certain extent of the agricultural slaves of the ancient world, and nevertheless the first step of their emancipation, that of their transformation into serfs, was not, I believe, the result of their own efforts but of the interest of their masters backed by the moral authority of the church. It is only since they acquired serf status that their progress up the social scale has been essentially the result of their own efforts . . .

Bibliography

Arnaud, Pierre, *Politique d'Auguste Comte*, A. Colin (1965).

Arnaud, Pierre, *Auguste Comte, textes choisis*, Bordas (1968).

Arnaud, Pierre, *Sociologie de Comte*, Presses Universitaires de France (1969).

Arnaud, Pierre, *Pour connaître la pensée d'Auguste Comte*, Bordas (1969).

Arnaud, Pierre, *Le 'Nouveau Dieu' (Préliminaires à la Politique positive)*, Paris: Librairie Philosophique J. Vrin (1973).

(*See also* Carneiro)

Aron, Raymond, *Main Currents in Sociological Thought*, vol. 1, chapter 2, London: Weidenfeld and Nicolson (1965).

Barnes, H. E., *Introduction to the History of Sociology*, University of Chicago Press (1948).

Bridges, J. H., *The Unity of Comte's Life and Doctrine*, London (1866).

Bulletin de la Société française de Philosophie, Numéro spécial (1958). (*Célébration du Centenaire de la Mort d'Auguste Comte.*)

Caird, Edward, *The Social Philosophy and Religion of Comte*, Glasgow (1893).

Carneiro, Paulo E. de Berredo, *Auguste Comte: Nouvelles lettres inédites*, Paris (1939).

Carneiro, Paulo E. de Berredo and Arnaud, Pierre (eds.), *Auguste Comte: Correspondence Générale et Confessions*, vol. 1, 1814–40, Paris: Mouton (1973).

Carneiro, Paulo E. de Berredo and Arnaud, Pierre (eds.), *Auguste Comte: Écrits de Jeunesse, 1816–28 (Suivis du Mémoire sur la Cosmogonie de Laplace, 1835)*, Paris: Mouton (1970).

Charlton, D. G., *Positivist Thought in France during the Second Empire, 1852–70*, Oxford: Clarendon Press (1959).

Comte, Auguste, *Cours de Philosophie Positive*, 6 vols., Paris (1830–42).

Comte, Auguste, *A General View of Positivism*, translated by J. H. Bridges, London: Routledge (1877).

Comte, Auguste, *The Catechism of Positive Religion*, translated by Richard Congreve, London: Longmans Green (1858).

Comte, Auguste, *System of Positive Polity*, 4 vols., London: Longmans Green (1877).

Comte, Auguste, *A Discourse on the Positive Spirit,* translated by E. S. Beesly, William Reeves (1903).

Durkheim, Émile, *The Rules of Sociological Method*, New York: Free Press (paperback edition 1964).

Durkheim, Émile, *Socialism and Saint-Simon*, translated by Charlotte Sandler, edited by Alvin W. Gouldner, Yellow Springs, Ohio: Antioch Press (1958); Collier paperback edition (1962).

Eisen S., 'Herbert Spencer and the Spectre of Comte', in *The Journal of British Studies* (1967), **7**, 48–67.

Evans-Pritchard, E. E., *The Sociology of Comte: An Appreciation*, Manchester University Press (1970).

Fletcher, Ronald, *Auguste Comte and the Making of Sociology*, London: Athlone Press (1966).

Fletcher, Ronald, *The Crisis of Industrial Civilization: The Early Essays of Auguste Comte*, London: Heinemann Educational Books (1974).

Gouhier, Henri, *La jeunesse d'Auguste Comte et la formation du positivisme*, 3 vols., Paris: Vrin (1933–41).

Gould, F. J., *Auguste Comte* (a biography), London: Watts (1920).

Hankins, Frank, 'A Comtean Centenary: Invention of the Term "Sociology"', in *American Sociological Review* (1939), **4**, 16.

Hubert, R., 'Comte', in *International Encyclopedia of the Social Sciences* (1930), **3**, 151–3.

Konig, R., 'Auguste Comte', in *International Encyclopedia of the Social Sciences* (1968), 3, 201–7.

Lévy-Bruhl, Lucien, *The Philosophy of Auguste Comte*, translated by Kathleen de Beaumont-Klein, New York: G. P. Putnam's Sons (1903).

Lewes, George Henry, *Comte's Philosophy of the Sciences*, London: Henry G. Bohn (1853).

Littré, E., *Auguste Comte et la philosophie positive*, Paris (1863).

Manuel, Frank, *The Prophets of Paris*, Harvard University Press (1962).

Martineau, Harriet, *The Positive Philosophy of Auguste Comte*, 2 vols., London: Chapman (1853).

Marvin, F. S., *Comte*, London: Chapman and Hall (1937).

Mill, John Stuart, *Auguste Comte and Positivism*, London: N. Trübner (1865).

Mill, John Stuart, *A System of Logic*, London: Longmans Green (1843).

Roberty, A., *Comte et Spencer*, Paris (1892).

Simon, Walter, M., *European Positivism in the Nineteenth Century*, Cornell University Press (1963).

Spencer, Herbert, *The Classification of the Sciences to which are added Reasons for Dissenting from the Philosophy of M. Comte*, London (1864).

Style, Jane M., *Auguste Comte: Thinker and Lover*, London: Kegan Paul (1928).

Whittaker, Thomas, *Comte and Mill*, London: Constable (1908).

Index

Index

(Major text sections indicated by bold figures)

Absolutism, *see* Relativity
Alexander the Great, 147
Alienation, mental, 144
Andreski, A., 3, 4
Apollonius, 52
Archimedes, 52
Aristotle, x, 13, 43, 62, 82, 129, 133, 134, 135, 136, 184
Attila 147

Bacon, Francis, 41, 43, 62
Bentham, Jeremy, 196
Berthollet, Claude Louis, 42
Bichat, Marie François Xavier, 12, 95
Biological analogy, *see under* Methodology
Blainville, Henri Marie Ducrotay de, 47, 138
Bonald, Louis Gabriel Ambroise, Vicomte de, 10, 11, 12
Bossuet, Jacques Benigne, 13
Brazil, advance of positivism in, 32
Broussais, François Joseph Victor, 141, 142, 187

Cabanis, 61, 149
Caesar, Gaius Julius, 147
Cervantes, Miguel de, 142, 143
Charlemagne, 147, 196
Civilization, *see* Social evolution
Classification, of the sciences, **50–9**; *see also* Methodology
Classification of the Sciences, The (Spencer), 32
Communism, 177, **178–88**
Comparison, as 'third method' of sociology, 18, 21, **106–14**
Comte, Auguste, xiii–xiv, 177, 191–2; life and significance of, ix–x, **3–33**; correspondence with Mill, **193–210**

Comte, Caroline, 26
Condorcet, Antoine Nicolas Caritat, Marquis de, 6, 9–10, 11, 12, 34 n17, 95, 111, 140
Co-operation, as origin of social force, 126–8, 134, 135, 185; *see also* Social organization
Cours de philosophie positive (Comte), *see* Positive Philosophy
Criticisms, of sociology, **25–9**

Darwin, Charles, 32
Descartes, 13, 43
Determinism, 28, 29
Division of Labour in Society, The (Durkheim), 14
Don Quixote (Cervantes), 143
Dunoyer, M., 185
Duration of life, as social influence, 156
Durkheim, Émile, xiii, 5, 6, **7–8**, 14, 30
Dynamical study, of sociology, **93–5**

École Polytechnique, Paris, 8–9
Edinburgh Review, 195
Employments, distribution of, *see* Labour, division of
Encyclopédists, 6
Environment, as influence on mind, 148–9
Evolution, Darwin's theory of, 32
Experiment, as 'second method' of sociology, 18, 21, **105–6**

Family, the, in sociological theory, 14, 107, 119–21, 133, 134
Fatalism, as charge against positive philosophy, 79–80
Ferguson, Adam, 13, 99, 141
Frederick the Great, 147
French Revolution, 24, 25, 187; and relation of positivism to, **81–4**

Galilei, Galileo, 43
Gall, 61, 119, 149, 187, 206
Godwin, William, 202
Gouhier, Henri, 9
Gouldner, Alvin, 6–7
Government, basis of theory of, 125–6; as cohesive social force, 134, 135–6; origin of, 134–5
Grote, George, 195

Hegel, Georg Wilhelm Friedrich, 177
Hierarchy, of the sciences, 13, 14
Hipparchus, 64
Historical question, *see under* History
History, as 'fourth method' of sociology, 18, 75, 114–15; and preparing for the historical question, **172–4**
Hobbes, Thomas, 135, 136
Humanity, religion of, 26
Hume, David, 13

Individuality, in sociological theory, 119, 127, 130; influence on society, 141–2, 146–7; communism as a threat to, 185
Industrial form of society, the, 135; gradually supersedes the military period, 166, 168, 170–71; and industry's needs for 'captains', 185–6; *see also* Military period of society
Industrial Revolution, 25
Intellect, as controlling influence, 136–7
Investigation, methods of, 18, 21, 101–15; *see also* Comparisons; Experiment; History; Observation

Julian, 99

Kant, Immanuel, x, 13, 68, 69
Kepler, Johannes, 42
Knowledge, 40, 41; sociology of, 25; stages of, 59

Labour, function of in sociological theory, 15; division of, 122–5
Lagrange, Joseph Louis, 67, 95

Language, function of in sociological theory, 15, 147–8, 149
Law of Human Progress, *see* Law of the Three Stages
Law of the Three Stages, 13–14, 20, **39–43, 160–66**, 173–4
Leibniz, Gottfried Wilhelm von, 94
Lévy-Bruhl, Lucien, 31, 191

Maistre, Comte Joseph Marie de, 10, 11, 12, 35 n19, 83
Marathon, battle of, 111
Marrast, M., 197
Martineau, Harriet, x, xiii
Marx, Karl, xi, 177, 191
Materialism, as charge against positive philosophy, 77, 78–9
Mathematics, importance of in science, 57–8
Mental phenomena, subordination of, 148–50
Metaphysical period, *see* Law of the Three Stages
Methodology of sociology, 7, 8, 16, 17–19, 20–22, 62–5; and biological analogy, 14–15, 27, 128–9 130–32, 138–9; and logical method, 67–8; and scientific method, 68–9; and historical method, 75; and reaction of sociology on other sciences, 75–6; *see also* Classification; Methods
Methods, of sociology, *see* Comparison; Experiment; History; Observation
Military period of society, 166–70; *see also* Industrial form of society
Mill, John Stuart, xi, xiii, 5, 26, 30–31, 191, 192; correspondence with Comte, **193–210**
Montesquieu, Charles-Louis de Secondat, x, 6, 13, 18, 139
Montpellier, 8
Moral weight, necessary in government, 137
Morals, science of, as ultimate goal of sociology, 9, 15

Napoleon I, Bonaparte, 99, 147

Natural sciences, relationship of sociology to, 45, 65–7, 71–3; classification of, 51–8; moral science as part of, 58–9

Natural laws, conception of, **65–7**; and human development, 94–5; social phenomena subject to, 90

'Normal type', concept of the, 18; and modification of social variations, 145

Observation, as 'first method' of sociology, 18, 21, 101–5

Order, theory of, 24

Parsons, Talcott, 33 n1

Pascal, Blaise, 100

Peel, J. D. Y., 3

Perfectibility, notion of human, 95–6

Philip II, 99

Plato, 13, 62, 184

Population increase, as social influence, 156–8

'Positive', meaning of word, 80–81

Positive method, application of, **87–115**

Positive period, *see* Law of the Three Stages

Positive philosophy, nature of, **39–50**; relation of sociology to, **70–77**; *see also* Positivism; Social forces

Positive Philosophy (Comte), x, xiii, 3, 4–5, 9, 16, 17, 19, 20, 21, 22, 23, 26, 27, 31, 128, 129, 193

Positive Polity (Comte), x, xiii, 3, 9, 10, 11–12, 14, 17, 18, 24, 25, 26, 27, 31

Positivism, 11, 24; and 'positivist sociology', 27; dissemination of, 32; intellectual character of, **77–81**; social aspect of, **81–4**; as rival to communism, 180, 181, 183–4

Principles of Sociology (Spencer), 3, 8

Progress, theory of natural, 24, **153–72**; role of positivism in, 82–4; as agent of change, 147; *see also* Law of the Three Stages

Property, social need for control of, 177, 180, 181–4

Prospectus des travaux scientifiques nécessaires pour réorganiser la société (Comte), 26

Pythagoras, 95

Race, declining influence of, 146

Reaction between social groups, 139–41

Recherches sur la vie et la mort (Bichat), 12

Relativity, move towards from absolutism, 80, 89

Religion, function of in sociological theory, 15

Reorganization of society, need for, 48–9

Revolutionary theories, modern, nature of, 133, 143–4; *see also* Communism; Socialism

Rome, Imperial, 131, 132, 168

Rules of Sociological Method, The (Durkheim), 7

Saint-Simon, Claude Henri, Comte de, 6, 7, 9, 30, 34 n10 and n12

Salamis, battle of, 111

Say, Jean Baptiste, 13

Scheler, Max, 28, 29

Schutz, Alfred, 28, 29

Sexual inequality, Comte and Mill correspond on, 191–2, **198–210**

Slavery, of producing class, 167–8

Smith, Adam, 13, 163

Social dynamics, *see* Progress

Social evolution of man, 16–17, 139–40, 153–6, 158–60

Social existence, theory of, **148–50**

Social forces, positive theory of, **126–38**

Social organization, theory of, 133–4

Social phenomena, provision of, 89–90; modifiable possibilities for, 96–101

'Social physics', 6, 34 n5, 44–5, 56–7, 101

Social science, in early stage, 88; spirit of, 90

Social statics, **119–26**

Social variation, limits of, **138–48**

Socialism, 177, **178–88**

Socialism and Saint-Simon (Durkheim 6

Society, in sociological theory, 119, 121–2

Sociological element in human society, **59–70**

Sociology, foundation of, 3–8; development of method and theory, 8–22; vocation of, 15–16; sociology of, 23–5; criticisms of, 25–9; Comte's importance to, 29–33; invention of term, 34 n2; relation to positive philosophy, **70–77**; *see also* 'Social physics'

Speciality, in human development, 45

Speculative class, institution of a, 161–2

Spencer, Herbert, 3, 4, 5, 8, 30, 31, 32, 33

Spontaneous order of human society, theory of the, *see* Social statics

Statical study of sociology, 90–93; *see also* Social statics

Système de politique psotive (Comte), *see Positive Polity*

Territorial property, political influence of, 129

Thales, 95

Theological period, *see* Law of the Three Stages

Tierra del Fuego, 109

Traité d'anatomie générale (Bichat), 12

Traité de politique positive (Comte), 31, 193

Turgot, Jacques, 6, 10, 12, 34 n18

'Utopian socialism', 177

Valat, Paul M., 9, 31

Vaux, Clothilde de, 26

Ward, Lester F., 30

Weber, Max, 25

Westminster Review, 32–3

Whitehead, A. N., 3

Wollstonecraft, Mary, 202

Women's social position, *see* Sexual inequality